PENGUIN BOOKS

DAYS *of* DARKNESS

Days of Darkness is based on Hazel Riseborough's doctoral thesis presented at Massey University in 1987. After graduation she wrote a report on the Taranaki raupatu claim for the Waitangi Tribunal, and taught nineteenth century New Zealand history at Massey University. In recent years Dr Riseborough has lived in the bush overlooking Lake Taupo, and divides her time between hiking in the bush and mountains and looking at the view from her study while she does further research for the Waitangi Tribunal and the Crown Forestry Rental Trust.

DAYS *of* DARKNESS

Taranaki 1878–1884

Revised Edition

Hazel Riseborough

PENGUIN BOOKS

PENGUIN BOOKS
Penguin Books (NZ) Ltd, cnr Airborne and Rosedale Roads, Albany, Auckland 1310, New Zealand
Penguin Books Ltd, 80 Strand, London, WC2R 0RL, England
Penguin Putnam Inc, 375 Hudson Street, New York, NY 10014, United States
Penguin Books Australia Ltd, 250 Camberwell Road, Camberwell, Victoria 3124, Australia
Penguin Books Canada Ltd, 10 Alcorn Avenue, Toronto, Ontario, Canada M4V 3B2
Penguin Books (South Africa) (Pty) Ltd, 24 Sturdee Avenue, Rosebank, Johannesburg 2196, South Africa
Penguin Books India (P) Ltd, 11, Community Centre, Panchsheel Park, New Delhi 110 017, India

Penguin Books Ltd, Registered Offices: Harmondsworth, Middlesex, England

First published in 1989 by Allen and Unwin New Zealand
This Penguin edition first published in 2002

1 3 5 7 9 10 8 6 4 2

Designed by Mary Egan
Typeset by Egan-Reid Ltd
Printed in Australia by McPherson's Printing Group

ISBN 0 14 301814 0

www.penguin.co.nz

CONTENTS

LIST OF MAPS

PREFACE

THE CONFISCATION OF LAND IN THE NORTH ISLAND OF NEW ZEALAND following the wars of the 1860s created a sense of grievance among the local tribes which continues to affect relations between Maori and European to this day. Maori frustration resulting from confiscation has been variously expressed over the years by further armed resistance, by pacific resistance to the enforcement of the confiscation, and by the presentation of a series of petitions to parliament. This book briefly examines the confiscation and then concentrates on the government's reactions to the pacific resistance offered by Maori to the survey for sale and settlement of the lands between Hawera and New Plymouth before the government had made any effort to delimit the reserves promised by the acts and proclamations of confiscation. It is a study of policies and personalities at a time of intense feelings and reactions resulting from cultural misunderstanding and racial intolerance. In refusing to consider Maori grievances, the government helped create in Taranaki a centre of disaffection which they perceived as a threat to the colony, but the discord that arose there between the government and Maori is better explained in terms of political and financial expediency, clashes of personality, and ideas of racial and cultural superiority than by any physical threat posed by the resident tribes. Nevertheless, Maori protest at the government's failure to set aside the promised reserves was interpreted as a challenge to the confiscation and was treated as a sign of fanaticism and infatuation, even as a manifestation of Maori determination to establish themselves once more as the dominant race.

This study does not seek to probe the philosophy behind Maori responses to injustice; that story remains to be told by those who have the right to tell it. But it is clear that successive governments found it expedient to misinterpret reasonable Maori demands. They then chose to deal with the ensuing situation not by granting reserves, but by passing some quite iniquitous legislation which enabled them to imprison without trial two prominent Taranaki chiefs and several hundred of their followers for a period of up to two years in South Island gaols. The injustice done to the Taranaki people stemmed more from a determination to force Maori to submit to European law and admit to European supremacy than from a greed for land. The Europeans already possessed the land through confiscation, and the government was determined that Europeans would occupy it. But much more than land was at stake. The government's aim was to end Maori isolation by settling a close European population in the area in an effort to destroy Maori separatism and self-determination. By separating the Maori people from the land they sought to destroy their mana motuhake, their distinctive Maori identity.

This dark period in New Zealand's history has been referred to in the literature as the Parihaka incident or the Parihaka affair. But the long-standing grievance of the Taranaki people and the expression of their frustration over government injustice was no incident or affair of the moment. Indeed the Parihaka years might be said to extend from 1860 to the present. The Parihaka people never did submit, and although the stand they took in defence of Maori rights was finally vindicated, the grievances remain. A deeper knowledge of the years in question is important to an understanding of the continuing efforts to have those grievances righted.

The complications of the Parihaka years would never have grown to the proportions they assumed if chiefly mana had been recognised and if successive governments had been prepared to consult with those chiefs they could not overawe. It is perhaps too much to expect that this could have happened, given the implicit belief of Victorian New Zealanders in the superiority of their race, reinforced as it was by the pseudo-scientific doctrine of social Darwinism. But it is not too much to expect that some lessons might have been learned between the attack on Waitara in 1860, which led to war, and the destruction of Parihaka in 1881. The first has been the object of a great deal of historical scrutiny; the second has been largely neglected, the case supposedly closed by the award of 'just and ample' reserves. But as the situation of the 1880s grew out of that of the 1860s, so the situation of the 1980s grew out of that of the 1880s.

The story of the Parihaka years shows that present day Maori claims to land are based on real and lasting grievances; yet the story has been largely consigned to the darkness. Had the 1926 Royal Commission on confiscated lands had a more extensive study of the injustice done to the Taranaki people on which to base its decision, it is very probable that compensation greatly exceeding that granted would have been recommended. A detailed reassessment of those years is long overdue: the situation has been passed over too lightly by historians and it is one of great moment to Taranaki. The present is offspring of the past and the story needed re-examining a hundred years later, as a reminder of the issues which lie behind today's attitudes and actions. Hayden White speaks of the burden of history and quotes those who say history justifies anything and teaches precisely nothing.[1] Indeed history is a burden, but it must be borne, and it must be used to teach, not justify, and to expose, not hide, events of the past which continue to impose their burden on the present.

A word of explanation is needed on the terminology employed in this study. Taranaki is used in European documentary sources to refer to a wider provincial district rather than a tribal area. As such it comprised seven main tribes tracing their descent from at least three canoes; yet it has the cohesion of a tribal district, a cohesion which stems from a cause, a grievance: land confiscation. One of the tribes, Te Ati Awa, is always referred to in the documentary sources as Ngatiawa, so this term has been retained. Ngaruahine were referred to as a hapu of Ngatiruanui, although in the twentieth century they were recognised as a tribe in their own right. 'Natives' and 'native affairs' are inescapable terms in reference to nineteenth century New Zealand. The emotive terms 'rebel' and 'loyal native' describe the views of the Europeans who bestowed the terms rather than those on whom they were bestowed.

The Appendices to the Journals of the House of Representatives and the New Zealand Parliamentary Debates are a rich source of information on the period under study, and the reports of the Royal Commission appointed under the Confiscated Lands Inquiry and Maori Prisoners' Trials Act 1879, are especially valuable. Unfortunately many papers such as police files have simply 'disappeared', and the important Maori Affairs Department files known as the West Coast Papers were destroyed by fire, so a vast body of material has been lost to researchers. What remains is scattered through lands, police, legislative, justice, prime ministers' and governors' files in the National Archives and especially in various ministerial papers in the Alexander Turnbull Library. A certain amount of material never published in New Zealand was printed in the British Parliamentary Papers; the Irish University Press series (here abbreviated to IUP since the pagination refers to that series and not the original) is a useful source of information not otherwise easily accessible.

I wish to express my gratitude and my aroha to Sir Makere Rangiatea Ralph Love, whose approval I sought before I began this study, and to Professor Ngatata Love of Massey University. During the research and writing of the thesis on which this book is based, I received encouragement and advice from many people. I would like especially to thank Te Pakaka Tawhai, Dr Kerry Howe, Professor Colin Davis, and Dr J. M. R. Owens of Massey University; and Dr Mary Bitterman, Dr David Wu and the staff of the Institute of Culture and Communication, East–West Center, Honolulu.

I am also indebted to Professor W. H. Oliver, editor of the *Dictionary of New Zealand Biography* and Karen Puklowski, cartographer at Massey University; and the staffs of Massey University Library, especially Courtney Carpenter; the Alexander Turnbull Library, the General Assembly Library and the National Archives, Wellington; the Hamilton Library, University of Hawaii at Manoa; the Bernice Bishop Museum Library, Honolulu; the Auckland Institute and Museum Library; the New Plymouth Library and the Taranaki Museum; and the Massey University Computer Centre.

My special thanks are due to Bridget Williams and the staff of Allen and Unwin, and to my colleague John Bevan Ford, tohunga whakairo of Te Ati Awa descent, who appropriately has given this work its moko.

I am grateful to the University Grants Committee, the East–West Center and the New Zealand–United States Educational Foundation for the grants which enabled me to undertake this study.

INTRODUCTION TO 2002 EDITION

On 5 November 1981 thousands of people gathered on the marae at Parihaka to commemorate the centenary of the invasion of the village. The grief of the people was palpable and I wondered at the gap between the reality and the meagre accounts in the history books used in schools and universities. In late 1984 when I began the study on which this book is based, I hoped that in writing about government action that impinged on the people of Parihaka in the 1880s, I might forge a weapon that those of the 1980s could wield in presenting yet another petition to parliament in their endless search for justice. At that time the Waitangi Tribunal was limited to hearing claims dating from the passing of the Treaty of Waitangi Act 1975, and the Taranaki people were still limited to presenting petitions; several hundred had been presented between the 1880s and the 1980s. However, one year later the 1975 Act was amended to allow for claims dating from the signing of the Treaty in 1840 and I found myself working on a topic that would obviously become part of a claim to the Waitangi Tribunal. Then in 1989 I was commissioned by the Tribunal to write a background report for the Taranaki Raupatu claim covering a much wider period, from 1863 to the present.

The opening hearing of all the Raupatu claims took place at Owae Marae, Waitara, in early September 1990, and hearings continued all over Taranaki for the next two or three years. It was both harrowing and inspiring to sit in the many meeting houses and hear the people articulate their grievance and their efforts over the years to seek redress. When the Tribunal process began there was no pool of trained historians among the people to do the research needed in presenting their claims. But everyone knew their history, everyone had sat at the feet of the elders and heard the stories, and from each hapu there emerged researchers determined to learn to find their way around local and national archives so they could write a report that would satisfy both Tribunal and Crown scrutiny. These home-grown historians did an impressive job.

At the first hearing at Parihaka in October 1991, Crown counsel presented a dramatic letter to the people from the Minister of Treaty Settlements. The Crown conceded that the question of the sacking of Parihaka was not disputed, and that it was ready to discuss 'any proposal whereby the mana of Parihaka might be restored'. 'It is my duty' said the minister, 'to apologise to the ancestors of Parihaka. I now do so'.[1] The Crown's hope was that the two sides might resolve the matter by direct negotiation, but Taranaki was not ready to accept the Crown's offer. This time their story would be told in full, in public; the nation would be made aware of the depth and legitimacy of their grievance.

The Tribunal finally sat at Parihaka in October 1992 to hear the academic historians present their reports, and most importantly to hear 'the Parihaka story' as told by the iwi themselves. It was an emotional occasion, and an historic one, when the Parihaka people found themselves before a full Tribunal of nine members, under Chief Judge Edward Taihakurei Durie, charged with enquiring into any action of the Crown which was prejudicial to the claimants and inconsistent with the principles of the Treaty of Waitangi. It had been a long time coming; there had been endless commissions over the years since the confiscations had been implemented, but only the Sim Commission of 1926, confined within very narrow terms of reference, had actually been authorised to enquire into claims arising from confiscation.

At the end of 1995 the Crown officially accepted 'that events relating to the implementation of the confiscations leading up to the invasion of Parihaka in 1881, the invasion itself and its aftermath, constituted a breach of the principles of the Treaty of Waitangi'. They accepted that the confiscations 'constituted an injustice . . . and had a severe impact upon the welfare, economy and development of Taranaki iwi'; they did not accept that the confiscations were unlawful.[2]

The Tribunal's Taranaki Report which was released in Wellington and at Parihaka on 14 June 1996 was a chilling document, an indictment of a century and a half of Crown actions in Taranaki which were 'the antithesis to that envisaged by the Treaty of Waitangi'. The invasion and sacking of Parihaka, the Tribunal said, 'must rank with the most heinous action of any government, in any country, in the last century'; and the leases in perpetuity of the lands supposedly returned to the people were the 'unkindest cut of all', for they ensured that as each generation succeeded to lands they could never live on or use, they would inherit 'the history of war, protest, imprisonment, and dispossession'. The people were denied 'even the right to forget'; and, as the Tribunal said, generous reparation would be needed to improve the lot of Maori, restore the honour of the Crown, ensure cultural survival, and re-establish effective interaction between the Treaty partners.[3]

By the early twentieth century, after the death of Parihaka's charismatic leaders, and with the government's reserves policy in place, Parihaka's landlessness was reflected in increasing poverty and deprivation. The village declined; by the 1930s most of the people could no longer maintain their homes on the marae and had to move away to find work where they could, in dairy factories or in contract gangs they established to labour for farmers throughout Taranaki. The Parihaka block, supposedly reserved for the benefit of its owners, was not in their hands but in those of the Department of Maori Affairs and by mid-century was badly run down and had accumulated thousands of dollars of debt – a debt which passed intact to the owners when the land was returned to their control in 1981. Yet the spirit of the village never died. The monthly meetings and special half-yearly meetings have been held without fail, probably since the founding of the village in the mid 1860s; and Te Raa o te Paahua, the anniversary of the invasion of Parihaka, has been commemorated every year since 1881.

The 1960s and 1970s were decades of protest around the world: protest over political, nuclear, environmental and racial issues. In New Zealand protests over Vietnam merged with the anti-nuclear stand; protest over apartheid in South Africa led to an increasing awareness of racial issues at home. The question of Maori land loss was highlighted by the 1975 Land March from the Far North to the steps of parliament and by the 1976 occupation of Bastion Point. And in that decade it was determined that Parihaka would once again be a centre of learning and teaching. Te Niho o Te Atiawa, the house on Te Whiti's marae, was opened to 'the students and teachers of the world', and a series of seminars was organised 'aimed at nurturing identity and bridging cultures'. The centenary of the invasion of Parihaka was approaching; Parihaka was on the move again.

Twenty years later the Tribunal hearing 'stirred the spirit of their tupuna' within the people and they decided to mount a new series of seminars to commemorate the example set by their kuia and kaumatua. I was asked to deliver the first of the 1993 Parihaka Seminars, and in February we all gathered again in Te Niho o Te Atiawa where I had presented my report to the Tribunal a few months earlier. The lecture, entitled 'Parihaka and the Historians', set out to show how 'the Parihaka story' had been presented in the literature, and especially how their revered leaders had been – and unfortunately still were – portrayed by historians. And I reminded them it was up to them to put the picture right – to tell the story only they could tell, from the sources available only to them – their oral sources, especially their haka and waiata.[4] Some of those waiata had been heard at the Tribunal hearings but they were not for 'public consumption' so to speak. But now, over a hundred years since the invasion of their village and the loss of the land, I hoped the uri, the descendants, would be ready to free Te Whiti from the bonds with which the historians had bound him.

At the end of the decade and with the approaching dawn of a new millennium Parihaka was ready. In collaboration with the City Gallery they had spent two years planning the Gallery's millennium project: the Parihaka Exhibition. It opened in Wellington on a blustery winter day in August 2000; 'the tears of the tupuna' were blessing the occasion. There were other tears that day – tears of grief as well as tears of joy and of release, and for some of the visitors who thronged the gallery tears of anger over a history that until then had been hidden from them.

Essays, paintings and poetry had been commissioned for the exhibition from academics and from leading artists and poets, and over two hundred existing paintings and sculptures had been borrowed from widely scattered collections at home and abroad. Many of these dated from the 1970s: artists had been galvanized by Dick Scott's *Ask That Mountain*, published in 1975. The poet J.C. Sturm, J.K. Baxter's widow, recalled that the publication 'sent a tremor right through the literary and visual arts community'. New paintings and earlier ones shared wall space throughout the gallery with lines from poems. Sturm's own poem said 'If you haven't heard of Parihaka,/ Be sure /Your grandchildren will / And their children after them,/ History will see to that'; and Roma Potiki's said 'It's mid-afternoon /a pale sun rings the mountain, /a little more snow melts'.[5] Paintings by Darcy Nicholas, Shane Cotton, John Baxter, Michael Smither and others told the story on wood and canvas, and sixty or so photos of Parihaka dating from the 1870s joined a collection of documents, manuscripts and artefacts. And in pride of place in the entrance hall were the photographic portraits of Te Whiti and Tohu, enlarged from snapshots taken in Nelson when they were held in exile in the South Island. The photos had never before been displayed in public, but had been kept under embargo in the Taranaki Museum.

The exhibition moved Parihaka back into the forefront of the nation's consciousness, and the publication of the 'catalogue' *Parihaka: The Art of Passive Resistance* is a lasting tribute to its leaders and people and a memorial to the injustice they suffered. The chapter by Te Miringa Hohaia 'Ngaa Puutaketanga Koorero Moo Parihaka' is a treasure house of whaikorero of the two leaders, of traditional waiata and haka, some composed by, some for Te Whiti and Tohu; and of the tapu 'poi manu', the chants accompanied by the beat of the poi for the recitation of whakapapa and karakia. In the decade after the return of Te Whiti and Tohu from the South Island much of this oral history was recorded with great care in manuscript books which are still held by descendants of the people of that time. It was taught to selected people under strict conditions and performed on special occasions, but until now it has not been released to public scrutiny. There is much still held by families loathe to release such tapu material, but records are gradually being made available and the vision of today's leaders involves the establishment at Parihaka of a traditional waananga, or school of learning where the teachings of the past can be shared with the generations of the present.[6]

I am grateful to Te Miringa Hohaia, Parekaitu Tito and the people of Parihaka for their aroha and their trust in me; and to Geoff Walker of Penguin who was enthused by my colleague Dr Danny Keenan of Massey University with the idea of a new edition of *Days of Darkness*. I am glad it will see the light of day again in a new millennium. A few corrections were needed; for instance in the earlier edition on page 66 I wrongly named Robert Studholme Thompson's wife as Kuini Wi Rangipupu. She was his second wife. His first wife, a close relative of Titokowaru, was Hana Taukawa, of Ngati Kaipoa and Ngati Maranga hapu of Te Kopanga. My thanks for this information are due to Aroha Houston of Hawera, a great-grandaughter of Hana Taukawa and R.S. Thompson.

Hazel Riseborough
Pukawa
September 2001

CHAPTER ONE

The Parihaka Years

The true character of a man is not easy to discern when the evidence exists in the records of his prosecutors.[1]

TO MANY HISTORIANS, THE NEW ZEALAND WARS ENDED IN 1870 WHEN the last imperial troops were withdrawn from the country. But from 1879 events in Taranaki kept the west coast and at times the whole colony in a ferment until on 5 November 1881, in 'one of the more eloquent moments in New Zealand history',[2] 1,500 militia and volunteers invaded the largest and most prosperous Maori village in the country, the undefended settlement of Parihaka at the foot of Mt Taranaki. Its unresisting chiefs, Te Whiti and Tohu, were arrested, their followers dispersed and their village and surrounding crop lands destroyed. While not a shot was fired, it was yet a continuation of the wars, a further manifestation of the determination of the Europeans to assert their supremacy and force Maori into submission.

Before the first Taranaki war, the two chiefs had lived at Warea on the coast near Cape Egmont. They were both deeply spiritual men and mission educated, having studied and worked under the Lutheran missionary Riemenschneider who established himself at Warea in 1846.[3] After their village was destroyed in the early days of the war, they called themselves king's men for their sympathies were with the anti-land-sellers. But their inclination was to settle their differences with the governor by negotiation, not war, and as early as 1862 Te Whiti's chiefly mana and lack of hostility toward Europeans was evident when he ensured the safety of the passengers from the wreck of the *Lord Worsley*.[4] In the late 1860s, Te Whiti came to the government's notice after he and Tohu had withdrawn from contact with both Europeans and warlike Maori and established themselves at Parihaka. As more and more Maori became disillusioned by warfare and loss of land and joined those already at Parihaka, European concern grew, and what had at first been seen as a potentially disruptive community controlled by pacifist leaders finally came to be treated as a threat to civilisation itself. Te Whiti would not cooperate with the government and permit the spread of colonisation to his district. He had not objected to the settlement of confiscated land to the south of the Waingongoro river – he had 'shared his blanket' – and now he expected that Maori and European would live peacefully, each on their own land on either side of the river. At that stage he had every reason to believe that the promises regarding the confiscated lands *would* be fulfilled, but in the face of increasing European pressure he could see that unless Maori took a determined stand they would receive no consideration from a government bent on replenishing their coffers from the sale of Maori land. Thus government attempts to 'enforce the confiscation' north of the river met with a continuing series of non-violent protests staged by the people of Parihaka at the behest of their chiefs.

It might be thought that Maori invited arrest in order to bring their grievances to the consciousness of the whole colony. It was believed at the time that Te Whiti sought to have the question of confiscation investigated in the courts, but he had more than once expressed his mistrust of the functioning of European law. From the available evidence it would seem that Te Whiti was not challenging the confiscation itself, but rather protesting the government's failure to set aside the promised reserves. There is no evidence to show that he changed his stance over time or reduced his demands. From the first, his demand was to be allowed to live peacefully on the land of his ancestors; his expectation was that the land occupied by Maori would not be taken from them – and from the assurances given them over the years it seemed that this would include all the land between the Waingongoro and Hangatahua rivers. The west coast people could do nothing except protest against the survey of the Waimate plains, and once most of the land there had been sold to Europeans and reserves set aside for Ngatiruanui, Te Whiti concentrated on attempting to preserve the land of his own Taranaki people in the Parihaka block. To the north and south, settlers had built their homes, and there, he said, they should stay, Maori and European living side by side in peace. But he would protest to the end the action of the government in breaking all the longstanding promises and taking his best agricultural land, the seaward Parihaka block which had been cultivated for generations by his ancestors.

Te Whiti's grievances never were investigated or redressed. He was dismissed as intransigent and obsessed; his determined stand over the question of broken promises was treated as part of a nationwide movement, a threat to the authority of the Queen – and to the supremacy of the white race. Te Whiti may have seen the issue as a moral war; the settlers and their government were determined on a less virtuous one. Finally, baffled by their inability to force the west coast people either to give in or resist, they had recourse to violence themselves. Fifteen years of peaceable pursuit of justice were brought to an end by a display of military might lauded by the press as a blow struck for freedom, the final blow designed to teach Te Whiti and Tohu the salutary lesson of submission and obedience.

Hundreds of words were written about the Parihaka years in official publications and contemporary newspapers, but the subject was soon forgotten once the crisis was over and the colony could concentrate once more on the momentous question of the opening up of the King Country and the provision of a route for the main trunk railway. Twentieth century history books also focused attention on Waikato and the King movement, and 'the Parihaka affair' was often mentioned only briefly or omitted altogether. Te Whiti was generally portrayed as a religious rather than a political leader, founder of an 'adjustment cult' outside the mainstream of New Zealand history, and the determined stand which he and his followers took against injustice was described either as madness and infatuation or as a grandiose challenge to the confiscation. More recently it has been seen as passive resistance – despite the fact that it was indeed very active resistance, although pacific in nature.

The European informant in the best position to report the doings and sayings of Te Whiti was R. S. Thompson, who had access to Parihaka through his wife, a relative of Titokowaru. But Thompson complained that nothing had ever been told him straight at Parihaka and he was therefore limited to inference. This did not prevent him from conjecturing as to Te Whiti's purposes, and through the reports he wrote while acting as interpreter with the survey parties on confiscated land,[5] inference and conjecture reached and certainly influenced the government. Other interpreters, government agents and the settler press had even less access to fact and more recourse to fiction, while

Maori informants were usually in government pay and therefore hardly objective observers. As Thompson said, those who would talk knew nothing, and Te Whiti's confidants would not betray his counsels.

James Cowan wrote more fully and sympathetically of the expedition to Parihaka in 1881 than any other writer; but he had received hospitality and friendship from Te Whiti, had stayed in his village and conversed at length with the old chief.[6] He was one of the few writers who had first-hand acquaintance with Te Whiti. William Baucke was another, and he described him as a traditional Maori leader, deeply versed in the lore of his ancestors, and one who taught his people to live in love and peace.[7] There is a marked difference in the writing of those who actually knew Te Whiti and those who 'knew' him through their own prejudices, or by hearsay. For years such writing as was undertaken on the 'Parihaka affair' tended to follow the accounts of government officials and the settler press, with their emotive and negative interpretations of Te Whiti's stand.

The story of the Parihaka years has been covered to any extent only by G. W. Rusden, whose *History of New Zealand* resulted in a libel trial and the suppression of his book; and more recently by Dick Scott, whose writing has been criticised in academic circles.[8] Rusden's three-volume history arrived in the colony in the middle of 1883 and from the start caused comment and controversy. Rusden lived in Australia and relied for his information on public documents, New Zealand newspapers, especially the *Lyttelton Times*, and on two brief visits to New Zealand in 1878–79 and 1881, during which he came to know such prominent Europeans as governors, bishops and parliamentarians, as well as several Maori chiefs, of whom he thought highly.

As the events at Parihaka moved to a climax, Rusden's indignation grew and he devoted about half of the third volume of his history to the events surrounding the infamous invasion of Parihaka on 5 November 1881. Rusden's sympathies were firmly with the Maori people who he believed had been most unjustly treated, but in condemning successive ministries, especially for their continued efforts to get possession of Maori land, he inevitably exposed himself to attack. As a non-resident and an infrequent visitor to New Zealand, it was easy to dismiss his views as ill-advised and uninformed.

The events at Parihaka did not form part of the actual libel in the case subsequently brought against Rusden by John Bryce, native minister at the time of the Parihaka raid, although Rusden's counsel made every effort to highlight them and so justify Rusden's description of Bryce as cruel and callous.[9] To the great satisfaction of many in both New Zealand and England, the verdict in the case went against Rusden and resulted in the suppression of his history and the award of £5,000 to Bryce.[10]

Contemporary writers who dealt with the Parihaka question were mostly politicians or military men who could not be expected to treat the question objectively, or journalists whose approach was dictated by their particular newspaper.[11] Most were hostile, and those who were not were generally anti-government, rather than pro-Maori. Even they accepted that Te Whiti was mad, or at least foolish, but they explained his actions as being due to Maori despair or excused them as a response to incompetent government, unjust legislation or European provocation.

W. P. Reeves was one politician and writer who expressed a liberal view of the Parihaka question; he was also one of the few who had actually met Te Whiti. In his general history of New Zealand published in 1898, he dealt with Parihaka in half a page,[12] but his was perhaps the most influential opinion ever expressed on the subject. It became the basis of the judgment of the Royal Commission of 1926 which vindicated the Taranaki tribes' original contention that the confiscation was unjust, and decreed that compensation should be paid for the wrong done to the Parihaka people when their village was invaded and destroyed.[13]

As time went on and the myth-makers did their work, the whole question of Parihaka acquired a more romantic aura, and such opinions as were expressed on Parihaka appeared for the most part in popular histories, notably in a series of books and articles by Cowan.[14] It was not until the 1930s that other scholarly histories of New Zealand began to appear, and those written in the following thirty years dealt with the pressing concerns of the time, which were other than racial matters. Maori issues were usually dealt with in a separate section or chapter, apart from the mainstream of New Zealand history, and the period from the wars until around the turn of the century received scant attention. As a result, Parihaka was often overlooked altogether.

A disturbing feature of this neglect is the treatment given to the Parihaka years in history books used in schools. J. C. Beaglehole's *New Zealand: A Short History*, published in 1936, relegated the 'provocative Parihaka incident' to a footnote.[15] J. B. Condliffe and W. T. G. Airey in their *Short History of New Zealand* described Parihaka as a 'communist village' where after 'curious and amusing scenes', the prophet Te Whiti was arrested and the 'threatened trouble ended in a burlesque at which the whole colony laughed'. In a later revised edition the paragraph on Parihaka was omitted altogether.[16] W. P. Morrell and D. O. W. Hall's version of Maori history was indicative of the subtly racist views of the 1950s, when the Maori urban migration had resulted in a visible Maori presence among the dominant European population; it had not however aroused an awareness of past and present inequalities in the law nor awakened any concern for Maori identity and culture.[17] It is an unhappy thought that such material was still offered in New Zealand schools at that time.

About 1960 there appears to be a watershed in twentieth century historical writing touching on the Parihaka years, at a time when New Zealanders were taking stock of race relations and rethinking Maori–European issues. The publication of the controversial Hunn report was both a product of and a catalyst for this new climate of debate.[18] Two of New Zealand's leading historians seemed firmly implanted on either side of the divide. Keith Sinclair's *History of New Zealand*, published in 1959, gave a fatalistic view of Te Whiti as a religious leader, a millenarian, impotent in the face of European might, whose village and influence decayed and apparently passed without trace.[19] W. H. Oliver's *Story of New Zealand*, published in 1960, looked at the social effects of Te Whiti's faith and works. It is a positive view, a balanced picture of Te Whiti as 'a man of religion as well as a land reformer'. Oliver thought Te Whiti 'the most striking leader in the post-war years', a man who served as something of a model for later leaders.[20]

Despite changing attitudes, some still regarded Te Whiti simply as a religious leader and a prophet.[21] Bernard Gadd's account of the 'prophet's teachings' is based on the sayings of Te Whiti or Tohu as reported in the *New Zealand Herald* and the *Lyttelton Times* of 1880 and 1881. Only four of his references are from more direct sources: from Te Whiti's conversations with Cowan and Baucke, and Te Whiti's testimony in court. These references suggest that Te Whiti advocated pacifism and from this it may be inferred that he advocated Pai Marire, that is, 'good and peaceful' teachings (as distinct from Hauhau teachings which developed from Pai Marire), but it is insufficient evidence on which to style a man a prophet and a religious leader. Since Te Whiti had a Christian as well as a traditional education, he could be expected to be a deeply spiritual man, a religious man, even though he was not bound to any religion. There was little if anything in the ritual or observances of the Parihaka monthly meetings suggestive of 'religion in the strict sense'.[22] The 17th of the month, the day the meetings were held, could hardly be compared to the Sabbath, since it commemorated the source of the grievance which underpinned the 'Te Whiti movement': the outbreak of the war that led to the loss of the land. What Gadd described as 'rites of worship', the oratory, poi and feasting that marked the day, were essentially traditional elements adapted to the theme of grievance and injustice. Clearly the monthly meetings were similar to traditional hui, of which a strong spiritual element, expressed in ancient or modern form, was an integral part. Maori did not distinguish and divide the sacred and the secular. Like other Polynesians, they lived in a world 'where the natural is supernatural but the supernatural quite natural'.[23] Te Whiti was a great student of the *Bible* and his biblical knowledge had become incorporated into his world view, but both Baucke and Cowan stressed Te Whiti's accent on peace, not religion. The newspaper reports of Te Whiti's teachings may be the only ones readily available to the European researcher, but they are a European source, and a European construction of Maori thought and actions. Until we have more reliable sources, we will not be in a position to comment on Te Whiti's beliefs, philosophy and teachings. The subjective translations of interpreters and the views of newspaper correspondents are not a good basis from which to start.

Dick Scott's *The Parihaka Story* (1954), the first full-length book on Parihaka, was followed in 1975 by an expanded and illustrated version, *Ask That Mountain*. The later book is not the 'rich store of oral history not before entrusted to a pakeha' of the publisher's blurb, although it does include some treasured recollections given to the author by kindly elders. Scott was a sympathetic visitor who received the kindness and hospitality traditionally given such people at Parihaka, but he was neither linguist nor Maori scholar, and it cannot be expected that Parihaka's taonga or treasures will be entrusted to such as he. Scott confidently reported Te Whiti's words and inner thoughts, although his sources were simply the usual government communications and local newspapers. Perhaps gravest of all was his insensitivity to Te Whiti's own wish that no photograph or likeness of him be made. The book contains every available likeness, created from 'surreptitious shirtcuff sketches' and similar sources known to be in existence. Scott's books have been dismissed as one-sided and unfair to the settlers, but they were, as he himself said, 'an attempt to redress a hitherto overwhelmingly one-sided record'.[24]

By the 1970s, the view of Te Whiti as a political opponent of the government was established in the literature. John Williams did follow convention and style Te Whiti 'the Parihaka prophet', but he recognised him as primarily a political leader with rational aims directed at the here and now rather than the hereafter. He was not convinced there was any evidence that Te Whiti's political activities 'were directed toward bringing about millennial goals'.[25] The events at Parihaka continued to attract little mention but this lack was compensated for in part by Alan Ward's *Show of Justice*, which provides a comprehensive coverage of Maori–European interaction throughout the nineteenth century and throughout the colony. It is particularly valuable for its treatment of the post-war period and the place in it of the Parihaka question, especially in comparison with the central role which the government accorded the King movement and the opening up of the King Country.[26]

Harry Dansey, the only Maori so far who has published work on the events at Parihaka, was not a historian but a journalist and playwright, and New Zealand's first Maori race relations conciliator. Having accepted the responsibility for writing about Parihaka placed upon him by the elders, Dansey methodically read himself into the period and found, like others before and after him, that 'the official documents contain enough to reduce even an objective student . . . to a state of either apoplexy or tears'. His play is the story of Te Ua 'the prophet' and Te Whiti 'the man of peace' and their differing reactions to European encroachment. 'In material terms both lost', but Dansey's aim is to show 'that even in loss there is victory' or, in Maori terms, even in mate there is tupu. *Te Raukura* is both a lesson and a warning, for it is the story of those who can forgive and of those who can never forget. Dansey illustrates the dichotomy of the Maori world through the use of two narrators: Koroheke, the elder, and Tamatane, today's youth: the one wearing his maoritanga like a cloak, the other wielding his like a weapon.[27]

Koroheke feels deeply the loss of the land and the injustice done to his people, but he accepts and practices Te Whiti's teaching of peace, love and brotherhood – 'in common toil to build the common good'. Tamatane does not want to hear of brotherhood. The rape of Parihaka, 'the nation's last armed land-grab . . . carried out not by British Imperial forces but by true New Zealanders . . . determined to . . . take over the square miles of fertile cultivated gardens', was not something to forgive and forget, but a thing to expiate, a cause to embrace:

Across the years I hear the voices call;
I hear the widows' cry, the sickening crash
Of rafters falling in the burning homes;
The people driven out like drafted sheep.

The men who broke, and bent, and turned the law
Have done great evil, not alone to those
Of that far time, but also to our own.
And so I hold their sons to answer for
The fathers' sins, and thus I justify
What I may do in this my day and age.[28]

Dansey's lesson and warning are to be taken seriously on several levels. It can no longer be considered a legitimate exercise for a European, dependent on European sources, to seek to interpret the Maori world. Maori feeling about such activity is understandably negative and would be well expressed in the words of Keri Kaa: 'waiho ma matou tonu e tuhituhi a matou korero'.[29] Archival material is a totally inadequate source from which to draw a 'Maori' perspective of the Parihaka years. There are no Te Whiti papers or letter-books available from which to glean ideas about the ideology and philosophy of the Parihaka people. They were rightly suspicious of the art of writing, given the fraudulent use to which Maori signatures had been put over the years. Whatever Te Whiti thought and said, he said to the people at great public hui on his own marae and in the relative privacy of his own wharenui in the evenings. What he is purported to have said, and more importantly to have meant, has come to us almost exclusively through European reporters dependent on European interpreters of varying ability and persuasion.

Interpreters are marginal people, standing between two worlds. They are mediators whose situation is ambiguous and ambivalent, and this may be reflected in their interpretation, rather than translation, of the spoken word. The interpreters who worked on the west coast were used rather as whipping boys by politicians. They were accused of being on the side of the Native Office or being pro-Maori, or of producing translations to order;[30] when the message was unacceptable the messenger could always be blamed. But when the government sought an excuse to arrest Te Whiti, they were only too willing to accept the translation of the government interpreter as proof that Te Whiti had wickedly, maliciously and seditiously contrived to disturb the peace.[31]

Licensed interpreters varied widely in competence and integrity, but even the best of them could be expected to perform well only in a one to one situation. There was a vast difference in the messages which emerged from conversations between Te Whiti and European friends or officials, and those which emerged from reports of Te Whiti's speeches given at public hui. Interpreters were almost invariably out of their depth in the marae situation where they found the language of oratory difficult to interpret. 'In the Maori world the speaker speaks. Understanding is the business of the listener.'[32] Te Whiti's Maori listeners would have heard a positive message rooted in the past but serving as an aid to survival in the present; a message unconcerned with historical chronology and accuracy, with distinguishing fact and fiction, a message of inspiration which affirmed and reinforced their identity. His European listeners heard, or at least reported, a negative message of madness, superstition and fanaticism. He spoke in his terms; they heard in theirs, and it is this latter message which persists in English in the documents and in the newspapers. This is no basis on which to judge the man or his message.

Documentary sources may enable us to say what Te Whiti did, but not why. Elaborating the 'why' is a task for his uri, his descendants, using sources properly available only to them and giving a Maori view of the years in question, the obverse of the coin tendered to date by historians. The message which inspired the people then lives on in the waiata and haka and the chants which accompanied the poi, such a notable feature of the hui at Parihaka. It is for the uri of Parihaka's leaders, past and present, at their elders' urging and with their blessing, to avail themselves of these taonga and write a life of Te Whiti and Tohu and the story of Parihaka. This is not to imply that we would thus get an unbiased account, a definitive version of the Parihaka years, but that at last we would get a Maori interpretation, a necessary counterbalance to the version derived from archival sources. There are references in the archival sources themselves which suggest the existence of a body of oral literature on which those with the liberty to do so might draw.[33]

Maori poetry and chant are a valuable source for our understanding of Maori history, yet they are a source as yet largely untapped. Only by returning to the power of the Maori word can we really hope to gain access to the thinking behind the action. But Keri Kaa's warning must be taken to heart. This is a task not for the interpreter, but for the tohunga, for one who is qualified in a very special way. Te Whiti's story remains to be written, but the 'archives' are there from which the Maori scholar might work.

While that story cannot be written from documentary sources, those sources are adequate for a study of European actions and reactions to this man and his time, and of the government's response to the development of a large and prosperous village headed by charismatic leaders, whose assertion of mana in rejecting European authority and whose moral stand over the non-fulfilment of the promises regarding the land confiscations of the 1860s drew thousands of followers to Parihaka and infused them with pride in their identity.

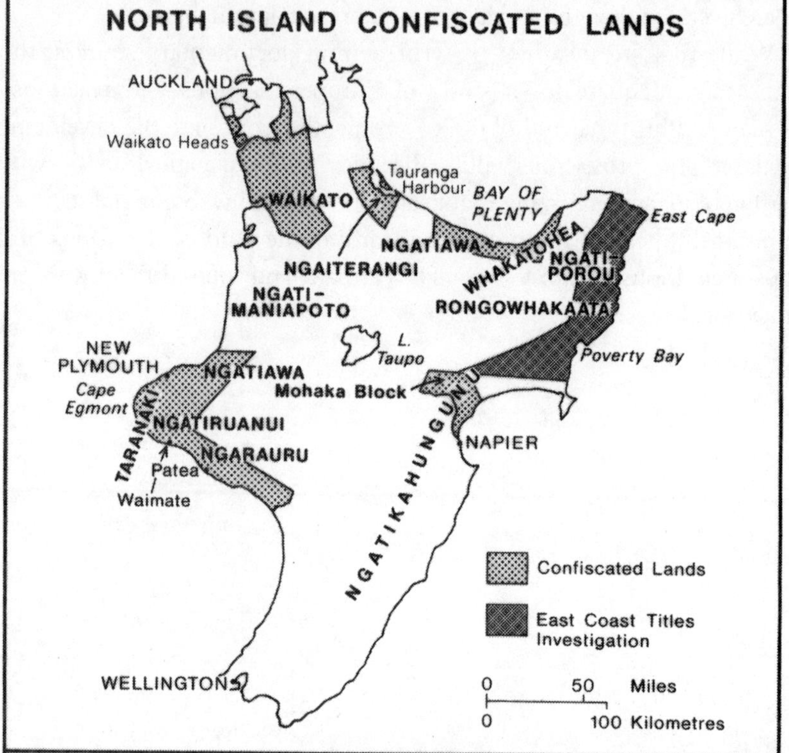

CONFISCATED LANDS (ACRES)

	Waikato	Tauranga	Opotiki	Taranaki	Totals
Compensation to Friendly Natives	221 979	9 822	48 967	91 667	372 435
Reserves for Returned Rebels	25 000	2 616	110 000	(a) 21 866	159 482
Land given back to Owners	15 000	63 346	40 832	180 000	299 178
Missionary and School Claims	4 867	800	—	—	5 667
Immigrant's Allotments	26 171	—	—	—	26 171
Military Settlers	214 884	26 701	(b) 70 485	95 118	407 188
Lands Sold	94 017	211	—	46	94 274
Lands Unsold	490 147	96 852	132 716	563 751	1 283 466
Lands Unsaleable	125 372	13 652	37 000	291 852	467 876
Totals	1 217 437	(c) 214 000	440 000	1 244 300	3 115 737

Total of Confiscated Lands 3 490 737 acres. Including Mohaka Block Established, 375 000 not yet dealt with.

Note (a) The engagements amount to nearer 50 000 although all not Gazetted.
(b) 40 000 to Arawa Contingent.
(c) 164 000 really returned and the Total includes a purchase as well as the Confiscation.

Based on: IUP vol 15 facing p126

CHAPTER TWO

Muru Raupatu: Confiscation

1863–1865

If the blood of our people only had been spilled, and the land remained, then this trouble would have been over long ago.[1]

On 17 December 1864, Governor Grey announced his intention to confiscate 'in the country between Wanganui and New Plymouth, and in the Province of Taranaki, such land belonging to the rebels' as he might think fit. What land he thought fit was detailed in an order in council dated 30 January 1865 declaring a relatively restricted area, designated Middle Taranaki, to be a 'district' under the New Zealand Settlements Act 1863. This was followed by another order in council of 2 September 1865 which declared a much larger area, designated Ngatiawa and Ngatiruanui, to be districts under the same act, but also promised that no land of any loyal inhabitant would be taken except as necessary for the security of the country, and then only against payment of compensation. It further provided that all rebel inhabitants who came in within a 'reasonable time' and submitted to the Queen's authority would receive a 'sufficient' quantity of land within the named district, under crown grant.[2]

Confiscation had been a hotly debated issue for some time and became a source of contention between Grey and his responsible advisers, each accusing the other of originating the idea. According to William Gisborne it was the premier, Alfred Domett alone and unaided, who devised the scheme of confiscation and military settlement. The first mention of confiscation came in a Domett minute to Grey of 5 May 1863 in which he advised that the land between Omata and

Tataraimaka, the property of those implicated in the Oakura ambush, should be declared forfeit and utilised as a site for a military settlement.[3] As the outbreak of war looked certain, Domett suggested one way of guaranteeing the future peace and security of the country would be to confiscate as much enemy territory as necessary on which to establish European settlements. He even considered bringing Ngapuhi down 'to act in concert' with the Europeans against Taranaki and Ngatiruanui, on the promise that they could keep any land they might conquer. The following month ministers 'cordially concurred' in a plan put forward by Grey for the defence of the southern frontier of Auckland province, which included the confiscation of 'the lands of the hostile Natives, part of which . . . would be given away and settled on military tenure . . . and the remainder sold to defray the expenses of the War'.[4]

In July, the governor issued a proclamation notifying the Waikato chiefs that those who remained peaceful would be 'protected in their persons, property, and land', while those who waged war against the Queen would 'take the consequences of their acts, and . . . forfeit the right to the possession of their lands guaranteed to them by the Treaty of Waitangi'.[5] Although this proclamation was dated 11 July, it was not made known to the Maori community until two or three days after General Cameron and his troops had crossed the Mangatawhiri stream on 12 July, and it was hardly sufficient warning of things to come. The government itself had not determined exactly what was to come. From a comparatively modest proposal to introduce 5,000 military settlers, put forward in Domett's memo of 31 July, within a few weeks the number of settlers and the extent of the confiscation had quadrupled.[6]

The government considered the Waikato tribes the most powerful, influential and warlike in the country, and thought that if they could be taught a lesson, one 'so severely felt and so much dreaded' as the confiscation of their land, then other tribes would take heed – especially those who at the time were considered to be wavering in their loyalty. According to this ministerial reasoning it was the paucity of the European population and the Maori's lack of respect for settler and government power which had led them to rebel, so the solution would be to introduce a sufficient European population to overawe Maori and secure peace. Ministers thought the confiscation of land would settle the difficulty with the Waikato tribes and a similar plan could then be applied to the 'rebellious tribes of Taranaki'. But since the 'civilization and improvement of the native race' was, they claimed, their prime concern, they undertook to respect the rights of those who had not rebelled and to leave, even to those who had rebelled, 'amply sufficient' land for all 'useful purposes'.[7]

Just what was amply sufficient land for a Maori and to what useful purposes he was required to put it were not then spelled out, but it soon became obvious that a civilised Englishman required a more ample sufficiency of land than was deemed good for a Maori. Within a few months, the colonial secretary and native minister William Fox stated his own conviction that it was most prejudicial to the native race for them to retain possession of large tracts of land which they neither used nor allowed others to use. But European and Maori ideas of what constituted land 'use' differed markedly. Fox himself delighted in over 3,500 acres of choice land between Marton and the Rangitikei river.[8]

Grey summoned the General Assembly for 19 October 1863 so that it might consider a plan for the introduction of military settlers which had been framed by his responsible advisers, but was based on that which he had adopted in British Kaffraria. So far it would seem that governor and ministers were in accord on the proposed confiscation. Even before parliament met, Grey had agreed that the first 2,000 of the proposed 5,000 military settlers possibly from the goldfields of Australia and Otago should be enrolled for service in the Auckland province, after which they would be allotted 50-acre farms to be held on military tenure.[9] In apprising the superintendent of Auckland of the scheme, Domett mentioned in passing that the formation of the planned settlements would probably involve the acquisition of land from 'friendly Natives, which must be bought in the usual way'.[10] The problem of distinguishing and separating the land of loyal and rebel natives was passed over very lightly in 1863, but it was a problem that was to bedevil successive governments for years to come.

When parliament met, Domett laid before the General Assembly a 12-page memo on how the necessary roads and military settlement were to be created and paid for. Already 8,000 men were deemed necessary for about 40 settlements, to be located on 190,000–200,000 acres of prime Taranaki land from Waitara to Waitotara, and 20,000 men and 1,000 miles of road were required overall. By a financial sleight of hand, Domett felt able to justify the raising of a £4 million loan, £1 million of which would be required for expenses of war and could be repaid from revenue raised by the sale of confiscated land. Domett felt it would be 'only just and reasonable' to take all the Waikato and Taranaki lands best suited to European settlement, leaving the rebellious tribes 'the valleys and plains further up in the interior'. The government, he declared, would banish Maori to the interior, but not 'drive them to desperation and the mountains'; indeed 100,000 acres could be left to the resident tribes of Taranaki.[11]

Although Domett resigned soon afterwards, the new Whitaker-Fox ministry adopted in the main Domett's elaborate scheme for raising money and confiscating land. Henry Sewell, a former premier and attorney-general, condemned the scheme as a proposal founded on wrong. He said it startled everybody, as it passed far beyond the proposal outlined on 31 July and would inevitably result in a collision and conflict of races.[12] The former chief justice, Sir William Martin, wrote a long and thoughtful paper on 'the plans now proposed for terminating the troubles of the Colony', which he sent to Fox with the request that it be submitted both to the colonial government and to the secretary of state for the colonies, the Duke of Newcastle. Martin pointed out that the imperial government exercised with great caution the right to take for purposes of defence or other national concerns the land of those who were represented in the legislature, and questioned the right of the colonial government to take in an unlimited and arbitrary fashion, the lands of those who were not so represented.

Martin's paper was a cry for justice for a wronged and oppressed people who 'are not attached to our system, because it has presented so little to be attached to', who 'have not fallen short of their part in the original contract more than we . . . have of ours', and who 'have not, as a nation, sinned more against us than we, the superior and protecting power, have against them'. He warned that the present policy would leave behind it the seeds of future war and would increase rather than diminish distrust.[13]

These prophetic words went unheeded. Fox enclosed a memo setting out his views on 'Sir William's able and elaborate paper' when he forwarded it to Grey. His overall assessment was that Martin's argument boiled down to a question of whether or not the Assembly had the power to confiscate land from those in rebellion. Martin had not talked of rebels or rebellion but of widespread distrust or disaffection and opposition to government; of the small turbulent minority and the large number living at peace. His paper was in the main an exposition of European injustice to Maori. Knowing full well that he would be accused of bias, he admitted that his statement was in some sense one-sided: 'it is the setting forth of that side of the question which is constantly dropped out of sight, while the other is made as prominent as possible'.[14]

The act which gave the Assembly power to confiscate land, euphemistically entitled the New Zealand Settlements Act, was finally passed by the Legislative Council on 17 November 1863, the day after Martin sent his paper to Fox, and came into law on 3 December. Defending government action, Fox declared that the government proposed 'to confiscate (that is, to take without compensation) no lands except those of which the owners have been engaged in open rebellion'. He stressed that the new law gave the government no power to *confiscate* other lands, but it did give power, on payment of full compensation, to *take* other lands, Maori or European, for such public purposes as the establishment of military villages.[15] This nice distinction would be cold comfort to those Maori who had never fought but who would now lose their land, but it would not be lost on Europeans. They stood to lose no land for 'public purposes'. There were no Europeans living 'on the frontier' where it was proposed to form military settlements; the whole purpose of establishing such settlements was to introduce Europeans to the area.

In moving the second reading of the bill, Fox observed that its primary aim was to aid in the suppression of the existing rebellion by introducing 'so strong a population into the disturbed districts . . . that the Natives might be deterred from all hopes of successful resistance to the establishment of law'. This of course meant that the government must have land on which to settle this population; and the land was available: it was that of 'those tribes who have been in rebellion'. About 4 million acres were available on which to establish 15,000–20,000 souls. J. E. FitzGerald, MHR for Ellesmere, and former superintendent of Canterbury, labelled the bill 'a repeal . . . of every engagement of every kind . . . which has ever been made by the British Crown with Natives', and expressed the fear that no sooner would Maori get to hear of the bill than every last one of them would be driven to a state of hopeless rebellion. Fitzgerald's spirited speech made some impact, for Fox added clauses to his bill with the object, among other things, of reassuring 'really loyal natives' that they would be dealt with 'as Europeans', and that only the lands of those in rebellion would be confiscated.[16] There was no question in the government's mind but that the Taranaki tribes were among those who were in rebellion. Sixty-five years later, the Sim Commission declared that they were not in rebellion in the first Taranaki war, and that in the second, which was only a continuation of the first, they were forced into the position of rebels within the meaning of the New Zealand Settlements Act and in the circumstances should not have been punished by the confiscation of any of their land.[17]

The effect of the New Zealand Settlements Act was to proclaim confiscated land to be crown land, freed from all other title or claim, by declaring it to be a district within the provisions of the act. Such districts, within which were the lands of any people deemed to have been in rebellion since 1 January 1863, could be proclaimed from time to time as the governor in council thought fit, and set apart for the establishment of settlements.[18] Compensation would be paid to those with 'title, interest or claim' to such lands, provided they had not themselves been in rebellion or aided, assisted or comforted those who had; and to those who, having been in rebellion, should come in, deliver up their arms, and submit to trial within a specified time.

The New Zealand Settlements Bill was accompanied through the House by the Suppression of Rebellion Bill and the New Zealand Loan Bill. This latter was to enable the government to raise £3 million, partly to help defray the cost of suppressing the rebellion and partly to pay for the introduction of settlers and the creation of settlements. The sum of £100,000 was to be set aside to compensate 'loyal Natives for land which may be required for settlement'. According to the colonial treasurer, Reader Wood, the 'rebel districts' in Waikato and Taranaki contained about 8.5 million acres, half of it of suitable quality for settlement. Deducting from the 1.25 million acres required for settlement of both European and Maori, there would be a balance of 3 million acres, about half of it available for sale. By judicious handling, Reader Wood thought this land would realise at least £3 million – but he would be sorry if the House supposed that the government 'looked upon this as a commercial undertaking'; it was just that details of the monetary transactions involved needed clarifying to show that the proposed loan could be repaid 'without any difficulty whatever by the sale of land'.[19] Early in the new year, Reader Wood set off for England to argue the colony's case for the loan with the imperial government.

Meanwhile the ministry received Newcastle's despatch of 26 November, stating that he did not disapprove of the measures outlined to him by Grey on 29 August and that he thought aggressors such as Waikato might 'properly be punished by a confiscation of a large part of their common property'. However, he warned against wholesale confiscation as a measure which would excite the cupidity of both old and new settlers eager for the acquisition of land and make Maori desperate, since they might view the measure 'not as a punishment for rebellion and murder, but as a new and flagrant proof of the determination of the colonists to possess themselves of the land at all risks . . . and at any cost'. Ministers were at pains to assure him they felt no apprehension that land confiscation could not be 'confined within wise and just limits', and said they had taken particular care to inform the tribes that the property of innocent persons would be respected and that punishment would be proportionate to guilt.[20]

Grey's letter to Newcastle of 6 January 1864, sent with the copy of the New Zealand Settlements Act, appeared to agree with the intentions of the act, but in fact Grey was already beginning to evince alarm at his ministers' real intentions. While he believed that this rebellion required more severe measures (including the confiscation of land) than any previous ones, he maintained that 'acting upon the principle of the great wisdom of showing a large generosity towards defeated rebel subjects', he would not carry the system too far. That others were suspicious of ministers' intentions was also made clear by the Aborigines Protection Society when, early in 1864, they sent Grey an address 'very numerously and influentially signed'.[21] The society expressed itself 'alarmed by the pertinacity with which . . . it has been proposed to confiscate the Lands of all contumacious and rebellious Natives'. They could see clearly what the ministry was determined to ignore: that confiscation in New Zealand, as elsewhere, would only intensify disaffection and perpetuate 'the strife of the races . . . through successive generations'. Grey assured the society that he would do his best to ensure that the confiscation of a 'considerable portion' of the territories of those in rebellion would be carried out in a 'spirit of liberal generosity, and of mercy'. But he persisted in his view that such punishment would 'deter others from embarking in a similar career' and added that it was the government's intention to 'secure to that numerous part of the Native population who have taken no active share in the present war, the whole of their landed possessions' – although he must have been aware that under the act of confiscation this would be impossible wherever loyal and rebel natives held land in common.

Grey was a master of the art of manipulating the written word, but ministers, especially Fox and Frederick Whitaker, who had been attorney-general in the Domett ministry, were apt pupils. Fox entirely concurred with Grey's observations and saw no reason to 'offer any on the part of the Ministry', yet a month later (perhaps at Whitaker's urging) he had concocted an amazing reply to the society's address which, he said, had 'impugned' the government's confiscation policy. It was a masterpiece of mis-statement, selective reporting and the 'monstrous falsehoods' of which he accused Maori. It also stressed that the object of confiscation was not punishment or retaliation but simply that of ensuring peace. He explained that Maori were fond of war, and if they could have 'the excitement . . . of a summer's campaign when it pleases them, with liberty to retain their lands when it is over without suffering any losses except their wretched dwellings and a season's crops . . . they will not easily be deterred from renewing hostilities'.[22] He did not add that their wretched dwellings and a season's crops were all Maori possessed besides their ancestral lands, the very foundation of their being, of which full, exclusive and undisturbed possession had been guaranteed them by the Treaty of Waitangi. Fox insisted that the war must be carried on until the Maori community was really convinced of European superiority. While he may have been alluding to military superiority, the superiority of the white race was certainly implied.[23]

Fox's letter to the Aborigines Protection Society was challenged even before it left New Zealand. Grey, wishing to clarify the Maori view on confiscation in his own mind, referred the letter to the Reverend Richard Taylor, whom Fox had wished to quote as corroborating his own view. The 'memorandumiad'[24] – the 'endless exchange of lengthy documents of an increasingly petty and futile description'[25] – between the governor and his responsible advisers over land confiscation had begun. There was no love lost between Fox and Grey. As the man on the spot in the New Zealand Company's settlements in Nelson and Wellington, Fox had felt that the governor's 'imperfect perception . . . of circumstances at a distance' impaired his ability to cope quickly and efficiently with day-to-day situations. Fox blamed many of the deficiencies and inefficiencies of early colonial government on Grey personally. The fact that Grey seemed to take the part of the Maori people and of the Colonial Office against colonists and their 'selfish desire to seize Maori land' led to what his biographer, Rutherford, described as the 'popular pastime of Governor-bating'. Not satisfied with attacking the public figure of the governor, Fox and others descended to attacking Grey personally in print.[26] Fox followed this up on later visits to England with a series of communications with Earl Grey, then secretary of state for the colonies, and with two books on New Zealand which were quite vituperative in their attacks on Governor Grey and his policies.[27] While Grey's use and misuse of information was often as selective as Fox's, he generally managed to maintain his dignity in print and refrained from personal attacks. In a despatch to Secretary of State Edward Cardwell of 29 September 1864, he even described Fox as 'a very kind hearted and benevolent man, from whom I am very sorry to differ'. Fox was, as Rutherford says, more provocative than provoked, although according to Alfred Saunders his tongue and his pen were guided by the far stronger will of Whitaker.[28]

If Grey had a cunning animal to deal with in Fox, he had a veritable wolf by the tail with Whitaker as premier and attorney-general. The Whitaker-Fox ministry, which took over in October 1863, was dominated by Auckland capitalists, notably Whitaker and Thomas Russell, his partner in a successful legal practice which concerned itself largely with speculative land dealing. Russell, a founder of the Bank of New Zealand, was Whitaker's minister of defence and it was impossible to distinguish where their political involvement ended and their business involvement began.[29] Together they constituted a formidable force in favour of confiscation of rebel land – for profit, not punishment.

In April 1864, Whitaker submitted to Grey a draft proclamation declaring that 'Chiefs and Tribes of Waikato' had 'justly forfeited all their land', and reiterating the peace terms they were prepared to offer Waikato and other rebel Maori should they submit before 1 July. The proclamation was the subject of considerable discussion between the governor and his ministers both before and after Grey hesitatingly signed a Maori version of the draft on 30 April. The paper war Grey generated over the proclamation finally led to the ministry's decision not to proceed with its publication.[30] Some of the disagreement was over the question of whether or not rebels who chose to submit should be obliged to surrender their arms, the ministry believing that they should and Grey that they should not. However, a much more serious disagreement arose over the question of confiscation itself, with Grey and his ministers accusing each other of being the originator of the scheme. Grey questioned the legality of the ministers' opinion that the rebel natives had forfeited all their lands, but Whitaker was satisfied that in point of law they had, despite the Treaty of Waitangi whose provisions, ministers believed, could last only so long as Maori fulfilled their obligations under it. And 'if there were any doubt on this point . . . the New Zealand Settlements Act . . . would virtually justify' the proposed declaration and 'afford ample means of . . . carrying it into effect'.[31]

This was too much for Grey, who felt that by signing such a proclamation he was being made to trifle with the 'whole future destiny of the Maori nation' and made the means of reducing from wealth to poverty generations of loyal and rebel Maori alike. When his ministers denied that it was on *their* advice that the rebels were to be informed they had forfeited all their lands, Grey felt the whole responsibility for confiscation was being thrust upon him – a situation that would suit the wily Whitaker very well, since his definition of confiscation was 'appropriation of land by the governor'. Grey argued that the New Zealand Settlements Act could hardly be construed as an act intended to deprive present and future generations of the Maori race of all their lands when their crime was perhaps no greater than 'comforting a parent, a child or husband, who had borne arms against the Queen'. His request that the proclamation be revoked brought forth an outburst from Whitaker, who felt that the governor in 'his zeal for the Maori . . . appears to forget the European colonists'.[32]

It was becoming very clear that Grey and Whitaker had quite different schemes of confiscation in mind. Grey conceded that his views had never varied on the 'propriety and necessity' of confiscating territory from Waikato, Ngatimaniapoto and Ngatiruanui, but insisted that the extent of confiscation should vary in proportion to the degree of guilt of those tribes. Whitaker, on the other hand, admitted the justice of confiscation as punishment for rebellion but qualified his views by saying it would not necessarily be 'proper and expedient' to confiscate, even though such a penalty might have been justly incurred.[33] He was obviously planning a scheme of confiscation based on government expedience rather than Maori guilt – one that confiscated productive land rather than rebel land.

The ministry now tried repeatedly to pin Grey down and have him proclaim districts under the New Zealand Settlements Act, and he as often managed to procrastinate. He was stalling for time while awaiting instructions from Newcastle; they were anxious for 'political and financial reasons' to get their hands on confiscated land – desirable Waikato and Tauranga land. The act required them first to establish military settlers on the land; having done that they could at last start replenishing their coffers through the long-awaited land sales. Before Grey would put the act into effect he wanted a clear statement to be issued as to the extent to which confiscation would be carried, for he believed it was essential that rebel natives who 'came in' should understand clearly what land they would forfeit and what land they could retain.[34]

This request foreshadowed the instructions received about this time from the secretary of state. Cardwell, who had succeeded to this office, was not as compliant as Newcastle. He recognised the need to inflict 'a salutary penalty upon the authors of a war' but objected to the powers of the act being permanently embodied in the laws of New Zealand and forming 'a standing qualification to the Treaty of Waitangi'. He urged that the guilty be carefully distinguished from the innocent, and that punishment be commensurate with crime. He felt that it was justifiable to recoup some of the war expenditure from the sale of confiscated land, but since most of that expenditure had been outlayed by Britain he insisted that confiscation or cession of land be limited to ensuring peace and maintaining British honour. The imperial government desired that cession of land be a condition of peace, but if this was found to be impractical Grey was to allow implementation of the act subject to certain restrictions: that its duration be limited to two years; that the land to be confiscated be promptly defined in area and location by a specially constituted independent commission; and that it be clearly understood that Grey's 'concurrence' in any forfeiture would be withheld unless he was personally satisfied that confiscation was 'just and moderate'[35].

Grey had pointed out, and Cardwell underlined the fact, that former wars in New Zealand had resulted in no extensive confiscation of land and therefore no smouldering legacy of resentments which had driven Maori to take part in later conflicts. Grey claimed as a virtue the fact that he had not confiscated land after the northern war of 1845–46, although, as James Belich pointed out, Heke and Kawiti never submitted but rather made peace with their Maori antagonists, a peace which the governor was then invited to share; Grey had not been in a position to force northern Maori into submission and to impose confiscation.[36] However, the point remains valid that there was no confiscation in the north, and no 'smouldering resentment'. The pity is that Grey did not remember the lesson. Cardwell now accepted Grey's reasoning that this occasion called for measures of severity which were however still to be tempered with 'generosity towards defeated rebel subjects'.

The arrival of Cardwell's despatch may have decided the ministry to provide Grey with some sort of an answer to his queries. They finally did so on 25 June, when they outlined the extent of the confiscation they proposed in Waikato and provided for possible subsequent confiscation of Maniapoto land. In Taranaki they proposed to confiscate sufficient rebel land 'on both sides of the Town of New Plymouth, including land of the Ngatiawa, Taranaki and Ngatiruanui tribes' to allow for the establishment of military settlements 'at such points as will provide for the security of the Town and the settled districts around it . . . and to afford a substantial contribution to the expenses of suppressing the rebellion'.[37] This was a conveniently vague description. Whitaker went on to say that it was also proposed to confiscate rebel land 'from the Waitotara River to a convenient distance, 10 or 20 miles to the North of the Patea River, including Waimate'. In effect all rebel land from the Waitara to the Waitotara was to be confiscated, yet ministers did not consider it would be 'necessary to interfere with the properties of the Loyal Natives, except in some special cases where they hold lands in common with Rebels'. In such cases loyal natives would be allotted their share of land, which they would then hold on crown grant. Lest these proposals not be vague enough, Whitaker provided that should circumstances 'modify' ministers' views, or the conduct of the natives 'render it just and expedient to go further than is now contemplated', ministers would reserve the right 'to alter or modify' their proposals.

In attempting to abide by Cardwell's instructions that the governor was expected to act on his own judgement if ministers' opinions as to peace terms should differ from his, Grey continually came into conflict with Whitaker. When his ministers naively declared that *as yet* practically 'no difference of opinion' existed between the governor and his advisers,[38] Grey suggested to Cardwell that the secretary of state could judge for himself that 'considerable differences of opinion' had arisen from time to time on subjects 'of great Imperial concern'. This despatch of Grey's was a very calm and rational statement of the difficulties he faced with an Assembly that met infrequently and then only for brief periods, ministers who were mostly absent from the capital, manipulation by Whitaker and Russell, and a provincial and racist European population engaged in a 'civil war' with the country's main landholders, who were unrepresented in the legislature.[39]

In the weeks that followed the paper war continued, with Grey resisting actual confiscation of land and ministers pressing upon him the urgent need for it. Each claimed their course was designed to give effect to the instructions issued by Cardwell. The main issue was complicated by side issues, such as the surrender of arms and the escape of prisoners, and finally resolved itself into a question of cession as against confiscation of land. On 7 September, Grey submitted to his ministers a draft proclamation which offered a free pardon to any rebel (but not murderer) who would, before 22 October, take the oath of allegiance and cede such territory as would be notified him by the governor and the military commander.[40] Whitaker replied that if the ministers were to agree to such a proclamation they wished to dictate its terms, especially in regard to the amount of land to be either ceded or confiscated. Grey refused to meet the

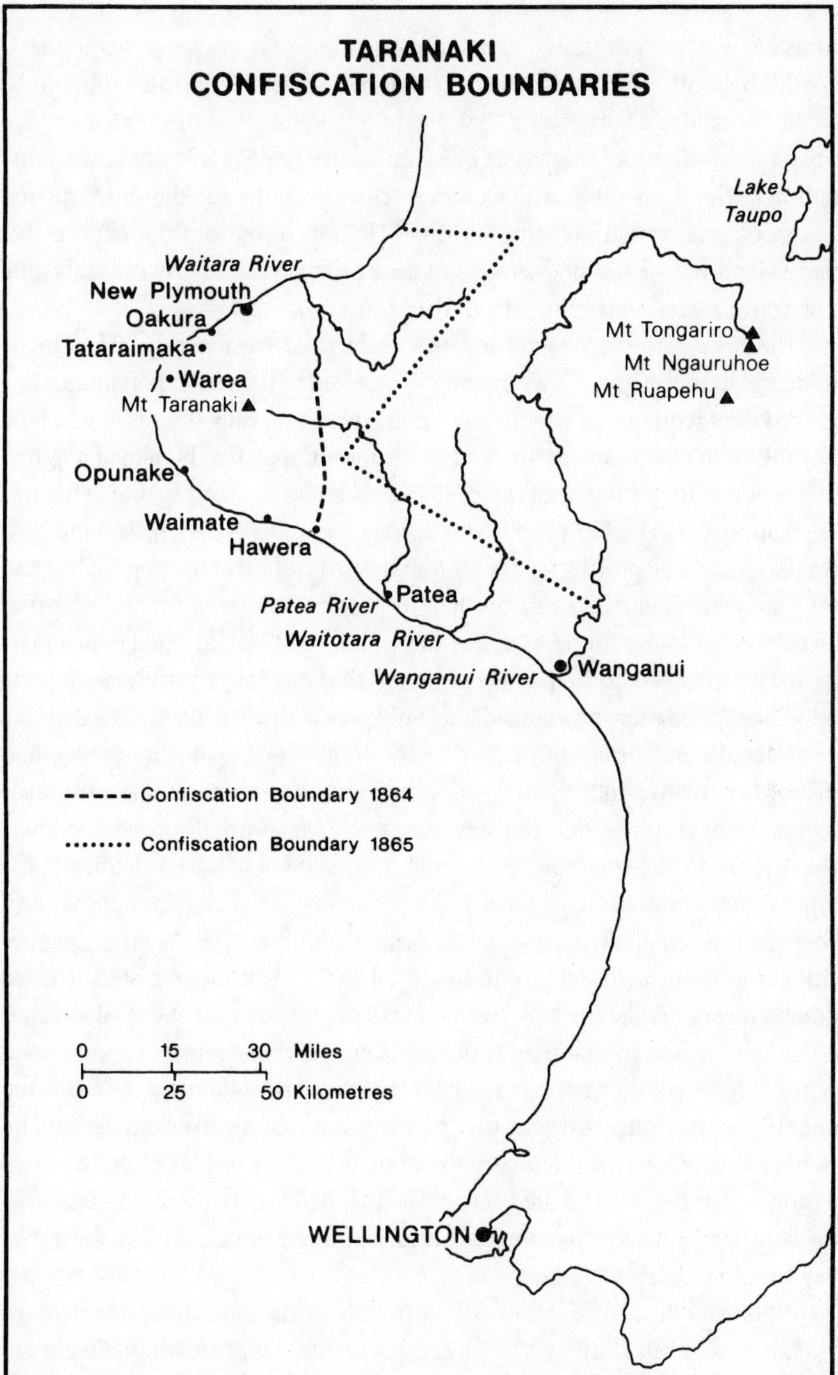

Based on: J. Rutherford, *Sir George Grey*, p525

ministers' wishes, and they declined to 'acquiesce' in the proclamation as it stood. Above all, they would not agree that mere cession of territory should be deemed a 'sufficient submission'. They required nothing less than that every last rebel should surrender his arms. Grey would have none of it, and declared that with or without his ministers' acquiescence he would issue the proclamation as it stood. He was still fencing for time. He hoped, but did not expect, that many Maori would accept the terms of the proclamation, but by promulgating it he could at least delay the start of the 'summer campaign'.

The governor's responsible advisers, feeling they had lost their 'legitimate influence' in the affairs of government, now asked to be relieved of office. Grey ignored their request and continued to press them to specify the amount of land they meant to confiscate. By the end of the month they finally named a figure: 1.6 million acres, 600,000 of them in Taranaki, and near Wanganui. This was less than they had earlier proposed, but they had modified their demands lest they be accused of 'prolonging the war for the acquisition of territory'. They had not suffered a change of heart but had been stirred to action by the return of the colonial treasurer from London with the news that he had failed to negotiate the loan which was to help solve so many of the colony's problems. Reader Wood had found there was considerable disquiet at the Colonial Office over the government's intentions with regard to the confiscation policy, and attributed this partly to interference by Grey. Now, with their honour in question and their financial policy in tatters, the governor's advisers formally tendered their resignations on 30 September.[41] Grey still contrived not to accept them, and the pinpricking correspondence continued for almost another two months until November, when a new ministry was formed with Frederick Weld as premier and Harry Atkinson as defence minister. On 6 October, the ministers tried to induce Grey to invoke the New Zealand Settlements Act over the Waikato land in their possession so that they could settle emigrants – and tap 'an important source of revenue': they hoped to sell £100,000's worth of land by the following January. Grey reminded them that according to Cardwell's instructions he should not bring the act into operation until and unless he had failed to obtain cessions of land from 'defeated rebels'. It was therefore necessary to issue his proclamation; ministers need not acquiesce in it nor be responsible for it, but they should publish it.[42]

When the proclamation finally appeared in the *Gazette* of 26 October 1864, it gave rebels until 10 December to submit, take the oath of allegiance, and cede so much of their land as Grey and General Cameron should decide.

When Grey tried to involve the ministers in decisions relating to required cessions of land, Whitaker replied coldly that they had not countersigned the proclamation so the responsibility was not theirs. 'Where there is the power, there must rest the Responsibility. The Governor has assumed the power, and thereby released the Ministers, the General Assembly, and the Colony from Responsibility.'[43]

It was clear that the governor's and ministers' views on the 'forfeiture of land' were far apart – and that they always had been, despite ministers' protestations to the contrary.[44] Each accused the other of not fulfilling Cardwell's instructions, but those instructions were quite clear: Grey was not to agree to any forfeiture of land unless he was 'Personally satisfied that the confiscation was just and moderate'. The ministers' proposals were never that, and Grey resisted them with all the guile at his command. The wrangle filled pages of print and months of time, but it had achieved one thing: no Maori land had yet been confiscated. Grey had procrastinated to good effect. Yet within a month, and just one week after the day of grace named in his previous proclamation, he was ready to sign a new one for Weld.[45] The reasons for Grey's change of heart were manifold and complex, and were dictated to some extent by General Cameron's actions and by questions of responsible government. There are also suggestions that it may have been an effort on Grey's part to boost his diminishing mana, or even that it was simply 'the acquiescence of an opportunist'; but it had been a long struggle and Grey was not in good health. Although he had foiled Fox and Whitaker, his attempt to obtain cessions of land had failed. He had agreed to Weld's conditions on taking office and knew he would face further ministerial resignations should he and his new responsible advisers fail to agree. However, he did believe Weld's confiscation policy would be more moderate than that of his late ministers.[46]

The proclamation Grey signed on 17 December 1864 designated as confiscated all the land in military occupation in the Waikato and as much rebel land in Taranaki as he should think fit. It also provided that the lands of those who had not been in rebellion would be secured to them, and that those who chose to surrender would have some part of their land returned to them. It did not require that every Maori surrender his arms. This proclamation is, broadly, a statement of Grey's position as it was from the start: land would be confiscated for punishment, not profit; punishment would be commensurate with guilt; the land of loyal natives would not be touched; and Maori were not to be totally humbled as Fox and Whitaker would humble them, for their word would be accepted as proof of their intention to surrender. But while the order in council of 30 January 1865 designated a comparatively modest area, 'Middle Taranaki' as a district under the New Zealand Settlements Act, in the Waikato, Grey's conscience had been 'stretched' by the Weld ministry 'from Ngaruawahia to Orakau', in the 'worst injustice ever perpetrated by a New Zealand government'.[47]

Cardwell expressed his concern that the 17 December proclamation announced a more extensive confiscation than he had anticipated, but he was satisfied that the promises it made to loyal natives and rebels prepared to submit would be faithfully observed. His faith in contemporary and future ministries was sadly misplaced, although in August, while planning the 'real instrument' of confiscation, Weld was still proclaiming that the intention of his ministry was 'to confine the confiscation of land taken from the rebel Natives within such limits as may inflict no undue hardship on the rebels, nor on those who have remained loyal'.[48]

But the government's intentions, as explained by the new native minister, J. E. FitzGerald, when appointing Robert Parris civil commissioner for Taranaki, were not simply to secure an area around the settlement of New Plymouth, but rather 'to confiscate the whole of the lands, to a distance of twenty miles or thereabouts from the coast, lying between the Waitotara River and the White Cliffs'. The Weld ministry could apparently believe this would inflict no undue hardship on Maori since it was not their intention either to hold or occupy all the land or to expel any of those tribes who were occupying it. Believing that the greatest mischief arose from delays in settling natives on the land, their stated aim was 'at once' to settle on 'sufficient' land all the local Maori who were willing 'to come in, accept crown grants, and promise to live peaceably under the law', and to return to the loyal natives 'as nearly as possible the exact land they are entitled to now'. Weld naively explained that this massive confiscation, which belied both the government's and Grey's professed intentions, would not be a source of further irritation to Maori since it would be clearly stated to them and immediately implemented.[49]

The actual confiscation was promulgated by order in council on 2 September 1865 and was accompanied by a proclamation of peace which declared prematurely that the war which commenced at Oakura was at an end. It went on to describe confiscation as punishment and a deterrent, and to promise that no further punishment would be inflicted on the rebels excepting those few involved in certain acts which the government considered particularly treacherous. It reiterated the promise to restore land at once to well-disposed natives and, most importantly, promised that commissioners would be sent forthwith to settle the people on the land and to 'mark out the boundaries of the blocks which they are to occupy'.[50]

The Weld ministry may have had the best of intentions with regard to their promises, but they were unable to withstand settler pressure to implement the confiscation policy in settler rather than Maori interests, and in any case by October 1865 they were out of office. Those who succeeded them were even more assiduous in their efforts to settle Europeans on 'conquered' land, and the non-fulfilment, by ministry after ministry, of the promises contained in the confiscation and peace proclamations was at the heart of the troubles which plagued the west coast and the whole colony for years to come. Confiscation left in its wake a bitterness which to this day has never been effaced.

CHAPTER THREE

The Survey of the Waimate Plains

1878

IN THE YEARS BETWEEN 1865 AND 1878, NO ATTEMPT WAS MADE TO enforce the confiscation north of the Waingongoro river. Most of the land remained confiscated on paper, but there was a world of difference to Maori between confiscation on paper and confiscation on the ground. The peace proclamation had assured them that no more land would be taken, but year by year, as funds became available, surveyors were moved onto confiscated land in other parts of the country to survey for sale or for military settlement. This 'creeping confiscation' of land belonging to loyal Maori or to returned rebels, who in many cases had occupied it peacefully since the wars, had led to unrest and interruptions to the surveys in other parts of the west coast and in Waikato and Bay of Plenty, and to a fresh uprising under the Ngatiruanui chief, Titokowaru, in 1868–69. But by 1878, the country had been preoccupied for many years with issues of colonisation and public works rather than Maori affairs. Maori were supposed to appreciate the benefits close European settlement was to bring them, and the government felt secure in the belief that they held the confiscated lands by conquest and were free to occupy them as and when they saw fit.

As the government had failed to occupy the west coast lands on two occasions – after the confiscation and again after Titokowaru's war – the local tribes had naturally come to see the confiscation as a non-event. This view had been reinforced from time to time by promises that those who remained at peace would be permitted to retain their lands, and by the curious system whereby the government paid Maori and accepted deeds of cession for land supposedly confiscated in 1865. The 1870s, the 'Vogel years', were a time of financial loans and public works, and it was obvious to each succeeding government that peace at any price was preferable to a renewal of the 'native difficulty' if loans were to be raised in the English market and settlement of the country continued. But as the colony's debt increased and as settlement proceeded, there was a pressing need both for a new source of finance and for more land. The great fertile Waimate plains lying 'idle and unused' in Maori hands were a prize no longer to be ignored. When the Grey government turned its attention to the plains and in July 1878, without the least effort to survey or even define the promised reserves for the resident Maori population, began instead to survey for sale, there was spirited reaction from the west coast tribes.

There had been many chances to put the matter of the confiscated lands on a more satisfactory footing. After Taurua's Pakakohe people who had been implicated in Titokowaru's war were returned from imprisonment in Dunedin in 1872, they were finally settled on reserves south of the Waingongoro, but no reserves were delineated north of the river for Titokowaru's people.[1] The native minister, Donald McLean, had decided 'he would not abandon the confiscation: but neither would he enforce it'. Rather he would try to extinguish Ngatiruanui claims in return for payment of compensation.[2] This was certainly not a situation conceded by the acts and proclamations of confiscation, according to which Titokowaru and his people had twice been in rebellion and had never 'come in and submitted to the Queen's authority'. But Titokowaru was still widely feared and the government, deprived of the presence of imperial troops and anxious to raise loan money in England, was in no position to risk another encounter with him. It was preferable to gamble on his remaining peaceful if he was permitted to return to his ancestral lands from exile with Ngatimaru, and then attempt to buy his cooperation.

Over the years, a succession of native ministers issued instructions to Robert Parris, the civil commissioner for Taranaki, with regard to the settlement of the confiscated lands. FitzGerald's instructions of 1865 to negotiate with all Maori of the Taranaki district and persuade them 'to come in at once and accept defined blocks of land within the confiscated territory' were followed in 1866 by those of J. C. Richmond, head of the Native Department in the Stafford government, who instructed Parris to induce absentee owners of Ngatiruanui and Ngatiawa to abandon their claims in return for reserves and monetary payment, and to settle the claims of loyal Maori and make reserves for surrendered rebels to the north of the Patea river. He was to settle the claims in 'the rest of the Ngatiawa Coast Block' by leaving all the land of the Taranaki chiefs Wi Kingi Matakatea and Arama Karaka, 'almost the only loyal men' in their area, and by making reserves of up to 50 acres per head, including 'kaingas, fishing stations and any other favourite spots', for surrendering rebels.[3]

The settlement of the question of the west coast confiscated lands was seen as the key to peace and prosperity in the area, so in 1872 instructions were again issued to Parris, this time by McLean who differentiated between the lands north of the Waingongoro and those south of it. A start had been made south of the river on allotting lands to military settlers and reserves to the local tribes, but awards of the Compensation Court still had not been defined. North of the river it was quite another matter, and in this regard McLean made his famous statement that the 'lands north of Waingongoro, as far as Stoney River, although nominally confiscated, are, with the exception of 1,400 acres at Opunake, quite unavailable for settlement, until arrangements are made with the Natives for lands sufficient for their own requirements'. Parris was to begin negotiations with Maori owners in the vicinity of the Oeo river and, in order that the lands might be free from 'all difficulties and obstructions', he was to pay them compensation at rates not exceeding five shillings an acre for all lands they might care to relinquish.[4] Despite all the earlier protestations that confiscation was in no way abhorrent to Maori, McLean admitted it to have been a very sore point with them, so much so that he had 'refrained from entering upon the subject', not wishing to 'open old wounds without the means of healing them'.[5] The long promised reserves and a little compensation were to be the salve with which to dress the wounds.

In 1876, McLean updated these instructions for Charles Brown, who in July 1875 had taken over from Parris as civil commissioner for Taranaki, and informed him that not only had Maori 'failed to recognise the reality of confiscation' but they had even got an inflated view of the value of their lands. Brown was now authorised to pay up to seven shillings and sixpence an acre but warned that 'everything like extravagant concession . . . should be carefully avoided', lest those who had lost lands south of the Waingongoro become dissatisfied.[6] It was vitally important for the government to 'acquire' the Waimate plains for settlement. It was 11 years since they had been confiscated – on paper – but Maori cared little for the Pakeha's pukapuka. Since there had been no action on the ground and they were now being offered money to 'relinquish' their land, it is hardly surprising they did not recognise the reality of the confiscation. Many times over the years, politicians lamented that the confiscation was a disaster and had cost the colony far more in blood, anguish, and money than it would ever have cost simply to buy the land, and McLean himself declared the confiscated lands to have been 'a very expensive luxury'.[7]

Meanwhile, the belief had grown amongst the west coast tribes that their land was to be restored to them, but in reply to a proposal to this effect, put to the House in July 1872 by Wi Parata, member for Western Maori, McLean declared that 'the land which had been confiscated after due proclamation by the Governor could not be restored'.[8] Then on 5 September 1872, in the debate which brought the Fox government down, Edward Stafford expressed the view that the best thing the government could do with the as-yet unalienated confiscated lands would be to divide them among 'the Natives who, after fair investigation, may be found to have an interest in them': not, he added, 'in answer to any demand of the Natives, but as an act of grace and as an act of policy'. This was enough for Wi Parata, who informed the west coast tribes that now there was a new government who would restore part of their confiscated lands to them. 'From Waingongoro . . . to Taranaki is in reality returned to the Maoris – this is quite decided.'[9] A month later though, in his brief reign as premier and native minister, the same Stafford declared it was 'not the intention of the Government to abandon the confiscated lands at all'. Fox, now safely in opposition, and Thomas Kelly, MHR for New Plymouth, needled Stafford with questions on his intentions with regard to these lands, but Stafford declined to commit the government 'to any specific action'. Kelly kept up the pressure and moved that the government act on the recommendation of the Native Affairs Committee to restore the as-yet unalienated lands to those owners who had remained loyal, or who, having rebelled, had returned to their loyalty. Stafford assured him it was exactly the government's intention to restore to the various hapu *some* land but not necessarily that which they had lost.[10]

This news was soon known on the coast, but within days another ministry had fallen and another promise was broken. Once again, 'sound principle was sacrificed to political expediency' and Maori were left more frustrated than before. Wi Parata reported the tribes anxious to know 'what was to become of them; whether they were to be well or badly treated; whether they were to exist or not'.[11]

Te Whiti also wanted the situation clarified.[12] He and Tohu, a fellow chief and a close relative, had probably never borne arms against the Queen and had certainly not been in rebellion in terms of the New Zealand Settlements Act.[13] In about 1866 they had moved inland from Warea and settled at Parihaka,[14] apparently with the aim of distancing themselves from European contact and from association with warlike groups of Maori. They soon gathered about them local Maori who had been displaced by the confiscation of their land, and those who wished to have no part of Titokowaru's war. From as early as 1869, Te Whiti was being seen by Europeans as a force to be reckoned with on the west coast. Initially Europeans took less notice of Tohu, and it was some years before his name began to appear in official documents.[15] When it did he was often referred to as Te Whiti's lieutenant or fellow prophet. According to those who acted as interpreters for Captain Knollys, Governor Gordon's aide-de-camp, Tohu described himself as Te Whiti's 'associate and equal'.[16] In December 1868, Parris reported visiting 'Pariaka, the place where the Warea Natives under the young chief Te Whiti all reside'. This was his first meeting with the Warea people since war had broken out in 1860, and it took place just when the threat from Titokowaru was at its height.[17] The following year he reported to McLean that the natives living between Umuroa and Waingongoro had agreed to open the road and commence flax operations, but that nothing could be done with 'the Warea Natives without going to Pariaka'. This he was loath to do because some of Titokowaru's followers had taken refuge there.[18] Parris would have done better to encourage them to be at Parihaka with Te Whiti than in the bush with Titokowaru, but that would have involved acknowledging Te Whiti's mana, and this he would not do.

The meeting at Parihaka in March 1870 attracted over 500 visitors from all the tribes between White Cliffs and the Waingongoro and even a 'deputation . . . from Tokangamutu', Tawhiao's headquarters in the King Country. Parris went to the hui hoping to 'reconcile Te Whiti's party to the necessity for the road to be taken through their district' and persuade them not only to agree to the road but to work on it themselves as the followers of other chiefs, such as Matakatea, Pihama and Manaia, were doing. Te Whiti knew full well that roadmaking was but the thin end of the wedge of European encroachment and warned the gathering to beware lest by agreeing to this first step, they lose their land and become homeless. 'Take the people with you,' he said to Parris, 'make the road, take them to town, let them have access to everything, and if they steal or get drunk, mind you do not imprison them.'[19] Reporting to McLean on the approaching August hui, Parris thought Te Whiti would recommend a peace policy, yet he was afraid he would 'dictate action independent of the Government which sooner or later must lead to collision' unless Maori confidence in the government could be restored by patience and 'conciliatory measures'[20] – an approach that would not meet with settler approval.

The September 1870 meeting at Parihaka lasted eight or ten days and was attended by up to 1,200 people, including groups from Waikato and Wairarapa, come supposedly to discuss 'the question of peace or war with the English'. Parris gathered a group of about 700 'friendlies' to accompany him, to counteract the presence of Titokowaru and his band of about 80 armed followers. However, Titokowaru declared that he would remain quiet unless interfered with, and Parris found 'hostilities emphatically condemned by all', especially by Te Whiti himself who for the past three years had been 'exerting his influence to put a stop to hostilities'. Parris commended Te Whiti's pacifism, his gentleness and his simple mode of living, but was concerned about his 'superstitious views' and reported to McLean that Te Whiti believed himself the only one who could restore order out of chaos.[21] The government was obviously more concerned about Titokowaru's influence than Te Whiti's and had sent HMS *Blanche* to patrol off the Taranaki coast while the hui was in progress.

There were many on the west coast who had faith that Te Whiti could bring order to their lives and to whom his pacifism appealed. His 'people' were no longer just from his own hapu or even the Taranaki tribe. Parihaka was already a haven for the dispossessed. The government, in taking land from loyal and rebel alike and failing to provide the long promised reserves, was building the very following for Te Whiti that they came to mistrust and fear. Ngatirahiri had fought as kupapa, or allies of the government yet at war's end they found their land confiscated, and Ngatimutunga returned from the Chathams when they found themselves excluded from Compensation Court awards. Both groups settled at Parihaka and became 'among the staunchest adherents of Te Whiti, and who can wonder at it?' The whole of Ngatitupaea hapu of Ngatiruanui, unwilling to join Titokowaru in 1868 and removed from their land by Parris 'to avoid unpleasant complications with neutral natives', sooner or later ended up at Parihaka. Since the government did not find it 'convenient' to settle them on their former territory south of the Waingongoro and Parris found it 'impossible' to locate them to the north, it was easier simply to 'defer' their case and leave them where they were. However, Parris admitted that if they took matters into their own hands and settled themselves where they chose, the government would find it expedient to provide land for them immediately.[22]

As Te Whiti's influence on the coast increased, the government was in two minds about him. They approved of his pacifism, but did not entirely trust it. After all, Titokowaru had professed peace in 1867 but made war in 1868.[23] This was put down to innate savagery, not justifiable grievances, and in the eyes of the government and especially of the settlers Te Whiti could be expected to act in the same way. The government feared Te Whiti's desire for peace would incline him to oppose works of colonisation in his district which were likely to lead to further discord. He had already intimated to Parris his view of what European civilisation had to offer his people, and the government, used to getting their own way with chiefs through bribes and promises, found him hard to cope with. He could not be bought; he had no desire for money or anything the Europeans had to offer him and was scornful of their vaunted progress.[24] There was a strange dichotomy in the government's view of the role of chiefs. McLean appreciated that they were 'the natural leaders of the people' and he believed that if governments had acknowledged the mana of chiefs and cooperated with them they could have halved the country's difficulties. He was happy to employ 'prominent chiefs to regulate and look after the people of their several districts.'[25] The problem was that Europeans took it upon themselves to decide who were the 'prominent' chiefs whose mana was to be recognised and whose cooperation sought or bought, and those who did not evince enthusiasm for European civilisation were hardly likely to be considered. Rather than meet such chiefs halfway and thus try to win their cooperation, the government ignored and insulted them and made every effort to reduce their sway over their people.

While Te Whiti's influence for peace was commended, fears were expressed that he was accumulating too much power and influence and this 'in one Native' was not desirable. As the days of war receded, a chief had to do more than just keep the peace; he had to cooperate with the public works policy. Parris watched Te Whiti's following grow month by month, boosted by 'the presence of Natives from other parts who have taken refuge under his fanatical ruling', and felt it could only end in the obstruction of colonisation in the district.[26] The problem could have been solved in 1872 by providing land on which the dispossessed could settle, and by acknowledging Te Whiti's mana and thus gaining his cooperation. But the one was deferred yet again and the other was never contemplated by Europeans.

On 8 October 1877, the Atkinson ministry resigned following a vote of no confidence and was replaced by the Grey ministry with John Sheehan as native minister. Saunders described Sheehan as 'a witty, profligate, self-indulgent spendthrift', and claimed that Te Whiti thought him to be 'governed by the basest of Maori women and stupefied by swallowing the strongest of fire-water'. The *Timaru Herald*'s view was that although Sheehan was of humble birth and had not had the advantage of a classical education he still had 'nothing whatever of the cad about him' but had all the 'high feeling, broad sympathy and courteous bearing of a good old fashioned gentleman'.[27] He was certainly something of a controversial figure, but then he was New Zealand born, a colonial and an Irish Catholic, and therefore slightly beyond the pale and a just target for sniping opponents. Despite this, the historian Alan Ward thought he deserved little sympathy since among other shortcomings he had 'little genuine respect for the Maori people and their sensitivities', even though he was a fluent Maori speaker and very much at home with the people – by many accounts far too much at home with Maori women.[28] Richard Woon, resident magistrate on the Wanganui river, reported the great satisfaction of the Wanganui people at the 'advent to power . . . of Sir George Grey, their former Governor and patron; and of the Hon. Mr. Sheehan, as successor to the late lamented Sir Donald McLean, like whom he is looked up to as their friend and protector'.[29] But like so many other prominent figures, Sheehan's views changed over time depending on whether he was in or out of parliament, in or out of government, or involved in a particular cause. As a lawyer working for the Repudiation movement he took a different line from that which he espoused as native minister.[30] In his first statement on native affairs, he advised the House that he intended to continue McLean's policy of avoiding conflict with Maori; that it was better to allow a few outrages here and there than always attempt to enforce the law and thereby imperil the peace of the country – and the chances of floating a loan on the London market.[31]

The massive immigration policy of the Vogel years had increased settler demand for land, and from the start the Grey government was under pressure to increase the purchase of Maori land. The government could justify doing this on the grounds that colonisation was in the Maori's best interest and the race was dying out anyway.[32] Grey and Sheehan set out to woo the chiefs where they could and to overawe them where they could not. They intended to start in the Waikato and open up the North Island to settlement by breaking down the aukati, the Maori frontier beyond the confiscation line, so 'you could go into the money market and borrow as much as you liked on reasonable terms'.[33] Having dealt with the Waikato they could then turn their attention to Taranaki.

In January and May 1878 Grey and Sheehan met Tawhiao and King movement chiefs at Te Kopua and Hikurangi,[34] and in June Rewi travelled to Waitara, 'the place where the troubles began', to meet Grey, Sheehan and the Taranaki chiefs and to 'finish the work begun at Hikurangi'. The newspapers had a field-day and filled pages with eulogies on Rewi, 'the well known and influential Maniapoto chief', who had 'always been dignified and courteous' – and whose presence at Waitara meant, it was hoped, the opening up of the King Country.[35] About 5,000 people poured into Waitara from the four winds, including all the leading chiefs from Wanganui, Wellington, Otaki, Waikanae, Heretaunga and Maniapoto territory. A public holiday was to be proclaimed in New Plymouth and surroundings, and the leading citizens planned a banquet and ball on 'a suitable scale' to commemorate the occasion.

But the great meeting did not begin. Firstly, Wi Kingi te Rangitake, who was 'old and feeble' did not arrive. Then it was reported that the Parihaka people were on their way, bringing 30, 40, 50 cartloads of food. Day by day they were reported advancing on Waitara, and day by day the meeting was postponed till they should arrive. At noon on the sixth day, the 'cavalcade' 600 yards long came in in a 'well formed line' with whips cracking and flags flying to a tremendous welcome. Te Whiti had not come to Waitara. He had no need to. A great chief had great storehouses. By provisioning the gathering he gave demonstration enough of his mana; and by accepting the gift of food the assembled chiefs acknowledged it. The meeting could now begin. Rewi had invited Grey to meet him at Waitara, but when Te Whiti's people formally presented the huge mound of food to Rewi for distribution amongst the tribes it was quite clear who was really the host at the meeting.[36] Three days later, to reinforce the message, they presented him with a gift of 'twenty five kegs and calabashes' full of preserved birds, a truly chiefly offering.

Grey and Rewi exchanged formalities. Rewi asked for the Waitara; Grey told him Waitara belonged to both of them: that there the struggle had begun and there it should end. 'Let the great chiefs come forward and help to make the laws for their own people, and help to administer those laws. Let them join in with the Government in making the colony as happy and contented as they can. Let them become Ministers to execute the laws.' Rewi agreed that there at Waitara he and Grey should plant the tree from which good would spring, a tree from which they could plant offshoots all over the island. Matene Te Whiwhi and Wi Tako Ngatata were in accord with the words of Rewi and Governor Grey, but Wi Parata and others had reservations, saying it was not enough to establish peace; the government should return some of the confiscated land to those who had been in rebellion.

The Taranaki settlers were delighted at the new accord between Maori and European. After four days of discussion that seemed to promise so well for the future peace and prosperity of both races, the mayor of New Plymouth proclaimed the day a holiday and the Europeans prepared a great feast for 'all the Natives at the Waitara'. Excursion trains ran, the band turned out and the 'Natives and Europeans . . . fraternised in a most cordial manner'. Rewi was not so sanguine. The problem ahead of him was to reconcile Ngatiawa, Taranaki and Ngatiruanui chiefs with the arrangements he had made with the government. Grey did not care to dwell on this aspect, but emphasised that with the aid of Tawhiao and Rewi he would carry out the great work which he had commenced of reconciling the two peoples of Taranaki and bring progress to the district. Grey could not have been serious in presuming that Waikato and Maniapoto chiefs were going to solve Taranaki's problems. In fact he wasn't. His eyes were not on Taranaki but on the King Country; his glittering prize was to be the completion of the main trunk railway. After ten days in Taranaki, with Rewi suitably flattered and appeased, Grey left by the government steamer *Hinemoa* for Wellington and despatched Sheehan overland to visit the Waimate plains and try to reconcile Titokowaru, Te Whiti and Tohu to the impending survey of the plains.

The Waimate plains had gradually been occupied by Ngatiruanui, especially from 1872 on when it seemed to Maori that the confiscation was to be abandoned. Even Titokowaru and his Ngaruahine people were tacitly permitted to return, since 'it would be politically undesirable, and . . . practically impossible, to attempt to prevent their occupying the country north of Waingongoro, the confiscation of that country having been abandoned by the Government'.[37] Titokowaru had returned to his land but not to his loyalty, but the government, claiming their policy of 'wise and salutary neglect', had caused him to 'give in', treated him and his people like returned rebels and paid them compensation, although they failed to settle them on defined reserves.[38] When this policy had sufficiently complicated the issue by reinforcing the view that certainly the confiscation must have been abandoned if the government was prepared to pay Maori for their land, the mode of 'acquiring' the land was changed. Charles Brown was ordered simply to offer 'gratuities' to the chiefs in recognition of their mana whenua, their land rights. This payment came to be known to Maori as takoha; the west coast commissioners called it secret bribery. Fox enjoyed himself hugely in exposing the scandalous use and misuse of takoha, £2,000 of which went to help pay for his old protagonist Grey's Waitara meeting and was spent on tinned fruit and salmon and lobster, good ale and wine and three-star brandy; even on costumes, chemises, fichus and shawls, ribbons, feathers, perfumery and trinkets for the women 'and portmanteaus to pack all their finery in'.[39]

When the commissioners questioned Brown, he explained that he 'awarded the takoha in two shapes. One was to cover the former tribal rights, which was publicly paid to the Natives interested; and the other to cover the *mana* of the chiefs, which was privately paid'.[40] Reporting to McLean in June 1876, Brown said he believed 'Titokowaru cannot see his way to taking the initiative in letting the plains go. But he is willing that they should go' and would even assist in the process provided his part in the action was not known to his people. 'I would suggest that £50 or £100 be given to Titokowaru . . . not that he is entitled to it.' Brown was quite happy to put the payment through under the signature of Nuku, 'a cousin or brother of Titokowaru', as he did not think Titokowaru himself would sign.

> The other natives who had claims in the Opako block would know nothing of it, as I have refused to pay "per acre" or to take a conveyance for it, because "it is confiscated land" – and I have promised something extra to a few, to make them swallow the confiscation, which they do very well when the pill is gilded at the expense of the others.[41]

Whatever the mode of paying, the tribes were not deceived by the change of name; they were still being paid for *their* land. Brown was pleased to tell McLean a few months later that Titokowaru had 'swallowed the bait'. He had written to Brown asking him to pay his debts amounting to £100 and had ended his letter 'kia puta ngaro mai, kaua e korero ki nga tangata katoa'. Despite this warning about the need for discretion, it soon became known that Titokowaru was receiving takoha and 'his people jeered at him for sitting on a new stool'.[42] He had the grace to stay away from Parihaka where Te Whiti described as Judas Iscariot those who took the pieces of silver.

McLean's instructions of 1872 and 1876 laid more stress on compensating Maori for lands they would relinquish, rather than on reserves *per se*. When asked by the west coast commissioners whether he had specific instructions to make reserves on the Waimate plains, Brown replied that he had 'general authority' under the instructions of 1876 and had been authorised to do what he 'thought necessary'. More than two years later, when he began to survey the plains for sale and settlement, he still had not thought making reserves necessary, although he said that by this time the people of his district understood the government would take all the land of the plains except for reserves 'which were to be made as soon as the chiefs had seen the Minister'. He expected opposition when he crossed the Waingongoro because of the lack of reserves and he later told the commissioners that he was sure there would have been no opposition to the survey had reserves been made. Yet he, who 'had "carte blanche" . . . to do whatever he liked in the matter', did nothing except later make excuses for his remissness.[43]

Apparently at one time Brown did propose a plan for making 'small reserves for each group of families', an early version of what came to be known in the 1960s as 'pepper potting'. R. S. Thompson, the interpreter employed by Brown to work with the survey parties, thought this an ideal solution to 'the native difficulty' as Maori would be detached from their tribe and their chiefs and absorbed into the 'great body of the rate-paying and loyal subjects of the Queen'.[44] The plan was scarcely practical since it would have involved much more time, effort and finance than the government meant to devote to the survey, and more to the point it would have involved attendance at the Native Land Court by those who had no intention of thus appearing to recognise the confiscation. Brown would have appreciated very well that his plan would not work, but by proposing it he could at least appear to be carrying out his instructions.

Brown was a devious character and certainly at odds with Grey. He was an old friend of McLean, and one of the first friends Grey's political opponents, the Atkinsons and Richmonds, made on their arrival in Taranaki.[45] He might have been in collusion with Sheehan; they were something of a type, in personal if not public morals.[46] Brown had come to New Zealand as a young man in 1841 and had long been active in public affairs. He had had several terms in the Provincial and General Assembly, was twice superintendent of Taranaki and served with the Taranaki Rifles in the 1860s. He received something of a mauling at the hands of the *Taranaki Herald* but was equal to the occasion; he helped found, and for a while edited, a rival newspaper, the *Taranaki News*, which took a strongly anti-Grey line, but turned a blind eye to Brown's shortcomings and supported his candidacy for the various offices he sought.[47] He contested both the 1881 and 1884 elections for the seat of New Plymouth, but despite the support of the *Taranaki News* he was not successful on either occasion; his reputation had suffered because of his notorious dealings with both Maori people and Maori lands.[48]

Brown was one of those McLean men who 'Partly because they genuinely liked them, and partly to secure Maori compliance with the survey of the West Coast confiscation . . . from time to time, took Maori mistresses'. Writing about his visit to Parihaka with Parris and Kelly for the March 1870 meeting, Brown told McLean he had been offered a small whare to himself but he did not like to leave his companions; he expected that if he had it would have led to 'a good-looking woman sharing my blankets'. Under the circumstances he had thought discretion the better part of valour. He was not always so discreet. Told that 'Timoti . . . one of Titokowaru's men goes into town who has eaten the eyes and hearts of Europeans', he reported that it 'would ill become me who have knowingly had cannibal bedfellows of the female gender to be squeamish at Timoti'.[49] After Brown's first wife died in 1875 he was 'offered' Lucy Takiora Grey, a first cousin to Hone Pihama's wife and a paid government informer. It did not suit him at the time and he told her 'if she served the government, I could serve her interests better, by her not being my mistress'. This rather reduced her willingness to assist him, and later when his planned remarriage was 'knocked on the head . . . I thought it well to tell her so. For if it is necessary for the acquisition of the plains, no woman shall be left out in the cold . . . I promised Lucy I would recommend her services for remuneration'.[50] As civil commissioner, Brown was in charge of native affairs in Taranaki for five crucial years from 1875, when he took over from Parris, until 1880 when Bryce abolished the position.

By May 1877, Brown felt that Maori were 'gradually but steadily improving in their feeling of submission' as a result of their defeat in war, and that the time would be right to cross the Waingongoro and settle the 'question' of the Waimate plains once he had finished 'carrying out the confiscation' to the south of the river. Brown's view was that the government had the right to do what it pleased within the boundaries of the confiscation. He ascribed the past and present difficulties in effecting the peaceful occupation of the plains not to the lack of reserves and the years of unfulfilled promises but to 'philanthropic advisers of the Natives' – men who professed not to be working in their own interest, but whose views did not coincide with those of the government; men who sought to unsettle Maori by raising doubts about the legality of the confiscation.[51] Maori had enough doubts of their own and did not need Europeans to raise them, but it was a common ploy to ascribe Maori dissatisfaction to the influence of evilly disposed Europeans.[52]

Brown was about to start surveying the plains late in 1877 when he was stopped by a telegram from Sheehan, the new native minister, who wished to take stock of the situation before proceeding with the survey. The following May John Ballance, the colonial treasurer, informed him that if the work was undertaken the government would support him with 'sufficient force'. The government obviously still had visions of Titokowaru the warrior, but Brown, like many another, felt himself adequately equipped to settle the west coast difficulty single-handed, and replied that he was ready to begin without any force to support him.[53] The survey and sale of the Waimate plains had become a pressing issue for the Grey government. James Macandrew, the public works minister and an ex-superintendent of Otago, in a minute to Cabinet of 22 May 1878 urged that there be no further delay in starting the survey – under the protection of a strong detachment of the armed constabulary. It was his opinion that the government had shown 'great remissness in not having had this land in the market now. It would have placed us in funds to a very large extent, and enabled public works to be carried on . . . irrespective of loan . . . it will place in the Treasury close on half a million sterling'.[54] After 13 years' delay the confiscation was finally to be enforced on the Waimate plains – for financial reasons.

Brown thought any opposition Titokowaru might have offered to the survey had long been bought off, but he knew Titokowaru wanted information on reserves before the surveyors crossed the Waingongoro. The government, anxious as they were to improve their finances, deferred any action on the survey until Sheehan had visited the coast. There is no record now of just what Te Whiti was told when Sheehan visited the area after leaving the Waitara meeting, for at a time when government officials wrote copious reports Sheehan wrote remarkably little, preferring to deal in oral communications.[55] But Brown, when questioned by the west coast commissioners in 1880, after some hesitation decided he had heard Sheehan tell Titokowaru and others that 'ample reserves would be made for them, comprising their fishing-stations, burial-grounds, cultivations, and settlements'. Titokowaru told him to go to Parihaka and discuss the question of reserves there.[56] Sheehan was well aware that

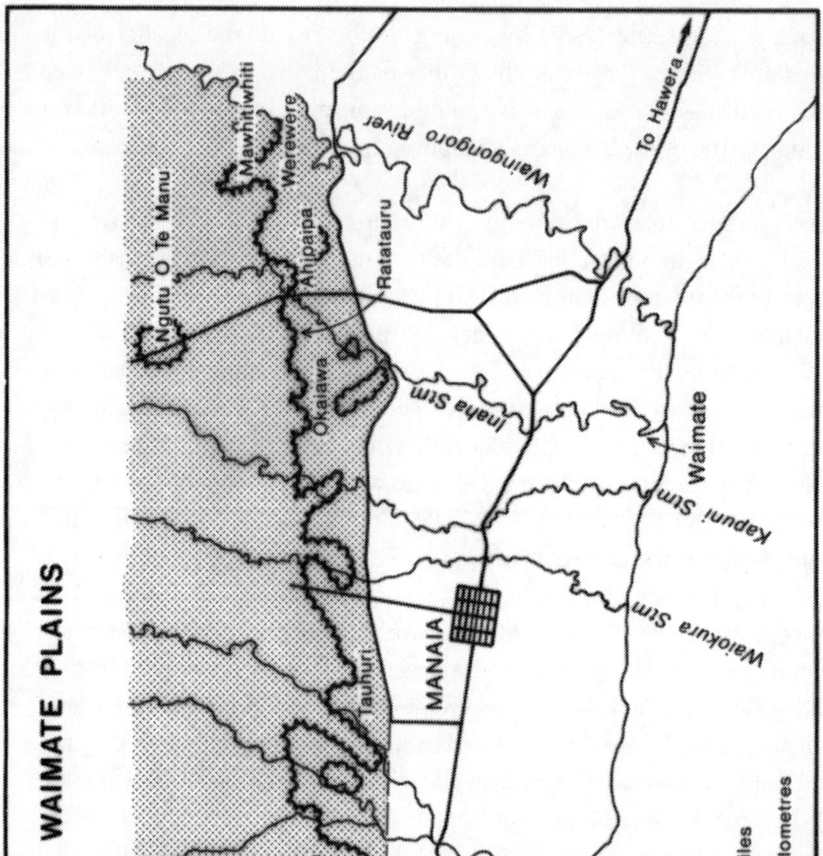

Based on: AJHR 1880 G2

non-fulfilment of promises to make reserves had led to trouble elsewhere including stoppages of surveys. Whatever Te Whiti was told or was given to understand, it was apparently enough to give him hope that the government at last meant to redeem the long unfulfilled promises about reserves for his people. Talk of takoha would have served little purpose. As Brown later told the commissioners, the nearer he got to Parihaka the stronger was the influence of Te Whiti and the less takoha could he disburse.[57] Te Whiti, 'anxiously promoting' the Maori race, wished to retain his land and his lifestyle and he condemned those who accepted takoha as betrayers of the people.

No sooner did Sheehan get back to Wellington than the survey of the plains was ordered. According to the chief surveyor, it was to be undertaken by the Survey Office under the direct control of Brown as civil commissioner. But when asked by the west coast commissioners whether the surveys were made under his direction as civil commissioner, Brown replied that they were made 'under the direction of the Survey Department'.[58] One controlled and one directed; neither accepted responsibility. On 29 July 1878, 'four strong parties crossed the Waingongoro'. They did not immediately begin the survey but started by simply cutting traverse lines with 'neither instruments nor chain on the ground', since Brown wished 'in this manner, to feel his way'.[59] Two weeks later, he reported 'the successful commencement and prosecution of the survey of the Waimate Plains, with every prospect of its peaceful continuance and completion'.[60] His optimism is surprising; he had experienced any amount of opposition to his work south of the Waingongoro and knew very well that the survey to the north of the river had been delayed for years because of the 'uncertain temper of the Taranaki Maoris'.

There was obviously also friction from the start between Brown and the survey office staff. It was a common cry that divided responsibility hampered the efficient administration of the confiscated lands. During his brief premiership in 1872, Stafford complained that he had 'the greatest difficulty in ascertaining the position of the confiscated lands, as . . . no one department knew the whole of the arrangements with respect to them'; the Confiscated Lands Department knew something, the Crown Lands Department held a few records, the Native Office was full of minutes and records.[61] Until after the abolition of the provinces the Native Office had their own survey department, which may have been a happier arrangement than that which existed in 1878 by which time the Crown Lands Department had responsibility for the surveys.

Brown had spread the word that the surveyors were about to start north of the river and warned local Maori not to meddle with survey pegs and trig stations. He sent Katene Tuwakaruru, a chief of that area and a native policeman, and William Williams, a licensed interpreter, to distribute and read to unwilling recipients a panui or announcement prepared by Sheehan about the coming survey. Brown reported that Katene did his work 'fearlessly and thoroughly' and doubted it would have been safe for any other of the native police to have attempted it.[62] It was quite clear that Brown's optimism about the 'peaceful continuance and completion of the survey' had nothing to do with Maori compliance; it was based quite provocatively on the use or threat of force. Despite Brown's protestations to the contrary he intended that Maori should be overawed into permitting the survey to proceed. Titokowaru's people were unhappy with the situation and with their chief. Te Ika and about thirty of his people protested peacefully, but said there would be no armed opposition. When Brown told him to petition parliament with his grievances Te Ika objected, according to Brown, that 'he could not acknowledge Parliament without denying the prophet Te Whiti'. However, he could and did petition the civil commissioner about the fate of his pigs and asked that they be spared the depredations of the survey party.[63]

It was not only Maori who were concerned about the survey.[64] The Europeans of the Normanby-Hawera area were more recent settlers than those around New Plymouth and were always manufacturing 'Maori scares'. In this case an 'alarm, commencing at Normanby, had extended to Hawera, that the Natives were going to fire on the survey party'. The Normanby settlers had even applied to the armed constabulary for arms and ammunition as they had heard that Maori were preparing to make a stand on the plains. Brown attributed such stories to his opposition, those who would 'poison the native mind' against him – and do the land deals themselves. Fox denounced these 'harpies' and 'rogues' who had 'infested the Coast for years', turning the Maori population against the government and baffling 'every endeavour after peace'.[65] Certainly the coast was not short of double-dealing land-sharks, and there was plenty of evidence of doubtful land deals and of unwitting Maori being taken for a ride. But the chiefs were not taken in by any plausible rogue and were quite capable of making up their own minds about the government's intentions and of judging the justice of its acts. And there were well-intentioned Europeans, with Maori interests at heart, to whom they could turn for advice if they wanted it, although officialdom looked askance at any European who gave advice contrary to that given by the government.

In the House, Fox wanted to know what Sheehan was doing about making 'the Queen's writ run' and vindicating the power of the law in Taranaki. Outrages had occurred, he said, and offenders had not been brought to justice; he asked if Sheehan had brought the subject to the notice of Titokowaru, Te Whiti or 'other influential chiefs . . . at his late interviews with them'. Sheehan was pained at the question and explained that he had not gone to the coast to ask chiefs to cooperate in apprehending offenders, but to 'preserve the peace of the country'.[66] He would not elaborate further and hinted only that he was taking a strong line, that matters were delicate and that progress was being made.

But despite Sheehan's posturing it was not he but Te Whiti who was in control of affairs on the coast. As a man of peace, Te Whiti decreed that the survey was not to be interrupted; enough blood had been spilled on that land. Brown misread as submission Te Whiti's willingness to trust the government to make the promised reserves, and concluded that Sheehan's strong line 'in dealing with the whole question' had convinced Te Whiti that opposition to the survey would be useless.[67] It escaped Brown entirely that Te Whiti was not submitting to the survey; he was permitting it. He would give the government the benefit of the doubt for the present and allow the surveyors to go onto the plains unhindered. As he had not been in rebellion, Te Whiti's lands were secured to him by the New Zealand Settlements Act and the proclamations of confiscation. If the government acted in good faith and began by delineating the promised reserves, *then* there was every prospect of the survey's 'peaceful continuance and completion'.

The reason for Brown's apparent optimism about the outcome of the survey now emerged. Before he had done more than make a relatively peaceful start, he wrote to Sheehan to say the time was approaching when his work – the survey of the plains – would be completed. He told Sheehan that he had accepted the post when McLean offered it to him in 1875 on condition that he could do the work in his own way, and that his claim to 1,000 acres of land on the plains, 'admitted by the Natives', should be 'given effect to on the peaceful completion' of the work. He was sure that Sheehan recognised his efforts on behalf of the government, approved his methods and would validate his claim to the land.[68] Brown did not mean to wait for trouble on the plains. He hoped his optimism would be persuasive and that he could get Sheehan's recognition of his claim before anything should happen to frustrate it. It was for these thousand acres that Brown had bullied and bribed and left no woman out in the cold.

Trouble over the survey came soon enough in the form of the murder of John McLean, the cook with a survey party on the Moumahaki block south of the Waingongoro.[69] Sheehan's immediate reaction to the incident was to ask whether the murder was connected with the survey, though he claimed to attach no political significance to the offence since the suspected murderer, Hiroki, was said to be a Waikato with no claim to the land. In fact his mother may have been Waikato but his father Ngarauru, and a former Waikato captive; Hiroki was born at Waitotara. Ngarauru claimed he was not one of them but belonged to Waikato, and described him as a bad character of a thievish nature.[70] The local people were obviously concerned that they would be tainted by association; some were afraid the Europeans would shoot them on sight. A group of leading Ngarauru men at Te Aro pa in Wellington assured Sheehan that had they been on the coast they would have captured Hiroki themselves. As it was, they would telegraph Waitotara to tell their people to capture him, and they begged Sheehan to publish their words 'that the Europeans may see them'. When it was believed Hiroki was heading for Parihaka, Sheehan suggested that Ngarauru could wash the blood of murder from the tribe by going there and demanding Hiroki from Te Whiti – despite the fact that Te Whiti had sent word he would notify the government if Hiroki sought refuge at Parihaka. Ngarauru gladly accepted the challenge, and a party of ten under their chief Aperahama Tamaiparea set off convinced they would find Hiroki at the Parihaka meeting on 17 October. Sheehan arranged a supply of food for them and told them he desired they 'should be strong in persuading the tribe to give up the murderer'. Te Whiti had stated publicly that he would not shelter Hiroki, and several messages had arrived from Parihaka that Hiroki was not there, yet on arrival Ngarauru ignored Te Whiti and proceeded to search the village. Te Whiti and Tohu were incensed; they had the Ngarauru band muru'd, or ritually plundered, to avenge the insult and ordered them out of the village. Brown met them back at Waitotara and congratulated them on Sheehan's behalf on having 'used every effort to relieve themselves of any imputation as regards Hiroki's crime'.

Despite the insult paid him, Te Whiti maintained his word. When Hiroki did arrive at Parihaka with a severe gunshot wound in the stomach from an encounter with one of the search parties,[71] Te Whiti sent one of his men to report the fact to Brown. He told him that had Hiroki died on the way that would have been the end of the matter, but since he had arrived and sought refuge Te Whiti was prepared to hear what Sheehan had to say about it. He requested an interview with Sheehan before anything else was done. Sheehan decided he would 'consider' the request, but meanwhile told Brown he 'had better go up and see Te Whiti'. He could thank him for notifying Hiroki's arrival and express his regret that 'the indiscretion of Ngarauru should have given his people offence'. Titokowaru expressed his opinion that no one should go to Parihaka until Te Whiti had had an interview with Sheehan, but Katene, who in government pay had so fearlessly proclaimed the coming survey, did not think it would be politic for Sheehan to see Te Whiti. Katene had an eye to his own mana, not that of Te Whiti. Brown went to Parihaka and the people gathered to hear Sheehan's message. They had no reply for him since the message was abundantly clear: the native minister obviously had no intention of going to Parihaka himself. Tohu told Brown not to send police of either race, 'as they would not understand him'. Tohu had no more faith in native than in European police.

These unnecessarily provocative actions of Sheehan's were typical of the ill-considered tactics that characterised relations between the government and Te Whiti and served to alienate him from them. Rather than acknowledge Te Whiti's mana and deal with him as a chief, they despatched their underlings to deal with him or used the tribes as pawns in a game to diminish chiefly mana and force submission to 'European law', which in fact meant European supremacy. By insulting Te Whiti and failing to consult with him, Sheehan missed the chance to have Hiroki surrendered, and a comparatively minor incident grew to major proportions and was to materially influence all further dealings between the government and the people of Parihaka.

CHAPTER FOUR

Challenge to the Confiscation

1879

THE SURVEY OF THE WAIMATE PLAINS PROCEEDED WITH LITTLE interruption for almost seven months, but it became increasingly obvious that Ngatiruanui would not meekly permit the survey and sale of their tribal land if the promised reserves were not first delineated. At the beginning of 1879, none of the west coast people whom the government viewed as having been loyal throughout the war and who had received Compensation Court awards on paper were yet secure on their land; none of those who, under the 1863 act and subsequent proclamations, had surrendered or 'returned to their loyalty' had titles to reserves; the confiscated lands which had been 'formally abandoned' by the Crown had not been legally relinquished by proclamation; and the assurances given to Titokowaru before the survey started appeared totally worthless when the survey lines came within a quarter of a mile of his village.

The survey was confined to Ngatiruanui land between the Waingongoro river and the Wahamoko stream, as it was not 'deemed prudent' at that time to carry it further north into Taranaki tribal land, where no takoha had been accepted.[1] But payment of takoha to Titokowaru in no way conciliated or restrained his people, and they finally took matters into their own hands. The first interruption to the survey came from Ngaruahine in December 1878, when the surveyors were turned back when they reached the cultivations at Taikatu, Titokowaru's pa. The surveyors profited by the absence at Parihaka of the people of nearby Omuturangi and carried the survey up to their cultivations before they too were turned back. These lines, once stopped, were 'never continued'.[2] They were obviously not essential. Far from being careful and conciliatory, the surveyors were trying the people to the limit. They 'understood' it was the duty of the civil commissioner to point out where reserves were to be made. Brown sent the interpreter R. S. Thompson ahead to 'discuss' reserves with the villagers, but on no occasion was a reserve marked out on the ground. There was further opposition to the survey at the other end of the plains in January 1879 when Charles Finnerty, an assistant surveyor, was told his work was that of a robber and a thief;[3] and in February when the women and old men first hindered and then stopped the surveyors who had actually cut lines through their cultivations. By March the survey pegs were being cut into kindling or pulled from the ground over miles and miles of surveyed land.[4]

It was in March too that trouble flared again over a road being surveyed towards Titokowaru's village. Titokowaru made a very reasonable request that it avoid his grass seed crop and burial ground and the Native Department officers agreed this should be done. But again the discord between Native Department and Survey Department surfaced and Finnerty, a particularly stubborn man, continued with his original plan because although he had been warned several times to stop he had not actually been obstructed or forcibly prevented from continuing his work.[5] The Native Department had spent a lot of time, energy and money in conciliating Titokowaru and Brown had warned the surveyors to treat him with extra courtesy, but it was all to no purpose. Titokowaru continually told government officers to go to Parihaka to talk about the confiscation, but they were determined not to allow that Te Whiti had the mana to deal with land beyond his own tribal area. They could not or would not appreciate that Titokowaru was a warrior chief whose mana toa, whose status as a warrior, was now checked by the mana Te Whiti exercised in the interests of peace on the length and breadth of the west coast. Provoked even to this extent, Titokowaru did not react with violence. Leaving his younger men to obstruct the surveyors if they wished, he left for Parihaka to lay his grievance before Te Whiti at the March hui.

That hui was largely ignored by Europeans, but a week later Sheehan saw fit to visit Parihaka. It would seem obvious he had gone there to discuss the question of reserves, but instead he began by demanding that Hiroki be surrendered for trial by the Supreme Court. Te Whiti, understandably mistrustful of the government, suggested that the court should sit at Parihaka since proceedings on the marae can be viewed from all sides and discussed in the light of day. When Sheehan proceeded to justify the government's actions on the plains as being 'in conformity with the intimation he had given to

Te Whiti before the survey commenced', he was interrupted by 'a violent torrent of words' from Te Whiti who accused the government of 'stealing the land' and generally being unworthy of recognition. Brown had never seen 'a Native speaker . . . so wanting in the usual courtesy to the other speaker, or who so completely lost his temper'.[6] The *Patea Mail* of 26 March 1879 explained Te Whiti's outburst as due to his attitude to Hiroki. 'We do not like the tone of the great prophet, and his violent action at the suggestion Hiroki be brought to justice clearly indicated that his feelings towards Europeans are not so peaceful as was thought.' However, it was not a question of Hiroki which caused the outburst, but the fact that there was obviously a wide discrepancy between what the government was now doing and what it had previously proposed. Sheehan of course would not allow this, but informed Te Whiti that 'as he had interrupted and would not listen to him, he would not now know what he intended to say'.[7] This effectively terminated the meeting, at least as far as Sheehan was concerned.

The native minister tabled a lengthy report of his visit to the west coast but it avoided all mention of his meeting with Te Whiti.[8] It was not until Fox, in the House, demanded information about the interview with 'Te Whiti and Hiroki' that Brown wrote his half page report, four months after the crucial meeting had taken place. Meanwhile Sheehan assured Fox that he was unable to report on any interview 'between Hiroki and himself at Parihaka, as no such meeting ever took place'.[9] Fox would have understood perfectly well that Hiroki's position at Parihaka was a humble one, even though some of Te Whiti's followers might look on him as a hero. Hiroki helped serve the food at the big public meetings; he did not confer with European guests. But political capital could always be made out of his presence there.

The end of his meeting with the native minister signalled the end of Te Whiti's willingness to accommodate the government. It was not Titokowaru's complaint and certainly not the question of Hiroki that triggered the issue, but the duplicity of Sheehan and Grey.[10] According to Parris, Te Whiti told him that when Grey met Rewi at Waitara he said he would 'plant a tree of peace whose branches would spread over the land'; but instead, 'in a very short time, he commenced stealing the land of the Waimate Plains'.[11] It must have seemed clear to Te Whiti from the way the survey was being conducted that government promises and those contained in the act of confiscation itself would not be kept, and that it was time to act lest the continuing provocation drive the people to retaliate and thus give the government an excuse to suppress them by force. Te Whiti peremptorily ordered his men to remove all the surveyors from the plains.

At dawn on 24 March, the day after Sheehan left Parihaka, the surveyors were told of Te Whiti's orders. None of the surveyors moved of their own accord, but none of them opposed their removal. It was obvious that Maori meant business; they quietly, thoroughly and good-humouredly packed up each survey camp, loaded horses and drays and carted everything back across the Waingongoro. The surveyors reported: 'I was very much pleased with their quiet behaviour', and 'with the exception of some tools that were out on the work . . . I have not lost anything'.[12] Te Whiti's message was clear: pacific, but not passive obstruction would be offered to any further attempt by the government to enforce the confiscation in this way. Brown, claiming 'the question of reserves has not been a material one' and finding a convenient scapegoat in Hiroki, explained the removal of the surveyors in terms which absolved him from all responsibility for the interruption to the survey.[13] The local press thought Te Whiti had the devil in him, that he had been stirred up against Europeans and might have had all the surveyors murdered but for the fact that he was 'a wily, cautious savage and feared the consequences'. The time had now arrived 'when the final blow' could be struck and Maori 'taught submission to the laws of the land.'[14]

It is hard to see the survey of the plains as anything but provocative; if not deliberately so, then simply through indifference to Maori sensibility and to justice and morality. Failure to make reserves on the ground was not just careless omission, but a reflection of a deeply rooted view that the Europeans could do what they liked in the country they governed, and that their actions in the interests of the colony were *ipso facto* in the interests of the Maori people. Parliamentarians, government officials, surveyors and interpreters were all of the opinion that it was injurious to Maori for them to hold large areas of land in common, and that the ideal was for a man to hold on individual title just sufficient land to support himself and his family. Judge Fenton of the Compensation Court had ordered that compensation awards should contain an inalienation clause, and there was thus an added reluctance to survey large reserves which might then remain in Maori hands and impede the progress of civilisation and settlement.

Such reasoning applied particularly to this part of the coast where the tribes were considered to be among the most troublesome and rebellious in the country. It was illustrated clearly in the case of the 'large reserve' to be made for the 'thoroughly loyal' Ngatiruanui chief, Manaia, and his people. Brown told the surveyors that a 2,000-acre block was to be reserved for them and that it should be excluded from the survey. The surveyor felt his job was to subdivide the whole district into sections and persuaded Brown that it was in Manaia's interests to have his land 'sectionised'. Manaia had not been told what land he was to have. As far as he or his people could tell, the whole area was being subdivided for sale. Nor had he yet been paid takoha. Brown had offered him first £100, then £1,000, but Manaia, 'more straightforward and upright' than other chiefs, had not taken the money then, feeling satisfied that his mana had been duly recognised and that he could have the money if he wanted it.[15]

Manaia never was paid his money. Although Brown's promise of £1,000 in takoha 'was as emphatic and precise as words could make it, and . . . nothing but the implicit confidence reposed by Manaia in this promise prevented the completion of the transaction then and there', Fox later felt that 'splendid provision' had been made for him in the way of reserves, and that the promised takoha, which was supposed to assist in fencing reserves and 'otherwise promoting . . . social improvement', could be 'fairly considered to have merged in the noble estate' of 1,500 acres bestowed upon him. Besides, Manaia had never again 'referred to Major Brown's promise, or intimated that he expected its fulfilment'.[16] According to Brown, Titokowaru at this time had accepted £900. In the House on 23 July 1879, Sheehan claimed Titokowaru had received £600 and by his silence had consented fully to the survey,[17] although Sheehan would have known that in the Maori world silence did not imply consent. The more troublesome a chief, or the more he was feared, the more attention was paid to him. Brown considered Manaia the first chief on the plains whose mana should be recognised, but since he was compliant his needs and sensibilities could be overlooked.

If it was not clear to the government, it was clear to the west coast commissioners who later enquired into its 'promises and engagements' with regard to the confiscated lands that the failure to make reserves was the root cause of the interruption to the survey.[18] But the commissioners contented themselves with condemning successive governments for their failure to honour long-standing promises and did not enquire into their underlying reasons for it. There were in fact several levels of reluctance to make reserves. One was simply the practical difficulty involved from the start, a difficulty which only increased over time: who was to have what land and where. The land had never been surveyed and when it was, land for sale and settlement took precedence. There was always 'a shortage of surveyors' when it came to dealing with reserves for Maori. The quality of land affected the ease of survey and the bulk of the land to be reserved for Maori was broken or bush covered. Dissension between the Native and Survey Departments exacerbated the problem. There were always financial constraints; the money that poured into the country in the early 1870s was not earmarked for Maori purposes. By the late 1870s, the indebtedness of the country and the state of the economy were such that no government would risk its electoral chances by further 'extravagance' in Maori affairs.

An added difficulty on the plains stemmed from Brown's attitude. Having neglected to make reserves for more than three years, he blamed a January 1879 telegram from Grey for the fact that none had been made at the time of the interruption to the survey. Grey had ordered him to submit proposals about reserves for government consideration before he came to any final conclusion about them or informed the people what land they were to have, and Brown told the commissioners that this even prevented his telling the people their cultivations and settlements would be reserved to them,[19] something they had been repeatedly promised over the years.

In the final analysis, all the 'reasons' put forward for the failure to make reserves on the west coast were nothing but excuses. In the commissioners' phrase, 'the troubles which . . . beset every successive Government might have been mastered at any time, if only scrupulous good faith had waited on steadfast counsels and a consistent purpose'.[20] The good faith was certainly lacking, but not the consistent purpose. That was from first to last to deny Maori their lands in an effort to diminish mana motuhake – Maori identity, Maori separateness, Maori pride. They wished to humble the Maori people, make them submit, and establish European supremacy throughout the land. As long as Maori held large blocks of land on the west coast, whether on original native title or on crown grant, they could retain an independence and a physical and spiritual distance from the European world which Europeans could not tolerate. Maori were to be civilised by having Europeans live amongst them. Inalienable reserves or those with communal title could frustrate this objective. There simply was no enthusiasm for making reserves north of the Waingongoro and failure to make them could be justified in a variety of ways.

The stoppage of the survey, this assertion of mana, was a new challenge. Brown described it as being 'very different from . . . previous occasions . . . when I have always been able to surmount the difficulty by delay, by temporising, and by a use of the compensation that was at my disposal'. He believed Te Whiti was still anxious to avoid bloodshed, but that he had been obliged to act as he had 'to maintain his position, and he is not in a position nor has he the will to prejudice it by retreating, nor can he choose what further steps he will take'.[21] Claiming to believe that Te Whiti's pacifism might be overtaken by his followers' fanaticism, the government decided to rush through the sale of some of this choice west coast land before their profit should be endangered by fear of 'another native outbreak'.

The very next day after the removal of the surveyors, the government took steps to arrange for the sale of the Waimate plains with the objective of putting 'a European population on the Plains as rapidly as possible' and the hope of putting Macandrew's half a million sterling in the Treasury. A preliminary advertisement notifying the sale of '16,000 acres of the well-known Waimate Plains . . . by public auction . . . on Tuesday, 6th May next' was to appear in New Zealand and Australian papers the following day, 26 March 1879. Even then there was still no move to determine reserves. The most the government would do, a week later, was 'reserve from sale' sections 'affected' by burial grounds, cultivations and fishing grounds. This involved an exercise on paper by which certain sections were marked 'withheld from sale'. It is hardly surprising that Maori believed the Waimate plains were to be sold with no provision at all being made for their requirements. The preliminary advertisement appeared as planned, but on 24 April a further announcement in the newspapers advised that the sale of the Waimate plains was 'postponed until further notice'.[22] The government had had second thoughts.

At the beginning of April, Sheehan had called Brown to Wellington and instructed him to point out on a map in the survey office some reserves in the surveyed section of the plains, bearing in mind 'that the Government had decided to return from 20,000 to 25,000 acres to the Natives on the Plains'. Brown accordingly coloured on the map about 3,000 acres to be set apart for reserves, comprising 'all the fishing-stations, and all the old pas and burial-grounds' he was aware of. These were the sections the Taranaki Land Board was then advised to withhold from sale. No one else was told of the 'existence of this coloured plan', and the fact of the reserves having been made at all was, according to the commissioners, still unknown to Maori 15 months later.[23]

In the meantime, James Mackay had been sent to the west coast as a special commissioner 'to report on the whole question of the Waimate Plains'. Francis Dillon Bell told John Hall that he had, months before, seen 'danger was ahead' if the government proceeded in the 'reckless course . . . of taking their survey right up to the wares and cultivations before even broaching the question of reserves'. He had warned Sheehan and others of the risk they were running but, he observed smugly, 'the mixed stupidity and conceipt of the lot made them disregard what I said. It must be pleasant for Sheehan and Brown to have had Jas. Mackay sent up by Grey to mend their broken kettles'.[24] Sheehan claimed he had specially requested Mackay to travel through the district, as the 'fact of his having no official connection with the Government gave him unusual facilities for acquiring a knowledge of the real views of the Natives'.[25] He was paid £300 for his trouble; another £50 was paid to his assistant, Captain R. T. Blake.[26] Mackay, another 'McLean man', had had a long connection with the government as a resident magistrate and assistant native secretary in Nelson and Westland and civil commissioner at Hauraki. He was a highland Scot, not unlike McLean and at times in virtual competition with him. He had a good command of the Maori language and a sensitivity towards the Maori people and their culture which was tinged with a certain ambivalence. In the end, his advancement counted for more than theirs and he was not above enriching himself at their expense. His official land buying was terminated in 1875, when 'some discrepancies in his . . . operations were exposed'.[27]

Mackay sent back a long and illuminating telegram to Sheehan about his visit to Te Whiti on 2 April.[28] Sheehan took care that this vitally important telegram, which too clearly expressed the 'real views of the natives', was not laid before parliament, but fobbed them off with a dull report, a sort of expurgated version which he had had Mackay write later, and which gave no particulars of the interview with Te Whiti.[29] Mackay had told Te Whiti that he was no longer in the service of the government, and tried to convince him that he had sought Sheehan's permission to assist Blake, who through his mother was related to Tohu,[30] with the mediation of the Waimate plains dispute. Te Whiti was not deceived. 'Is not Mackay a Government Commissioner?' he asked Blake. 'He and Parris are the celebrated men whom all the Maoris have heard of.' He spoke clearly and directly to those who had sent these commissioners:

> The Governor has no claim on the lands this side of Waingongoro. . . . Why did not you occupy them at the time of your conquest? According to Maori

> custom you should have done so. I am now in occupation: and even if the land had been taken, I, according to the same custom, having been allowed to reoccupy the land, have not lost my rights of ownership.

Mackay tried to cite examples of loss of land by conquest but carefully avoided the question of occupation, and when he said he wanted Te Whiti and the government to come to an amicable arrangement about the confiscated land, Te Whiti replied:

> I do not admit your right to survey it. My blanket is mine. . . . You want to cut my blanket in two. It will be too small for me then . . . I do not desire war. All I want is to be allowed to remain at peace on my own land . . . I gave up land from Waitotara to Waingongoro under the arrangements with McLean and Parris. That ought to satisfy you . . . I turned the surveyors off quietly, because they had no right on my land . . . tell the Governor not to persist in the survey, and I will sit down peaceably on my land.

Mackay understood the idiom – that it was the west coast people, not Te Whiti as an individual, who had given up land to the south of the Waingongoro and who claimed ownership to the north of it. He replied in the same idiom, suggesting Te Whiti let the government deal with these lands as Parris had dealt with others, a portion for Te Whiti and a portion for the government. But Te Whiti asked if they had not seen

> the line cut through the cultivation at the door of Titokowaru's house? . . . Where, then, is the piece to be retained by the Natives? Where are the promises of McLean and Parris that the land in the occupation of the Natives should not be taken from them? But for the surveyors being turned off, we should receive no consideration at the hands of the Government. The works of McLean, Parris, and the old Government were different from the acts of Sheehan, Brown, and the new Government . . . I asked Brown to remove his guns. He said he had, but he carries them up to Titokowaru's house. The surveyors were then taken off . . . to prevent evil. . . . The people might not sit down quietly and submit to their land being surveyed under their feet.

When Mackay tried to assure him the government did not mean to take all the land but would give back pieces, as promised by McLean and Parris, Te Whiti asked eagerly if Mackay was authorised to offer part of the land and agree for the government to take the other part. 'It seems to me . . . by the way the surveys have been conducted, you wish to take the whole of the blanket and leave me naked.' Mackay could make no such offer, but said he would report to the government and return to see Te Whiti if there was 'anything of importance to communicate'.[31]

Amazingly there was not, although Sheehan tacitly admitted the truth of Te Whiti's statement that but for the surveyors being turned off, his people would have received no consideration from the government. He told the House on 23 July 1879 that he was not aware,

> nor was the country aware, nor do I believe the House knows as a fact, what the exact position of those lands on the West Coast was. It has only been made clear to us by the interruption of the surveys. It turns out that from the White Cliffs down to the . . . . [Waitotara] the whole country is strewn with unfulfilled promises.[32]

Meanwhile Sheehan told Mackay that he recognised Te Whiti's 'desire to discuss the question and come to some settlement', but implied it was really Te Whiti's own fault that no reserves had been defined. Government instructions regarding Waimate had been, he said, 'of the most liberal character', but they had been unable to give effect to them because the natives would not point out the reserves they specially required. This had now been done for them and the sale map was 'speckled over with reserves'.[33] But on 4 April, the day he received Mackay's telegram, Sheehan told the Taranaki Land Board to withhold until further notice the advertisement regarding the sale of the plains.[34] He then hurriedly returned to Taranaki to confer with Brown, Parris and Mackay, to 'ascertain what foundation there was for the statements made in many quarters, and believed in a great many others, to the effect that important promises made by the Government in respect of the West Coast confiscated area had not been fulfilled'; and to determine whether such promises had anything to do with the interruption of the survey.[35]

Sheehan had no trouble in discovering justifiable 'feelings of insecurity and distrust' among loyal natives and those who had returned to their loyalty. Nor had he any trouble in exculpating both Parris and Brown, or in blaming for the present state of affairs past governments 'who had the control of this question at the time when the confiscation was first decreed'. He found the Waimate plains to be confiscated land about which 'no promises have been made to the former owners'. He was sure neither Parris nor Brown had ever disclosed to the tribes the instructions they had been given by McLean; yet he was in no doubt that the people were now 'generally aware' the government proposed 'to give both ample reserves and money payment'. As to the Parihaka block of about 80,000 acres, he could find no evidence that any 'promise of any character whatever, definite or indefinite, has ever been made to the original owners, for the return of the whole or any part' of it – a suggestion the west coast commissioners could not 'allow . . . for a moment'. Nor, he added, had 'any action ever been taken of an official character to justify even a suspicion that any intention to return the block had ever existed in the mind of the Government'.[36] This really was double talk. Certainly Sheehan had taken good care not to make any promise directly to Te Whiti. But in 1878, when Te Whiti had restrained 'the more turbulent spirits' from interrupting the survey at its commencement, Sheehan, according to Brown, said he had considered the question of returning the Parihaka block to Te Whiti but 'had come to the conclusion that it would be paying too heavily for Te Whiti's having kept the peace on the coast'. In 1879 though, he admitted that there would have been comparatively little land available for sale once provision had been made for the large number of people of the Taranaki tribe living on the block. Then in 1880, he told the west coast commissioners that:

> Te Whiti had done good work for years on the coast in preserving the public peace; and that I was disposed, in the event of his pursuing a similar line of conduct in the future, to recommend to my colleagues the restoration of the Parihaka Block to the original owners; that is to say, the whole of the . . . Block, extending down to the sea. This restoration was to be entirely dependent on good behaviour.[37]

As Te Whiti had kept the peace and Sheehan did not want to pay such a high price for it, he made him no promises, made no reserves, and then capitalised on the ensuing reaction. Te Whiti was no longer the 'singular man' of 'essentially peaceful and amiable nature' that he had been in 1872, nor did he deserve credit for his success in keeping the peace between the two races as he did in 1876.[38] Although still 'a remarkable man' because of the 'immense ascendency' he had obtained not only over his own Taranaki tribe but over all the west coast people, he was now an

> element of disturbance . . . and no settlement of the question in dispute can be discussed unless full allowance for this unusual and important element . . . is made. Year by year, for years past, he has been prophesying that at a time named by himself there would happen the resurrection of the dead ancestors of his tribe, the re-establishment of the Native people in possession of the whole island, and the disappearance of the Europeans and kupapas . . . like a 'swish' from the face of the country. Though year after year has witnessed the failure of these prophecies, still his influence remains without any sensible diminution. It is a moot point whether he is a believer in his own fanaticism, or whether he is not, under the guise of a prophet, endeavouring to become the saviour of the lands of himself and his own particular following.[39]

Sheehan's record of what Te Whiti is reported to have said over the years depicts Te Whiti as a fanatic and contrasts strangely with Mackay's report of an actual conversation with an apparently sane and rational man. The few instances of conversations with Te Whiti that come down to us in the documents almost invariably show him in this latter vein. Mackay's telegram to Sheehan was probably the most accurate and revealing record of Te Whiti's views the government ever received, and they suppressed it and ignored it. The message was too clear, and not what they wanted to hear.

Te Whiti's supposed prophesies and fanaticism emerge from the record of his speeches on the marae. Europeans found Te Whiti's oratory confusing, even unintelligible, steeped as it was in messages from the past and in biblical phraseology. The interpreters who sent their versions of his speeches back to the government did great violence to his words, and the government did itself a disservice in trusting licensed interpreters and other government agents whose knowledge of Maori was often quite inadequate. It was one thing for these officers to converse freely with the people of their district on everyday matters in situations where ambiguities and misunderstandings could be clarified and corrected. It was another to be part of a crowd listening to an oration on the marae of Tumatauenga, god of war. Europeans were then dependent for clarification of obscure points on the loyal chiefs like Hone Pihama who usually accompanied them.[40] These men, looking to their own mana, were more apt to put a negative than a positive aspect on Te Whiti's utterances. They were often divided among themselves on what was really meant, and they were generally not present in the evening in the meeting house, the marae of Rongo, god of peace, when Te Whiti and Tohu elaborated on and clarified the speeches delivered earlier in the day.

The English versions of those speeches, often reprinted in official government publications, are unreliable in that there are sometimes several versions of the one speech, and are misleading in that they are too literal and do not probe the thinking behind the words. Te Whiti was said to have complained that 'his utterances became public property once past his lips';[41] he could in fact be made to say what Europeans wanted or expected to hear. Te Whiti's actions were habitually explained in the press as being due not to his search for justice, but to his chagrin at the failure of some prophecy he was reported to have made. Those who could not understand him and could not explain his 'hold on the people' necessarily attributed it to fanaticism, and once expressed this view was endlessly repeated and used to dismiss his legitimate grievances.

Mackay's telegrams and reports showed clearly that there was great 'discontent and disaffection . . . among the majority of the Maori populations of the Provincial District of Taranaki' resulting from confiscation and the ensuing mismanagement by successive governments of the confiscated lands and the promises made in regard to them.[42] Sheehan dismissed Te Whiti's discontent as being due to a misunderstanding over the survey lines which had cut through Titokowaru's cultivations, and insisted that the promises alleged to have been made in the past had 'no existence in the official records'. Yet despite this, he was prepared to recommend that a quarter or more of the coast be set aside as reserves, that monetary compensation be paid, and that special consideration be shown to the chiefs 'in order of their rank'.[43] The *Taranaki News* of 19 April 1879 was indignant over the

> supposed discovery of . . . promises . . . hidden till now in the archives of the Native Office. . . . The cry of injustice to Natives is an old ruse. . . . Whatever promises have been made they cannot be pleaded by outlaws. By sheltering the murderer Hiroki, Te Whiti and his people have rebelled against the Government. . . . Our rapidly increasing population, the requirements of the public exchequer, the wants of the district as regards harbor accommodation . . . demand that these lands should no longer be retained by turbulent, semi-barbarous people, too idle to put them to any good use.

Mackay was now despatched through the district between New Plymouth and Wanganui to visit every hapu and every major chief and discuss their grievances – every chief, that is, except Te Whiti. Fox later explained to the House that Sheehan saw Te Whiti's mind 'opening in the direction of negotiation' and said he was prepared to stand by his offer. 'But he never said to Mr Mackay "You go and tell him so" . . . and Mr Mackay never did go and tell him so.'[44] Mackay did, however, report back to Sheehan that it would be 'useless, and . . . highly improper . . . to conceal from the Government that the Ngarauru, Ngatiruanui, Taranaki and Ngatiawa Tribes . . . are very discontented with their present position, and consider that injustice has been done to them in the matter of their lands'; that Ngarauru and Ngatiawa and some of the Ngatiruanui and Taranaki people would admit European 'right by conquest, but say we have not carried out our engagements about awards and reserves'; while Te Whiti's and Titokowaru's 'immediate followers . . . deny the right of the Crown to any confiscated lands'. He thought that if the less disaffected could be mollified by the award of reserves or titles to Compensation Court awards, they could be detached from Te Whiti and the strength of the 'hostile party' reduced.[45]

Mackay had advised Sheehan to inform Te Whiti and Titokowaru 'distinctly' that part of the Parihaka block and Waimate plains would be 'at once set apart for them and granted to the proper owners'. But this was not done, and when Mackay saw Titokowaru on 25 April during his journey through Taranaki he found him 'civil, but seemingly determined to make common cause with and be guided by Te Whiti only'.[46] It had been obvious to government officers for years enough that no settlement could be effected on the west coast unless it was agreed to by Te Whiti himself, and yet at this crucial point Sheehan chose to ignore Te Whiti altogether.

Robert Studholme Thompson, the interpreter working with the survey parties, attended the May 1879 hui at Parihaka. He was a European whose wife, Hana Taukawa, from the Waimate plains, was a close relative of Titokowaru. Thompson, like other interpreters, was a marginal man, with a foot in both worlds. He identified strongly with the European world, yet through his wife he had contact not only with Titokowaru and his people, but also with Te Whiti and the people at Parihaka. The government suffered him because of his usefulness to them, but he was classed among those who

> would obstruct every measure as long as they could, in order to compel the Government to give their Maori wives and half-caste children certain reserves . . . the men who are the obstacles to all Governments . . . the men who have sold their people, and who have used their Maori wives and half-caste children as levers to provide themselves with money.[47]

He regularly attended the Parihaka meetings and sent the government detailed reports about the state of affairs on the west coast. A collection of copies of some of these reports, written between August 1878 and October 1880, was sent to the House in 1880, as 'evidence of loyal service by R. S. Thompson'.[48] They are a valuable indication of the way Europeans interpreted Maori thought and action, or used their position as mediators between the two worlds to further their own ends. Thompson was a much more competent interpreter than many of those operating on the coast. Rewi had used him at the Waitara hui in 1878, saying he wished to have his own interpreter translate his words 'because I have seen what newspapers have done'.[49] Even so, Thompson was not averse to ingratiating himself with the government by proffering unsolicited advice and by telling them what he thought they wanted to hear, all the while claiming 'disinterestedness', considering 'how large a stake' he had, through his wife and children, in the confiscated land. It was, he explained, because he considered the struggle to be a national one that he clung to his own people, 'and not for the salary doled out to me. The interests of my children lead me the other way judging from the ruthless confiscation of their inheritance'.[50]

Reporting back to Brown on the May hui, Thompson said it was well attended, with a noticeable increase in 'the numbers from Whanganui and Waitotara', and was 'characterised by more direct reference to the land and less scripture than formerly'. Everything he heard and saw at Parihaka led him to the conclusion that it was the legality of the confiscation that Te Whiti intended to dispute.[51] Te Whiti had repeated that there would be no fighting, although there was yet one more thing 'the Europeans had to do to them and that was to "patu tatou katoa kia mate" '. Thompson left this untranslated, which was rather cunning since it would be sure to be taken to mean that Maori expected to be wiped out by force, although it might just as well have signified their spiritual death through total loss of land. Te Whiti also castigated te hunga he, those who had sold land, telling them they had brought trouble on themselves and all their people. Thompson doubted that Te Whiti and Tohu would speak their minds to any but Grey and Sheehan. He was right; they would not deal with underlings and they both expressed themselves 'very anxious to hear the whereabouts of the new Governor'.[52]

Thompson's advice to Brown was to use Hiroki as a lever with which to manipulate Te Whiti. Since Te Whiti had, in his opinion, 'made Hiroki and the confiscation one question', he thought they should refuse any discussion about the land unless Hiroki was given up. He was confident that Te Whiti would refuse to give Hiroki up, 'and then we should have to take him and whilst doing so would so cripple Te Whiti that he would never be able to raise the question of the confiscation again'. Katene was even more explicit: he wanted Te Whiti arrested as well as Hiroki. He assured Brown that no armed opposition would be offered and that Te Whiti's followers would 'crumble to pieces' as soon as Te Whiti was made prisoner.[53]

This sort of advice was just such as would appeal to both Brown and Sheehan and it cannot be doubted that they took note of it. Sheehan would turn a blind eye to an outrage or two as long as it suited him, but Hiroki's presence at Parihaka could be used as an excuse for action when needed. The Maori language newspaper *Waka Maori* urged caution: 'We cannot . . . think the Government will rush headlong into another Maori war. . . . It is certain that cities of refuge for murderers cannot be tolerated in the land, but all peaceable measures should first be tried'.[54] The government instead tried further provocation, and 'nothing more was done towards meeting the overture made by Te Whiti' when he had met Mackay at the beginning of April.[55] The government had ample opportunity to act; Mackay was busily employed on the coast from April until July, but he kept his distance from the one man through whom a settlement could have been effected.

But Te Whiti was not to be ignored. His response to Sheehan's studied neglect drew the attention of the whole colony to the state of affairs on the west coast. On Sunday 25 May 1879, in a symbolic assertion of proprietorship, he sent his ploughmen, unarmed, to cut his moko into the land at Oakura where the second Taranaki war began in 1863. In the next few weeks his men, always unarmed, ploughed confiscated lands held by settlers from Pukearuhe to Hawera.

The settlers were outraged. William Courteny,[56] on whose farm the ploughing began, telegraphed to Grey on 26 May: 'Five ploughs and 20 hostile natives are ploughing up my best field. . . . If Government do not remove them at once I will shoot their horses and the natives also'. Grey wired back that

Courteny would be wise to leave the case to be dealt with by the ordinary course of law, which though slow was certain, and that while his right to the land might be 'indisputable the shooting of horses or men would be a very grave offence'.[57] Telegrams flew back and forth. Colonel G. S. Whitmore, the colonial secretary, asked Parris on 27 and 29 May whether the natives who were trespassing merely meant 'to force trial by claim on title before Court or Commission or if they were armed and meant to resort to violence and, most importantly, whether it was true that 'one of the Natives ploughing at Tapuae and who has been a friendly Native through all the wars is influenced by having been deprived of the land he is ploughing by confiscation without receiving adequate compensation'. Parris replied on 30 May that he had been to Parihaka and had 'a long discussion with Te Whiti in the presence of about 200 of his followers', all of whom were very civil and dignified, and that there was 'no immediate danger or cause for alarm'. Te Whiti would not resort to violence but had ordered the ploughing and would persist in it in order to 'assert his right to the land'.[58] The local press saw savages on the war-path. 'The ploughing party and most of the natives at Oakura are in a state of excitement, having donned war mats embroidered with red, daubed themselves with war paint and decorated their heads with feathers.' The Auckland papers predictably were less emotional. They could 'hear of no single instance where a settler has been in any way threatened'.[59]

At last the government took notice of the fact that the unrest on the coast was due to widespread disillusionment over the lack of reserves or titles. It suited them to take notice: they could assure the settlers that the natives had no hostile intentions but were simply pacifically asserting their claim. One of the ploughmen was Bob Erangi (Ropata Ngarongomate) of Ngamahanga hapu, a close relation of Te Whiti and an original owner of the land south of the Hangatahua river known as the Stoney River Block, which had been granted as compensation to his hapu after their surrender in 1865 under Grey's peace proclamation. Fox described it as an 'informal restitution' as no title to the land had ever been confirmed.[60]

The settlers were not appeased; while Maori beat their swords into ploughshares, the settlers formed committees in New Plymouth, Hawera, Patea, and Manutahi, and passed resolutions stating that 'an exhibition of the power of the Government . . . with armed men would do more to make the natives act as peaceable subjects than any Civil action in a Court of law . . . dealing with quasi rebel natives who by force dispossess peaceable subjects of land held under Crown grant'.[61] They met Grey, who on 31 May had gone up to New Plymouth with Whitmore and the recently arrived governor, Sir Hercules Robinson, and demanded the government undertake the defence of the province. They told him they felt at any moment their wives and families might be murdered in their beds; they 'were living in a condition of constant menace . . . great uncertainty and anxiety prevailed . . . ruin stared them in the face'. Grey assured them the government would protect the settlers, but this reply was considered unsatisfactory. A further public meeting in New Plymouth declared that as long as the government 'allowed the nest at Parihaka to remain' there would be no peace; the settlers were without 'protection or arms and utterly at the mercy of the Natives', who were not even 'an organised body of armed natives who had made up their minds to declare war upon the Settlers, but fanatics whose mode of action they had no knowledge of'. They did not have just the ploughmen to deal with, nor even the whole of Parihaka, but all the natives on the west coast. They believed that the trouble had begun at Waitara with Rewi demanding the confiscated land, and was compounded by Hiroki, a murderer, being allowed to take shelter at Parihaka, and that if he had been arrested immediately they would not be menaced as they were now. Te Whiti might order them 'to be encircled tomorrow morning'.[62]

This was not the hysteria of new settlers but the reaction of those in the long settled district around New Plymouth, those whose agitation had finally forced the government to allow Titokowaru to leave their district and return to his ancestral lands on the Waimate plains. Settler insecurity was real enough in the face of the number of unsettled land claims in the province,[63] but this was not the fault of Maori. They were a great deal more insecure than the Europeans, and they had, after all, only armed themselves with ploughs. While Maori fought 'a new kind of war',[64] the settlers prepared for such a one as they remembered. It was 'the old fighting chief Titokowaru who was believed to be the most dangerous of them all'[65] that they really had in mind, and they reacted to the thought of Te Whiti and Parihaka much as they had done to Titokowaru and Te Ngutu o te Manu. They went back to the premier and told him they wanted an answer, some assurance before he went back to Wellington. Grey told them he would 'not be bullied', that he had received 'threatening telegrams', and that while he was determined to do all he could to settle the question, he would do nothing wrong: 'I have spoken explicitly and nothing will move me from doing what is right, with caution and prudence'.[66]

The ploughing was suspended while the dignitaries from Wellington were in the area. But they left without making contact with Te Whiti, and the ploughing resumed with the ploughmen 'very orderly and good-tempered . . . but still very earnest and determined to do their work, with perfect faith in the supreme power of Te Whiti and Tohu to bear them harmless through what is ordered to be done'.[67] Ngapuhi and Rarawa chiefs wrote to the governor and the premier on 5 June, asking that their handling of the troubles 'about to spring up in Taranaki . . . be good, and guided by patience, so that good may result, and that peace may rest upon the two races'.[68] But the settlers' minds were on war not peace. They began to enrol as volunteers and demanded the government issue them with arms and ammunition. Imagination was running riot. A 'suspicious vessel' was reported just off the Taranaki coast at the very time Maori people were collecting seafood nearby. The vessel had also been seen there some months before and there was 'reason to fear' she had landed arms – in fact a Maori cart 'containing arms' was reported to have been seen leaving the area.[69]

In the first week of June, telegrams arrived in Wellington from Manutahi, Patea, New Plymouth, Hawera, and even Thames, Christchurch and Timaru offering the services of the local volunteers 'in the event of a war with the Natives'. Whitmore was ready to receive all offers if the government could not 'avert hostilities without sacrificing its duty', but Grey cautiously instituted some enquiries, at last. On 7 June, he telegraphed Brown to ask whether Courteny's land which had been ploughed was 'confiscated land taken from rebel Natives or . . . land taken from friendly Natives under some arrangement of compensation being given in other lands' and if the latter, whether such compensation had been made and accepted by the natives, and titles issued to them for the land. The answer, inevitably, was that it had belonged to both 'rebel and friendly natives' and the latter had signed an agreement accepting other lands as compensation, but no titles had ever been granted for any of it. Some of the ploughmen were 'friendly natives who owned that particular piece' and who had 'signed the agreement on 2 July 1866'. This seemed to surprise Grey, who on 10 June telegraphed the information to Sheehan, Macandrew, Robert Stout and W. L. Rees with the opinion that the ploughing should be interpreted not as a determination to evict settlers from confiscated land but as a means of drawing the attention of the government and asserting a legal right. Sheehan solemnly replied that the news interested him exceedingly but did not altogether surprise him, and that he would 'take steps to have this view of the question made known to such of our friends as know how to use the information with discretion'.[70]

It hardly seems possible that the government, and Grey especially, should have to wait till large numbers of 'friendly natives' joined in Te Whiti's peaceable but insistent protests before they were convinced that Maori were suffering a sense of real injustice and not just exhibiting 'wilfull bounce'. There was political capital to be made now out of such an unexpected discovery. The embattled Grey government, so criticised by speculators in Maori land for its own large-scale buying of Maori lands in contravention of its avowed policy on succeeding to office,[71] and sensitive to criticism of its 'profligate' native policy, would welcome any excuse to justify its handling of the lands question and Maori affairs in general. A further meeting with Tawhiao in May had ended badly, and Fox made great play of the discomfiture of 'the great Pro-consul, the great Maori-tamer' of whom Tawhiao said 'I will have nothing to do with that man Grey'.[72] Fox, Harry Atkinson and Whitaker were vociferous critics of Sheehan and the government. Atkinson was prominent in the Taranaki group which hounded the government to mobilise the colony against local Maori;[73] Whitaker, a noted speculator in Maori lands, reputedly believed 'that any man who gets land out of the hands of the Natives and cultivates it is a public benefactor'.[74] If the government could show judgement in handling the grievances of the 'friendly Maoris' and then crack down hard on the 'rebels', they might yet assuage settler hysteria and turn the political tide.

War fever continued to grow, fuelled by Major Maillard Noake whose appointment had pleased the settlers and given them confidence that the whole of the settled district could be held by volunteers. However, they were strongly in favour of having 'the Ngatiporou sent to Parihaka' to do the fighting for them, since fighting was considered inevitable and it was expected 'the Maoris will strike the first blow soon'. Noake telegraphed Wellington on 9 June that he needed ample provisions in case of a siege: carbines and revolvers, repairs to the Manutahi blockhouse, a doctor and medicines, a clerk and stationery, four drill instructors and an experienced and intelligent adjutant. Whitmore replied tersely that such things were 'all good in their way but not yet essential', and that Noake seemed to be increasing rather than decreasing excitement in the district. He sincerely trusted Noake did not 'express to settlers as to me your conviction that war is inevitable', since as far as the government was aware nothing had as yet happened to justify that impression.[75]

The settlers did not need Noake's urging. Their sentiments were expressed editorially by the local press:

> Perhaps . . . the present difficulty will be one of the greatest blessings ever New Zealand . . . experienced, for without doubt it will be a war of extermination. Justice demands these bloodthirsty fanatics should be returned to the dust. . . . The time has come, in our minds, when New Zealand must strike for freedom, and this means the death blow to the Maori race.[76]

The *New Zealand Herald* was more cautious and was pleased to hear that the mayor of Wellington was to interview the premier 'to urge the necessity for preserving the peace, in view of obtaining the loan in the London Market'. Even a 'slight contest', the paper warned, 'would greatly militate against our obtaining a loan'. By the end of the month, the *Herald* was more outspoken and reported that the 'Atkinson party' were making political capital out of the native difficulty.[77]

Those who least considered war inevitable were the Maori of the district. Te Whiti's followers obeyed Te Whiti's orders and pacifism was his first requirement. Others were saddened or 'pouri because the Pakeha are holding meetings and asking for arms'. And there were a few notes of caution sounded by Europeans. Mr W. N. Syme, the settler living nearest to Parihaka, said there were 'many exaggerated rumours afloat', and while he agreed the situation was grave he could not agree with the excited talk about fighting. Robert Trimble, MHR for the Taranaki constituency of Grey and Bell, dared to inform a 'large and influential' public meeting that he regretted very much 'the line of comment . . . so frequently indulged in with regard to Te Whiti', who he believed was 'very grossly misrepresented'.[78] Trimble distinguished between the old settlers, who had suffered much yet had 'such kindly feelings' towards those 'who had made them suffer', and the great bulk of the inhabitants, the new settlers, who felt no friendship for Maori people and who would 'knock a Maori on the head just as they would a mad dog, if war broke out'.[79] This was useful old settler logic. It meant the ploughmen could still be dealt with severely 'in their own best interests' since it would protect them from this 'dangerous element' in the more recently settled districts. Too much can be made of the difference between the reactions of the old and new settlers in Taranaki. The old settlers prided themselves on their tolerance and good will towards Maori, but it only took a crisis like the ploughing to expose the deep racial bias and intolerance of the old settlers and this was freely expressed in the New Plymouth newspapers of the day. If there was a gulf between new and old settlers, it took the form of jealousy of the earlier settled provincial centre of New Plymouth rather than a difference of attitude towards Maori.

When ploughing started near Hawera on 21 June, the settlers were 'very excited' and resolved to remove the ploughmen 'tomorrow at 12 oclock' if the government would not take steps to do it. Grey asked questions instead: were the natives armed, had they occupied the land, was there any violence, had any damage been done? The settlers replied that they were armed with ploughs and had done violence to Mr Livingstone's lawn. That was provocation enough – although four days later the settlers had 'nearly completed regulating the turf by hand' and after being rolled it would 'not show much sign of damage'.[80] Inspector Foster Goring, of the armed constabulary, advised the government that the settlers had removed the ploughmen and 'carted them across the Waingongoro Bridge', and that the natives were gathering on one side and about a hundred settlers on the other. 'Majors Brown and Noake are there. Natives defiant'. Thompson telegraphed that Te Whiti intended to continue ploughing to force a settlement, and that there was a great desire that the governor should visit the district. But Te Whiti, the only one who could calm the situation, was the last person Grey would negotiate with. Mackay had 'not been near Te Whiti and Tohu yet', and Grey would have the settlers understand that there were no negotiations whatever going on with Te Whiti.[81]

The settlers were sure war would be commenced 'at any moment', but Captain Arthur Tuke reported the ploughmen 'perfectly good humoured' and with no warlike intentions, but an 'implicit belief in Te Whiti'. Grey told him if it appeared their actions would excite the settlers so much that a breach of the peace might ensue, he should have the ploughmen arrested by the police or armed constabulary and bring 'a charge of disturbance' against them. He advised the settlers that they, with the assistance of their friends, were quite justified in removing natives who might be ploughing their land, but he warned Tuke to see that it was done without 'insult or violence'. The Hawera settlers were furious: 'Bloodshed certain if Government continue passive advice. You use AC in future to eject ploughmen'. It still appeared that the government intended the Maori trespassers to be treated under the normal laws of the colony as any European trespassers would have been, but settler pressure – and the reassurance that extra troops had been despatched to the troubled district – finally overcame Grey's caution. The following day, 29 June, Grey wired

Goring: 'if the Natives plough again arrest them all'; and Sheehan instructed his officers and the armed constabulary officers throughout the district not to worry about the law: 'you take the men and the government will find the law'.[82]

Immediately the arrests began on 29 June, Te Whiti was said to have ordered that only men of mana should form the ploughing parties: 'Titokowaru, Te Iki and other leading men' were to be taken prisoner. Those who had been imprisoned or who had demeaned themselves by siding with the government were to 'repair to Parihaka and place themselves under his protection'. The ploughmen were not to be afraid of Europeans or sword wounds or death, and party after party were to be 'taken prisoner and replaced ten times'. No arms of any kind were to be carried and no resistance offered. The ploughing was not merely a ploughing of the soil but 'a ploughing of the mana of the Government' so that it might be 'irritated' into seeking Te Whiti at Parihaka. These directions were reported by Katene to have been issued at a meeting between Titokowaru, Te Iki and others, and a messenger bearing 'final directions' from Te Whiti. When Katene addressed the meeting, 'wishing to save them from the evils they were rushing into . . . Te Iki told him to sit down, such talk was not palatable to his ears'. Te Iki then went to 'examine the farms' on the Hawera side of the river and 'chose Mr Barrow's and Mr Gordon's both near Waihi. Titokowaru decided in favour of the former as there is firewood handy for cooking'.[83]

When Brown took Major Roberts to arrest Te Iki's party on 3 July, they offered no opposition, but Te Iki asked 'that they might not be bound', and promised to go quietly.[84] They were not felons to be arrested for a crime, but men of mana for whom imprisonment in such circumstances would mean tupu, not mate – or, in cultural terms, would be a positive not a negative outcome. But the government labelled them as fanatics in order to deny the justness of their grievance, and then felt free to imprison them to 'save them from themselves'. The *Taranaki News* comforted its readers with some statistics: there were 1,200 armed volunteers in the district and 400 armed constables, while it was thought that Maori had no more than 500 fighting men between Mokau and Waitotara; and assured them that Tawhiao had no part in these troubles 'between Te Whiti and Grey'.[85]

The first batch of 11 ploughmen was committed for trial on 5 July in the New Plymouth Resident Magistrate's Court, charged with malicious injury, forcible entry and riot. The ploughing and the arrests continued throughout the month; on 5 July 90 ploughmen were in custody, the next day 105.[86] In the

New Plymouth court on 24 July, Porana, one of the ploughmen 'indicted for having . . . unlawfully and maliciously broken the soil of a certain field the property of W. Jury and done damage thereto to the extent of £5', declared he had ploughed under the orders of his ariki: 'I am one of his spiritual ploughmen, and it is quite right that I should do his work. My weapon was a plough but yours [the arresting sergeant] was firearms'. Another, 'Mahoki', asked to sign the statement he had made, said 'I do not understand writing now, there is a spirit within me which hinders me from writing'.[87] Two days later, ploughmen who had caused damage estimated at five shillings were 'sentenced to two months hard labour in Dunedin gaol, each to enter into his own recognisance in the sum of £600 and to find two sureties in the sum of £300 each to keep the peace for 12 months, or to be imprisoned for 12 months in Dunedin gaol; sentences to run concurrently'.[88] Others of these desperate criminals were sent directly to Wellington to await trial and were held in Mt Cook prison, on which £750 was quickly spent for alterations and repairs and to build an encircling palisade. Platforms, sentry boxes, night lighting and 'properly disciplined guards' were still needed lest any of these prisoners escape. It was believed that if this happened or if any were 'set free by due course of law' it would be 'a serious disaster to the colony . . . as Te Whiti and the remainder of his fanatical followers would at once set it down to his supernatural power'.[89]

Mackay was now officially a government commissioner, having been appointed on 29 July 'Special Commissioner to investigate alleged unfulfilled promises of reserves or money for natives in connection with the settled blocks on the West Coast'.[90] He reported that the sentencing of Te Iki and Tamati Kuku to seven days' solitary confinement, and of 15 other Ngatiruanui to 'two days' confinement in cells on bread and water, as punishment for insubordination and general disobedience of the gaol regulations', had had a 'most salutary effect' and all orders were now promptly obeyed. Mackay had enquired into the fanaticism of these ploughmen and discovered some remarkable things: 'Ngatiawa . . . joined Te Whiti because they could get no land satisfactorily reserved for them'; Taranaki had 'stronger faith in Te Whiti', their grievance being that lands 'formerly verbally surrendered to them by Mr Parris . . . have not been placed on a satisfactory footing as regards title', and they were dissatisfied 'as to the uncertain tenure of the Parihaka Block'; Ngatiruanui had 'the most unbounded and fanatical reliance on Te Whiti and his supreme authority', deemed themselves 'martyrs to his cause', and complained their lands 'were never conquered and held by Europeans' and that they were offered monetary compensation for their land and promised reserves 'wheresoever they were occupying and cultivating the land'. Having heard all this, the singular conclusion of the special commissioner was that 'no disturbance would have arisen if the Native and Survey Departments had been acting in accord, and the controlling power been vested in the former'.[91]

By the time parliament met on 11 July, the 'self destroying Grey Government' was under extreme pressure both internally and externally.[92] The opponents of Grey and Sheehan's Maori land purchase policies had massed their forces, the economic situation had deteriorated alarmingly, unemployment had risen, and land sales had fallen off. In addition, dissension within the Cabinet had resulted in the resignations of Ballance and Stout, and Grey's leadership was increasingly questioned, partly on account of his handling of the west coast crisis. Ballance for one had advocated stronger action. As treasurer, he wanted 'native difficulties' out of the way in the interests of increased revenue from land sales.

Fox, newly knighted, to Grey's chagrin,[93] and newly elected leader of the opposition, quickly took command of the Address in Reply debate and moved a motion of no confidence in the government. In his speech, 'perhaps the most merciless . . . ever heard in the House of Representatives',[94] he mocked and derided Grey and Sheehan, 'these two Maori-tamers, these conjurors with their magic wands', for their personal and public behaviour and especially for their 'miserable mismanagement, attended with the most alarming, the most disastrous consequences to the country, of Native affairs'. The best possible thing they could have done with the 'King party' was to leave them to themselves instead of 'making love to them in the most violent manner'. As to the 'Waimate and Parihaka affair', they were 'so busy careering over the country and carrying on their political campaigns that they could not search the records of their offices' and discover the promises of reserves made to the tribes over the years. 'In the Waikato they go down on their very knees to the Natives, imploring them to accept their terms. Then the Native Minister comes down to Parihaka and shakes his fist in Te Whiti's face and defies him and Titokowaru.' The thought of the personal conduct of the native minister brought out the offended and enraged puritan in Fox. 'You cannot travel into any part of Maoridom . . . without hearing tales that make us blush for our country. . . . You may track the progress of the Government through the district in which they have travelled by the foul atmosphere and foetid odours they have left behind.' It was no wonder 'the great chiefs of the Maori race should stand aloof from the European'.[95]

Grey's defence of his government ran to ten pages in Hansard. He complained of a hostile governor;[96] of a hostile House; of land speculators and a 'certain number' of landed families enriching themselves at the public cost; of a Legislative Council which 'assumed all the airs of the House of Lords of England'; and particularly he complained of Fox, his 'one consistent enemy' who had dogged his footsteps 'with almost unexampled malignity'. He said almost nothing about Maori affairs or about granting land to Maori, but he would happily accept 'the vast tracts of fertile land still held by the Natives, and which they are from time to time willing to dispose of' and throw them open to auction instead of allowing them to fall into the hands of speculators.[97]

In the Legislative Council, Bell spoke forcefully and calmly, condemning the government for its handling of the situation on the west coast and saying that if the government had condescended to call the west coast tribes together to tell them what land was to be reserved for them, 'satisfactory arrangements might have been made with them'. He insisted that while they must maintain English supremacy and not 'yield to the rubbish which the fanatic Te Whiti' preached about ploughing the land, they must in justice 'give up at once the attempt to get that land except in strict accordance with the promises of the late Sir Donald McLean'.[98]

In the House, Sheehan replied to Fox's charges and bold faced declared that although he could not 'admit that the Natives had any right to the land or to reserves', there was 'abundant evidence in writing that there was every intention to make ample reserves'. He added that he had a plan showing that nearly 4,000 of the 16,000 acres surveyed on the plains were to be set aside as reserves, in addition to 'their burial-places, their pas, and the mouth of every stream running into their lands'. He did not admit that his plan of proposed reserves was not prepared until *after* the surveyors had been turned off and the land offered for sale, but maintained airily that it was 'understood' Major Brown, in whom he had the utmost confidence, should be in a position to make reserves of 25,000 acres out of a block of about 95,000 and this would make Ngatiruanui 'the wealthiest tribe in that part of the country'.[99]

Sheehan illustrated the dichotomy of thought pertaining to Te Whiti, which depended on whether things were going well or badly for the Europeans. Speaking of the time immediately preceding the commencement of the survey, he said that as 'Te Whiti had been a man of peace, and had by his religion been teaching the people for years that these matters must be settled not by force, but by an appeal to a Court of law, we thought we might very fairly go on with the survey of the Plains'. But then, after the interruption of the survey, Te Whiti suddenly was not a sane man, 'a man of the ordinary stamp . . . like Tawhiao, Rewi, or the chiefs in other parts of the country', but 'a fanatic, or something worse' who, when he 'had the fit on', would not 'talk business in a business-like way' but abandoned his senses and acted 'entirely upon his religious promptings'.[100] Rewi, the great fighting chief of Ngatimaniapoto, he who had defied the government's forces to the end, was the man in favour at this time. As he could do no wrong, so Te Whiti could do no right.

The debate in parliament dragged on for two weeks to its inevitable conclusion on 29 July, when the Grey government was shown to have lost the confidence of the House. Grey was granted a dissolution on the condition that he bring forward no 'contested legislation', and stayed on long enough to pass the Maori Prisoners' Trials Act on 9 August, the first of the infamous pieces of legislation brought down to 'settle the west coast difficulty'. Sheehan had promised his officers the government would find the law once the ploughmen were arrested, but he now claimed he was going to 'deal fairly' with them. There were 170 of them in gaol in Wellington and another 25 in Dunedin, and as he would not consider anything so disreputable as the *ex post facto* legislation Atkinson was advocating, he declared that the prisoners must be tried by the law as it stood when they were taken. Atkinson informed the House that Sheehan's posturing was quite unnecessary; the two of them had already agreed how the prisoners would be dealt with. They would not be punished, they would simply be detained, for if they 'were brought to trial, and if through a failure to convict, they returned to their district, war would be quite certain there'. He criticised the government roundly for their handling of the 'business on the West Coast', saying they could not be trusted 'with the protection of the lives and properties of the settlers'. But Grey marvelled at his criticism since 'Not a single life had been lost; not a drop of blood had been shed; and the greater part of the best fighting men of the Natives concerned were now in custody'.[101]

It was not only the best fighting men who were in custody and were to be affected by the bill about to be passed into law. Wi Kingi Matakatea, 'almost the only loyal Native on the coast', had been solemnly promised his land would never be taken, but it too was confiscated and later 'returned' to him, although his title to it was never confirmed. After thirteen disillusioning years he had joined the ploughmen and had been imprisoned with the rest. The Europeans wanted to think his arrest a mistake; he had not been ploughing, but only 'looking on'.[102] But when offered bail Matakatea refused to leave his men, and when about to be sent to Dunedin in January 1880 he would not accept the native minister's offer to be 'all but released', saying that 'if the Government wished to show him kindness he hoped they would do so at Taranaki' by settling the grievances of his people.[103]

The Maori Prisoners' Trials Act provided that the governor in council should fix the date and place of trial 'of certain Maori Prisoners . . . committed for trial at the Supreme Court at Wellington', and also that the place of trial could be 'any other place in the colony' where the Supreme Court sat. The act did not state that the prisoners 'must be brought to trial within three months of . . . passing this Bill' as Whitmore argued in the Council.[104] The governor could name whatever date his ministers advised, and as Sheehan had already agreed with Atkinson that no date should be named, and as the act was to remain in force until 30 days after the commencement of the next session of parliament, there would be ample time to bring in a new bill to ensure further postponement of trial.

The bill was debated in the Council before it was debated in the House.[105] Standing orders were suspended and the bill was not translated, despite the protests of Maori members in both the House and the Council. It was more important to rush the bill through on the last sitting day of the session than to worry about 'theoretical objections' and 'technicalities'. Since the bill stated that it was 'indispensable for the peace and safety of the colony that the ordinary course of law should be suspended', members of both government and opposition were prepared to accept that argument. They could not risk these men being 'liberated with the *imprimatur* of the Supreme Court upon them as guiltless' lest their prophet 'at once have a greater power than the Governor of the colony' and be hurried along 'to excesses, the end of which cannot be foreseen'. William Rolleston, MHR for Avon, thought it would be mischievous either to oppose the bill or discuss it. Fox agreed, saying no responsibility rested on opposition shoulders; it was simply their duty to allow the government to pass its bill.

But there was opposition, from both sides of the House, to people being 'incarcerated for an offence of nothing; to extraordinary and unjust' proceedings; to 'abominable measures' brought in at the last moment and 'pushed through unreasonably'. One member was ashamed that a parliament of Englishmen should pass such a bill, while another declared it was a denial of justice, a conflict with the principles of Magna Carta and a suspension of the Habeas Corpus Act.[106] Atkinson was in no mood for legal niceties and asked if it was possible to deal 'under the common law or the Statute law of England' with a native like Te Whiti who believed himself 'to be a Divine power'. The bill was 'in the interests of the Natives themselves' who required 'protection from their own infatuation', and he hoped the members of the Assembly would 'dismiss from their minds the idea that this action of Te Whiti had in any way been produced by the non-fulfilment of promises made by the Government'. The movement, he said, was a national one and sprang 'from the belief that Te Whiti is a supernatural power, and will again establish the Maoris as the dominant race'.

This sentiment was a telling one. The settlers and their representatives could still claim they lived in fear of their lives, and their emotional accounts of their dread of infatuated savages murdering them all in their beds could still strike a chord of sympathy. Aucklander William Swanson thought the bill a Taranaki measure pressed on the government by Atkinson, and this view was reinforced by an emotional outburst from Thomas Kelly (New Plymouth).[107] Ward described settler fear in the 1860s as very real but substantially unjustified. It was even less justified years later when the 'peaceful religion of Te Whiti was confounded with the bloody tenets of the Hau-Haus' in the 'excited imagination of the ignorant public'.[108] The ageing Titokowaru had long since surrendered his mana toa, his status as a warrior, and it was obvious that the Europeans could outnumber and outgun all the tribes of New Zealand, not just those of the west coast. After all the Maori race was widely believed to be dying out, and now 200 'of the best fighting men on the coast' were in custody, so talk of the settlers' fear of violence was simply an appeal to the emotions and a cloak for the real concern: the challenge to European supremacy.

Many knew that the majority of Maori on the coast were not in favour of war and that Te Whiti, who was 'idolised' by his followers, would not tolerate violence. But there were those who professed to believe Te Whiti to be essentially pacific but perhaps unable to control his 'violent followers' and those who professed to believe that although his followers might be unwilling to fight, Te Whiti might yet force them to do so. Either way the government could claim it was dealing with fanatics, and that it was legitimate to 'put aside the ordinary course of law', imprison these protesters and deny them the justice of a trial. Maori must be saved from themselves and the House was prepared to help the government do it. They might *talk* against the bill, but they would not *vote* against it, would not make it 'contested legislation' that would have to be thrown out of the House. The bill was read a second and a third time on 9 August, and with the 'native question' safely taken care of for the time being, the government could go to the country and fight an election that had more to do with personalities, economics and class issues than with racial ones. Maori lands were an issue, but not Maori people. The situation on the west coast had been a handy issue on which to force an election, but it had little to do with fighting one.[109]

CHAPTER FIVE

Response to the Challenge

1880

These are the days of darkness and the moon and stars give no light.[1]

THE NEW SESSION OF PARLIAMENT OPENED ON 24 SEPTEMBER 1879, BUT it was the end of October before the confusion of the 1879 election and the motions of no confidence were finally dealt with by the aid of the famous 'Auckland Rats' – Reader Wood, William Swanson, W. J. Hurst and W. H. Colbeck, former Grey supporters who went over to the Hall government and gave it a working majority in the House.[2] John Hall was then left as leader of a 'Conservative Government now compelled to be Liberal' with Whitaker, Atkinson, Rolleston and Bryce in his Cabinet. Whitaker's reputation had suffered as a result of his involvement in a dubious deal over the purchase of the Piako swamp and he had lost his seat at the election, but Hall called him to the Legislative Council and appointed him attorney-general.[3] In the governor's speech which opened parliament, it was stated that steps were being taken 'for the holding of a full inquiry into the existence and extent of all the alleged unfulfilled promises in regard to lands', and John Bryce, the new native minister, agreed that 'for the sake of our own reputation abroad and in the colony' an enquiry should be held as he believed there probably were some grievances 'of one kind or another' on the west coast. But, prejudging the situation completely, he declared that there were 'probably no grievances to speak of' on the Waimate plains proper and no mere adjustment of reserves would settle the difficulties that had arisen there. The real trouble, he claimed, was that almost all Maori on the west coast were 'deeply infatuated with the belief that Te Whiti holds supernatural powers, and that he will recover not only the reserves, but also the Plains, and everything else'. Bryce thought it a sad state of affairs when the peace of the colony had to 'depend upon the discretion of a man . . . far gone in insanity'. He explained that his sympathies were with his friends, the settlers, for he understood the state of anxiety in which they lived and felt they deserved the consideration and sympathy of the House 'on account of the noble manner in which they both acted and forebore from acting' at the time of the ploughing.[4]

Such comments were an indication of what was to come, of how the new native minister would react to the inquiry sparked by the actions of Te Whiti and his followers. He told the House that he aimed to improve the Native Department 'out of existence' and to give the Land Purchase Department special attention in order to promote the settlement of the country. He had 'pretty positive opinions' about the alienation of native lands and thought 'the greatest facilities . . . should be given to the Maoris for surveying the boundaries of their land' – not to enable them to settle it themselves, but to facilitate alienation.[5] Bryce lost no time in introducing extraordinarily repressive legislation to parliament, and the next few months were marked by a series of bills designed to keep some of 'the most turbulent Maoris on the coast' safely out of the way in South Island gaols while the native minister, in the face of opposition from the resident tribes, members of the House, his cabinet colleagues, and even the commissioners appointed to inquire into the alleged grievances, went about his plan of establishing a 'close European population' on the west coast.

Bryce was a typical settler who had fought in the wars of the 1860s. His views were hopelessly at variance with Maori aspirations but were quite suitable for the position of native minister in a government committed to reducing expenditure on native affairs. Bryce had a very different background from most cabinet ministers of his time. He had arrived in New Zealand in 1840 as a seven-year-old, the son of an immigrant Scottish tradesman. He had little schooling and from an early age worked in the bush, on farms and in the goldfields. According to Rusden, he was a 'self-opinionated, shrewd and callous' man who had begun life as a 'cow-boy' and whose later conduct as native minister justified 'the inference that he was of the inferior order of cow-boy'.[6] Others described him simply as stern and uncompromising, a man whose 'opinions on the Maori question were the orthodox views of the fighting frontiersman', or, more discerningly, as completely Eurocentric, 'thoroughly paternalistic, insensitive and unsympathetic towards the deeper Maori aspirations'.[7] Bryce claimed to be 'almost a New Zealander', but he was quite unlike Sheehan in that, despite having lived most of his life in close proximity to Maori, he knew little enough about them and found nothing to admire in them as a people. He had absorbed 'very little' of their language and nothing of their culture, which he saw as an impediment to progress, as something to be destroyed.

There was no comfort for the Maori people to be gained from Bryce's native statement. Henare Tomoana, member for Eastern Maori, felt he could not remain a member of Hall's government while his people were 'suffering . . . some . . . in gaol . . . and nothing done in answer to their prayers to alleviate their sufferings'. Wishing 'to go honorably' because he could not see what benefit his people could derive from the policy proposed by the native minister, he bowed to the House and crossed the floor to rejoin his colleagues on the opposition benches.[8]

Things on the west coast were quiet. The ploughing had ceased at the end of August and the local tribes were believed 'to be quietly awaiting the action of the Parliament and of the ordinary Courts of law' – a view perhaps based on the actions of a committee of nine prominent chiefs, led by H. K. Taiaroa, MLC, who wished to test in the Supreme Court the validity of the acts under which the land had been confiscated.[9] As government policy had impinged more and more on the west coast people, so Te Whiti's following had grown;[10] the half-yearly meeting at Parihaka in September was reported to be the biggest yet held there, with about 3,000 Maori and 15 Europeans present to hear Te Whiti's speech which was 'as ambiguous as ever and the Natives even did not understand him'.[11] R. S. Thompson telegraphed an urgent report to Whitmore and sent Sheehan a long account of the meeting, together with a 'literal translation' of the speeches and a commentary to explain the 'allegorical language'. At least part of the commentary derived from Te Whiti's own explanation delivered in the meeting house in the evening. He was said to have talked of his ploughmen, whom he had sent to plough the puku, the vital parts, of the government in order to strike deep at European passions and emotions, and of the consternation and confusion this had caused. The answer to the problem, he said, lay not in legislating but in conferring with him. Again he insisted there would be no fighting, that even if Maori and European together tried 'to create a war it would be in vain'.[12] According to Thompson, Te Whiti referred to his ploughmen again on the second day of the meeting, saying that the government's aim in imprisoning them was 'to bring them under the mana of the Queen'. But he proclaimed that there was tupu, not mate, in going to prison for him: 'You shall suffer imprisonment for my name I will give you a voice and wisdom you will not be abased'.[13] These were the words of a wise man, not a deluded fanatic, yet two months later, when all was quiet and 'nothing particular' had been said at the October hui, Thompson, harking back to the September speech, warned the government to be on their guard. He said Te Whiti had spoken of the end of his work and had predicted some future event. What it might be there was 'no way of discovering . . . because those natives who *will* talk know nothing of the matter, and his confidants . . . will not betray his counsels'. Thompson therefore was 'limited to inference for [his] conclusions',[14] and as usual when Te Whiti was not understood it was concluded that trouble must be brewing.

Had Te Whiti been seen as rational instead of mad, it might have been concluded that he had indeed 'finished his work' and that the future event he predicted, the 'day of death and quarrel', was not to be of *his* making, but the government's. It was as though he had recognised that he would not get justice from the government and he warned his people to be on the alert, but counselled them to have faith: 'be joyful, gently rest all of you'. The end of the world might come for them in the shape of further repression, but still they were to be peaceful and leave the resolution of the quarrel in his hands. There would be no war, for 'his word had gone forth'.[15]

With the change of government, there was a corresponding change in Thompson's reports on the Parihaka question. They became more militant – and more mischievous, as though they were pitched at Bryce, telling the new native minister what Thompson thought he would want to hear. The speech at the small November hui at Parihaka was, he declared, 'thoroughly rebellious . . . an uncompromising assertion of independence' and tantamount to a declaration of war, for although the Parihaka people still insisted they would not fight and relied on their 'non resistance as their safeguard', they believed they could do anything 'short of actual battle and murder without punishment'. Thompson now professed to believe that if they were attacked they would fight, but they probably would not strike the first blow. Charles Brown was happy to accept Thompson's view of the situation and advised the government that the report could be accepted 'as in the main correct'.[16]

All was quiet at the December hui. There were not many present; most people were busy cultivating their gardens and those who were there were waiting for the government's next move. By this time, the House was about to pass a bill to establish a commission to inquire into confiscated lands on the west coast. Thompson thought Te Whiti, who, he said, was 'well informed' of events in Wellington, would respond positively to any proposal put to him to discuss matters, but would also insist on the imposition of certain conditions. Since he would treat with no lesser person than the governor or his appointee, it would be necessary to 'flatter his vanity' by making it clear that the commission was 'fully empowered by the Governor personally as the representative of the Queen'. This unpalatable fact seriously troubled Thompson, who wondered whether 'we are justified by apparently lowering our dignity in appearing to treat with him'. He reluctantly came to the conclusion that they were, since there was so much at stake and Te Whiti's undoubted influence over so many potential troublemakers meant there was no other way of 'extracting evidence' from his followers.

Thompson even had words of wisdom for Bryce on the composition of the proposed commission: gentlemen of dignity and wisdom were required, none to be from Taranaki and none Maori; and on the place of its convening: only Parihaka would be considered a fitting venue by Te Whiti and his people. Thompson was 'aware that we concede a great deal' by agreeing to such a thing, and recommended the commissioners be accompanied by a good strong force of armed constabulary who would 'add to the pomp and circumstance' of the commission and protect it from 'insult and outrage' – and be on hand to carry out the odd arrest. They could even permanently occupy the rebel stronghold should that become necessary, or at the very least spy out the lie of the land while they had the chance.[17] Thompson had his audience summed up: this 'vigorous policy' was just Bryce's style. But he also had an ulterior motive: he was pressing his case for the raise which Sheehan had promised him and which Bryce had so far declined to pay.[18]

On 19 December, the Confiscated Lands Inquiry and Maori Prisoners' Trials Act was passed into law. This was the first of the curious double-barrelled pieces of legislation passed to deal with the 'Parihaka question'. It provided for 'Inquiry into alleged Grievances of Aboriginal Natives in relation to certain Lands taken by the Crown' (those between the White Cliffs and the Waitotara), and it enabled the governor in council to 'Postpone the Trials of certain Prisoners who have been committed for Trial for alleged Offences concerning such Lands'. The second part of the act repeated the provisions of the earlier Maori Prisoners' Trials Act which had now lapsed, and it was to remain in force until '60 days after the commencement of the next session of Parliament'. The act was passed just in time; there was to have been a special sitting of the Supreme Court in Wellington just before the end of the year. The ploughmen could now be legally held without trial until about the following August, when another bill could be introduced to further delay trials which the government really had no intention of holding.[19]

In moving the second reading of the bill on 2 December, Bryce explained that he did not attach much importance to the idea of inquiring into Maori grievances; indeed he was not really convinced that there were any unfulfilled promises to inquire into, and he intended to say very little about the bill because he 'held that it was inexpedient to discuss these matters in detail'. Magna Carta and *habeas corpus* were 'mere legal technicalities', 'mere form[s] of English law' for lawyers, not statesmen, to fall back on. There were, however, two points Bryce wished to clarify: there was no intention in passing the bill to provide for any inquiry into 'the validity of the act of confiscation'; and no one should imagine that the ploughing had anything to do with Maori 'asserting their legal right to the land'.[20] This statement went unchallenged, yet no one, least of all Bryce, had asked Te Whiti what his object was in ploughing.

There were those in the House, however, who were of broader vision than Bryce. They even managed to get the debate adjourned for a week so that the bill could be translated for the benefit of the Maori members, in accordance with standing orders. Some described the bill as 'legislation of a very dangerous and unprecedented character' and a means capable of 'grossly oppressing the Maoris because we happen to be a little afraid of them'. Several expressed the view that if Maori had committed a crime they should be brought to trial and if they had not they should be released forthwith. They questioned the double standards whereby Maori could be treated in a manner that would cause an outcry if applied to Europeans. But Bryce had his supporters – Sheehan chief amongst them. In a very revealing speech, he admitted that there were many unfulfilled promises and that the west coast people had grievances enough to justify all they had done, yet he declared he would vote for the bill since it was in the best possible interests of the natives to be kept in 'mild confinement' till the government had a chance to 'settle the question'. R. J. Seddon too was in favour of the bill and could see no injustice in it. He even thought the prisoners 'seemed to thrive very much better where they were than they would on their own native heath'.[21]

The bill inspired less discussion, less emotional debate than its predecessor had done. There was now a precedent for such legislation. Consciences had been dulled, and members were prepared to accept the view of the 'experts' that but for such a bill there would be war on the west coast. They were also consoled by the promise of a commission to inquire into 'alleged promises and grievances'. But Whitmore pre-empted the commission's findings by declaring that the commissioners should be chosen from 'competent and independent gentlemen', whose deliberations would show that although the government may have been for 15 or 16 years 'very negligent in issuing Crown grants and so on', it had not actually 'done any substantial injustice whatever'.[22] Although the ploughmen had not committed any crime which under the existing law would merit a long term of imprisonment, the majority of the legislators were not disturbed by the injustice of continuing to hold them in confinement while the government put its house in order.

Francis Dillon Bell had a more lively sense of justice and raised a prophetic voice of his own in the Legislative Council. He did not delude himself that after so many years the Maori community would accept as anything more than another government device to 'stave off difficulties' a mere commission of inquiry that did not have the power to make decisions and fulfil promises. He disagreed with the very preamble of the bill which stated that it was 'alleged' that promises had been made: he reminded the Council that, while the proclamation of 1865 confiscated 'the land of those in rebellion', it not only 'did not confiscate the land of those who remained loyal, it conserved their rights and made the express promise to them that their land should not be taken'. Clearly these promises had not been kept and they were 'absolute promises, whose fulfilment some day was a necessity on the part of the Government', no matter what the cost.[23]

Here was the rub. The government dared not run the risk of returning the prisoners to the land, but the cost in financial and philosophical terms of returning the land to the prisoners was one the colony was not willing to face. The thought of vast tracts of fertile land lying idle in Maori hands and mana motuhake, Maori integrity, undiminished, Maori separateness assured, was not to be contemplated. It was too high a price to pay for justice. With reason the prisoners were denied the opportunity to raise the legality of the confiscation in a court of law; with reason the commission was limited to inquiring into 'alleged' promises but not to fulfilling them.

On 20 January 1880, the governor, Sir Hercules Robinson, appointed William Fox, Francis Dillon Bell and Hone Mohi Tawhai commissioners under the act.[24] Bell was a relative of Edward Gibbon Wakefield and, like Fox, a former New Zealand Company man. His French education had provided him with 'charming and delightful manners', and his linguistic ability and long experience in New Zealand had made him a fluent Maori speaker.[25] Tawhai was a Ngapuhi chief and member for Northern Maori. Their commission required them 'to inquire into, examine and report upon' claims brought before them or initiated by them related to promises made or 'alleged to have been made' by the government regarding lands between the White Cliffs and the Waitotara river confiscated under the 1863 act or amending acts. All evidence given before the commissioners was to be 'fully and fairly taken down and transcribed in writing' and if necessary accompanied by a 'full and accurate translation . . . duly verified as correct',[26] a notable advance on the system so long in use of verbal communication through incompetent interpreters. Any two of the commissioners could, acting together, exercise the powers of the commission, and their written report was to be presented within four calendar months from that date.[27]

The west coast tribes were notified of the commission by a proclamation also dated 20 January 1880, which informed them that those with 'claims and grievances' were to bring them before the commissioners. Should they neglect the opportunity to do so, the blame would rest with them and not with the government.[28] Despite the promises of the acts and proclamations of confiscation that loyal natives should retain their land, they were now obliged to come before the commissioners in order to have these promises fulfilled.[29] The title 'loyal native' was not applied to those who had never borne arms against the Queen but who had fallen out of favour with the government, and the most loyal native, disillusioned by 15 years of broken promises, was on the same footing as the most intransigent rebel. Had colonial governments abided by the laws of their own making, there would have been 'no grievances to speak of'. Since they had not done so and were undoubtedly in the wrong,[30] they were morally obliged to return all land illegally confiscated – and, as Bell said, it did not require a commission to determine which that was. They could then 'as an act of grace' have inquired into the many verbal promises known to have been made over the years and, since the peace of the colony was supposed to be the aim of the exercise, settle the remaining rebels on defined blocks. If the much vaunted West Coast Commission was seen by some, both Maori and European, to be window-dressing or humbug, it is not surprising. As it was constituted under Bryce's legislation, it was aimed more at making an impression abroad than at dispensing justice at home.

On 23 December 1879, the governor issued a proclamation ordering that all those committed for trial under the Confiscated Lands Inquiry and Maori Prisoners' Trials Act and held in Mt Cook prison be tried in the Supreme Court in Wellington on 5 April 1880.[31] Early in the new year, however, these prisoners were quietly transferred from Mt Cook prison and shipped to gaols in Dunedin and Hokitika. Bryce reported their removal 'this a.m. by 6.15 while streets were empty'.[32] Many people found this dawn raid disturbing, and in the House Tawhai expressed the opinion that the prisoners had been sent to the South Island 'in order that they might be got rid of, and that they might perish there'.[33] He had not forgotten the fate of those taken prisoner after Titokowaru's war and kept confined in cells or who sheltered in caves as they worked on the road to the Otago peninsula between 1869 and 1872. Thirty or more of them had died in their southern exile.[34]

The West Coast Commission held its first sitting at Hawera on 11 February 1880 with just two commissioners, Fox and Bell; the one connected with the confiscation, the other with the Waitara purchase. Tawhai had asked to be relieved of his position as a commissioner with Bell and Fox, feeling he would be like a 'carthorse with blinkers on, driven by a man with a whip who pulls the reins which way he pleases'. Neither Hall nor Fox gave Tawhai the credit for deciding his resignation for himself, but put it down to 'the work of Europeans'. Fox told Bell there was no time to be lost in starting their work, as 'Mohi's advisers will be doing all they can to impede us and the less time we give them the better'.[35]

Tawhai described past governments, which had included Fox and Bell as native ministers, as the 'root of all evil'. He claimed he accepted office as a commissioner since he had fought neither against Hauhau nor the Queen, but when he learned his fellow commissioners were not impartial men but were 'the very men who had created the trouble on the West Coast' he resigned his appointment. Fox, in a scurrilous speech about Tawhai's resignation, accused him of 'cheerfully' accepting his position, asking for an advance on his expenses, and then disappearing for some days before publishing his resignation in the newspapers in language 'put into his mouth by some designing person'.[36]

The settler press was indignant at the suggestion from some quarters that the commission was appointed to inquire into the legality of the confiscation which, they said, had taken place 'by the right of might'. In their view the confiscation was an 'accomplished fact' not to be questioned, and assigning liberal reserves to the natives would not be a 'confession of a weak case but an act of pure generosity on the part of those who . . . are entitled to the whole. . . . The idea of turning the Waimate Plains into a vast menagerie for certain creatures to lie and bask in was never thought to be in the range of possibility'.[37]

Discussions were held between Fox, Bell, Bryce and others with regard to Tawhai's replacement on the commission. Katene's name was put forward but Bell was doubtful about his suitability because of his 'insufficient rank'. Fox, with fine disregard for Maori values, could not see that as a valid objection, but in any case was ready to go on 'either with Bell alone or with another European added'.[38] In the event, Tawhai was not replaced and Fox and Bell conducted the whole inquiry on their own. There was obviously dissension in the Cabinet about a replacement commissioner and Fox and Bell agreed to 'feel their way' for a while, by which time Hall thought that it would 'seem a mockery' to give them a Maori colleague. All the same, he was 'pouri as the Maori call it' about there being no third commissioner but admitted he was 'in a minority of one in the Cabinet on the subject'.[39]

Bryce was sorely put out by the appointment of this commission, which he felt would poach on his special preserve, and was determined that 'Justice to the natives was to go hand in hand with a thorough determination . . . to establish the authority of law upon the Coast'.[40] Robinson explained to the Colonial Office that by this Bryce meant that roadmaking and surveying on the plains would proceed while the commissioners held their inquiries, and if any resistance was offered the armed constabulary would be ready to march on Parihaka 'in order to destroy that headquarters of fanaticism and disaffection'. The governor was uneasy about this arrangement, but his advisers were 'strongly of opinion that it is desirable to take action before the turbulent and ill-affected natives now in prison are released'. And once again, financial expediency was to override political caution: the state of armed preparation then being maintained was 'as expensive as war', and the ministry could see no end to it if decisive steps were not taken.[41] Fox and Bell had even greater misgivings than the governor and 'positively refused to act' unless ministers were prepared to maintain the *status quo* with regard to claims, reserves and titles until the commission had held its inquiry and submitted its report. Ministers compromised: the commissioners went to the coast in January 1880 to begin visiting the various settlements, and on 29 January Bryce was permitted to move 'several strong detachments' across the Waingongoro to carry out 'repairs' to the old coast road across the Waimate plains. But the survey of the disputed land was not to be resumed 'for the present'.[42] The local settlers had hoped for more. 'The Government must strike a blow at the Maori and once more place the British flag on the Waimate and other confiscated lands, never again to be removed.'[43]

It is hard to see how the tribes on the west coast were to understand that their grievances were to be inquired into impartially when the government came bearing 'the olive branch in one hand and the rifle in the other', as Henry Scotland put it in the Legislative Council.[44] But true to his peaceful professions, Te Whiti offered no obstruction to the roadmaking. Bryce thought this was because Maori recognised it as an assertion of European 'right and power to occupy the Confiscated territory'. It was anything but that. When the armed constabulary roadmakers crossed onto the plains, Te Whiti sent several cart-loads of food as a present from the local tribes to the Europeans. Some time later, this was followed by a gift of food specifically sent from Te Whiti and Tohu to Colonel Roberts as 'chief of the Constabulary'. Again the significance of the gesture escaped Bryce, who was 'not inclined to attach very much importance to the fact of presents being thus repeatedly made' but thought they probably just indicated peace.[45] In fact they were an unmistakable assertion of the donors' mana over that land. This was the manaaki, the traditional hospitality of host to guest, and by accepting the food the guests accepted the manaaki and acknowledged the mana. The west coast commissioners, a deal more astute than Bryce, recognised this and proposed the native minister return the gift in kind to signify that the government rejected the assertion of mana and simply accepted the offer as an act of kindness: 'ko te atawhaitanga kua utua e te atawhaitanga'.[46]

Thompson, still trying to ingratiate himself with Bryce, gave it as his opinion that since Te Whiti and Tohu recognised Colonel Roberts as 'a fit recipient' of their gift they would also be prepared to recognise him as 'a person authorised to enquire' into the meaning of the disturbances. Thompson had not 'the slightest doubt' that if Colonel Roberts took the constabulary to Parihaka and *demanded* of Te Whiti his meaning, all would be explained to him. Fighting was 'out of the question' and thus the matter would be finally settled without 'compromising the dignity of the nation'.[47] Thompson followed up this advice with a direct appeal to Bryce 'even at the risk of being considered importunate'. He said the government should not let the occasion of the March meeting at Parihaka slip by without confronting Te Whiti and bringing the whole matter to a head. As long as Hiroki was at Parihaka they had ample excuse to send in the constabulary, for 'if the prisoners in Otago are worthy of punishment so is Te Whiti their master'. The affair could be settled with credit to the ministry, 'not to mention the "kudos" which would accrue' to Bryce personally.[48]

Brown, Sheehan, Mackay, Thompson, Bryce: each was sure he knew how to solve the west coast problem – and that he alone knew it. Bryce was not prepared to say Thompson's advice was wrong, 'but the risk would be too great'. If Hiroki was not surrendered on demand 'as is not unlikely . . . our failure would be complete'. He said Te Whiti had given no clear indication of wishing to give way, but should he do so it would be easy to give him an opportunity to 'withdraw with grace and dignity' as Thompson advised.[49]

Bryce was unable or unwilling to read the 'clear indication' Te Whiti had given, but the commissioners were not so obtuse. They notified the people gathered at Parihaka for the February hui that they would be sitting at Oeo[50] and would be glad to hear anything the Parihaka people had to say. Naturally the Parihaka people said that if the commissioners wished to talk to them they were welcome to go to Parihaka. The commissioners proposed going there, but this prospect disturbed Hall who told them that of course they would do as they thought proper but he hoped they would 'consider once, twice, thrice before accepting the invitation'.[51] In the end they did not accept it and they lectured the few Maori who 'embarked on the government canoe' and attended the Oeo sitting on 19 February about listening to Te Whiti's foolish words.[52] But only one of those who had listened to Te Whiti was there to hear the commissioners telling them it was the word of the governor that prevailed 'on both sides of the Waingongoro'; that the people of Parihaka could ignore the commission but its work would go on anyway; that despite their foolish absence their land would not be taken away, so long as they remained at peace and did not interfere with the work of the commission. Tutahau replied:

> I belong to Parihaka and have just come from there. I have only this to say to you, in answer to the statement you have just made. You throw all the blame upon my side. . . . The wrong you have done you say nothing about; you blame us for everything. . . . The dispute between yourselves and Te Whiti is on the question of your chieftainship or superiority. I have nothing further to say to you or before you, the Commission.[53]

It was a question of mana. The commissioners were 'adulterous men enquiring into their own sin', men whose hands were soiled with land confiscation, sent to treat with Te Whiti who had not been in rebellion against the Queen and whose land was guaranteed to him by the proclamation of confiscation. Their commission empowered them to inquire into *all* promises and engagements but, from the start, they 'refused to hear counsel who wished to question the validity of the confiscation'. Fox argued that 'harpies' and 'rogues' put Maori up to questioning the validity of the confiscation, and he wrote an 18-page memo dealing with the commissioners' decision not to listen to such arguments. He justified this decision on the grounds that the 1863 act was not *ultra vires*, and under English law conquest did not have to be validated by occupation as it would under Maori law. He ended lamely by contending that even if an inquiry were legally due to Maori, there were no moral considerations which would justify the panic this would cause to innocent settlers who had bought land from the colonial government.[54]

Fox and Bell were concerned that so few of the local people attended their early hearings.[55] At the end of the Waitara sitting on 8 March, they again lectured the loyal natives assembled before them, believing that their words would be reported back to Parihaka. If Te Whiti had complaints to make they would listen to them, they said, but if he made none they would 'tell the Governor that Te Whiti has spent so much of his breath in prophesying about those things that do not come true, that he has nothing at all to say to the Governor'.[56] This drew no response from Parihaka, so once more the commissioners proposed going there themselves. Bryce was so concerned he sent a coded telegram to Hall: 'Commissioners have decided to visit Parihaka. I can't approve but there is no help for it. They assure me they are doing it with the best intentions which I quite accept and will hope for the best.' Hall agreed with Bryce 'but as it would be improper for Government to do anything which might appear to interfere with independent action of Commissioners' he could only say he thought the step inadvisable and hoped it would be made clear to Te Whiti 'and everybody else' that such a proceeding would be one for which the government was in no way responsible.[57]

The commissioners did not visit Parihaka, but there were about 1,500 Maori and 50 Europeans at the March 1880 hui, the tenor of which was such as to calm local sentiments. The Europeans had as usual been given a friendly reception at Parihaka[58] and the 'happy faces of the natives' returning from the hui were striking evidence that there was no war spirit abroad. The Parihaka meetings were now reported to be doing good rather than harm, and were seen as a safety valve whereby Maori could release, in talk rather than action, 'any surplus anger they may have generated'.[59] The local press was a reliable barometer of settler feeling. When the government took decisive action and European dominance appeared assured, as it did at this time, the press could afford to be magnanimous. When Maori appeared to have the upper hand, the press became strident and racist.

Thompson sent a report of Te Whiti's speech, giving the Maori which he said was from his notes taken at the time, the English translation of what was said, and his interpretation of what was meant. 'Nothing', he admitted, 'has ever been told me straight at Parihaka', but he claimed Te Whiti wanted an area of Taranaki land reserved 'hei wahi tapu mo tenei whakatupuranga, te hunga tika me te hunga he' – which Thompson saw fit to interpret as meaning 'his end and aim is to form a settlement at Parihaka which shall be the head-quarters of the Maori people, not only of the tribes of Ngatiawa, Ngatiruanui and Taranaki but also of all the tribes of the island who shall seek refuge with him'. This settlement, he said, would rule itself, have its own laws and 'live at peace with the Europeans by a sort of International treaty'. Te Whiti would then arrange with 'someone appointed by the Governor' for the rest of the confiscated land to be settled by both European and Maori, the Maori 'on their reserves and the Europeans on the remainder, but the Maories being owners of the soil to receive "takoha" from the Europeans'. Thompson again expressed his view that there could be no peaceful settlement of the Waimate plains till Parihaka was broken up.[60]

A rather different version of Te Whiti's speech was given by the *Taranaki News* which reported him as saying that 'justice should be done to the Natives and in return they would give the Europeans hospitality'; that although the government had not fulfilled its promises and was ready to 'enforce its own will by the point of the sword' Te Whiti had no weapons and his people would not fight; that his people should not sell any more land, for the proceeds would only be spent on drink; and that while the Europeans spoke of him 'as a madman and a fool' they should 'judge by his sentiments whether he was mad'. The newspaper admitted that translation of Maori speeches was largely a matter of guesswork and that it was 'the exception rather than the rule for any two interpreters to give a like translation and meaning of a speech'.[61]

Thompson's concept smacked of European, not Maori thinking, but Bryce would have found the interpretation accorded well with his own view that Parihaka was a dangerous nest of fanaticism which needed breaking up. By mid April, he had about 600 armed constabulary and public works men pushing on the roadmaking towards Parihaka. He had expected opposition, especially when the roadmakers crossed the Waiweranui, 'the Rubicon of the Parihaka country', at the beginning of the month, but again no opposition was offered. Roadmaking to Bryce was an outward and visible sign of European power and authority, and was meant to overawe as much as it was meant to open up the country.

On 15 March 1880, the west coast commissioners had issued an interim report which stated unequivocally what had long been obvious: that the question of reserves was basic to the settlement of the west coast difficulty and that nothing should have been done or must now be done until adequate reserves were marked out on the ground for both the Ngatiruanui and Taranaki people. They recommended an immediate start be made to delineate a 'broad continuous belt of reserve' of about 25,000 acres on the Waimate plains between the Oeo and Waingongoro rivers, enclosing all the settlements and cultivations of the Ngatiruanui people. This reserve would be inalienable 'so long as the Natives live there in peace', but it would be anything but a Maori enclave. The commissioners advised that control of the whole reserve should remain in the government's hands until such time as the forest was cut back from the various settlements, leaving the inhabitants no escape route into the bush and giving Europeans the 'strategical command of the whole coast' – a recommendation highly reminiscent of the thinking of the late 1860s.

The commissioners' second main recommendation was to set apart for the Parihaka people 20,000–25,000 acres of their own tribal land 'so long as they live there in peace'. There was an element of blackmail in this proviso. The people had kept the peace for 15 years but were required to maintain an undertaking of indeterminate duration in order to qualify for the reserves which should have been theirs by right. If their grievances were legitimate, as the commissioners said they were, then the reserves should not have been the subject of bargaining and provisos. But the settlers had to be appeased, and knowing that their advice would be unacceptable to those many people whose aim was to destroy Parihaka, the commissioners took pains to point out that, like it or not, it was imperative to provide reserves for the Parihaka people. They

> are there, and they must have land to live upon; and, what is more, being there, they certainly will not go away. The sooner every one makes up his mind to that the better; and the sooner every one makes up his mind that any idea of appreciably replacing out of Parihaka land the vast expenditure going on is illusory, the better too.

It was obvious to the commissioners that the question of the plains and that of Parihaka were inseparable; that if an attempt were made to occupy the plains without Te Whiti being assured of his safety at Parihaka then it would be found that they could 'get neither Parihaka nor the Plains except at the price of a struggle which no one can doubt would then be desperate'.[62] Just as one could hear Fox's trenchant moralising in the preachment the commissioners made at the conclusion of their various hearings on the coast, so one could discern Bell's more temperate and realistic judgement in the words of the commissioners' report.

The report received a mixed reception. Hall 'substantially' agreed to the recommendations of the commissioners and wanted immediate steps taken to carry them out as far as was possible under existing legislation. Atkinson agreed that 'the question must be dealt with as a whole'; and thought 'ample reserves as ample as you like so long as other Natives are not made jealous' should be assigned immediately to Te Whiti and his people.[63] Bryce procrastinated, and when Hall urged him to make a start on the reserves he decided to begin not with reserves for the disaffected, but with those for Hone Pihama, who was present at every hearing of the commission, who spoke more than anyone else did and of whom it was said 'he is the West Coast Commission'. In addition Bryce wanted more roadmaking, around Normanby. 'This will be enough surveying for the present and in my opinion there will be risk of stoppage or worse. . . . It will not do to be hurried into scattering more survey parties over the country than are necessary to shew that we are going steadily on.' Bryce was not happy about the commission and its work and found various opportunities to question or belittle its labours, saying that he was aware of difficulties the commissioners were not aware of, and that he had not overlooked certain points but was sure the commissioners had.[64] Report or no report, he was determined to go his own way, for he had persuaded himself that the problem he was up against 'comprised mental conditions'; that the question of reserves was but 'a small matter in Te Whiti's eyes' and that the question of the confiscation 'held a very subordinate place in his mind'.[65] There was therefore no valid reason he could see for making reserves for this fanatic and his followers and his aim was simply to overawe them with an unmistakable display of European superiority and might.

Soon after the report was issued, it was decided Parris should superintend the laying out of reserves as recommended by the commissioners. He was also sent to Parihaka to inform Te Whiti about the conclusions they had reached. According to Thompson he received a warm welcome there, but as an individual, an old friend returning after a long absence, and not as an official of the government or a representative of the commissioners.[66] Parris simply said the people were 'civil and cheerful', busy with their crops, with no thought of fighting; the only hostility he encountered was from Te Whiti, who was 'vexed and sullen' so that it was 'impossible to reason with him'. Parris commanded that all the people assemble in the morning to hear what he had to say. Te Whiti refused; he was not about to listen to a proposal made by 'one person'. Parris decided Te Whiti was put out because the commissioners had not gone to Parihaka, although they had had discussions with Titokowaru. Parris was himself put out by the presence of another European expert at Parihaka, one S. Croumbie-Brown, who had been 'annoying Te Whiti . . . with proposals for him to go to Wellington and promised to raise £500 to pay his expenses if he would go', a proposal, said Parris sourly, which amused the natives highly.[67]

Croumbie-Brown was another who saw himself as ideally suited to solving the west coast problem. He was an experienced war correspondent who had been employed by the Edinburgh *Daily Review* during the American Civil War and the Fenian invasion of Canada and he was now earning an apparently precarious living as a special correspondent for the *Lyttelton Times* and the *New Zealand Herald*. He claimed to be 'actuated solely by a desire to do what little I may towards furthering the best interests of the colony', but the local press, riled by his very presence in their midst, condemned him as 'a disguised Duke or an undisguised snob . . . a writer of exaggeration, misrepresentation, persiflage and rot'. Croumbie-Brown had made several visits to Parihaka and claimed that he had 'gained an ascendancy' over the mind of Te Whiti, who, he declared, had told his people that Croumbie-Brown was the only European who had ever approached him in whom he felt confidence.[68] What Te Whiti would not have known was that Croumbie-Brown, under the guise of friendship and impartiality, was in fact spying for the government in return for money to pay his debts and in the hope of gaining more steady employment with the government. He had first offered his services to the Grey ministry and had agreed to do a report for Whitmore on a recent visit to Parihaka, but the change of government had prevented that scheme. At the beginning of November 1879 he approached Hall with another offer, claiming Te Whiti would now be more open to negotiations because of his decreasing influence and his people's increasing disillusionment, and that he, Croumbie-Brown, was the ideal person to do the negotiating. He asked for no reward 'beyond actual expenses' but hoped that if he succeeded the government and parliament would recognise his services 'in one form or another'. To substantiate his claim Croumbie-Brown offered Hall the report he had contracted to do for Whitmore, and he presented it on 13 November with a request for the 20 guinea fee for which he had urgent need to meet 'a certain liability next week'.[69]

This report, accompanied by sketch maps of Parihaka and the surrounding area, set out in great detail how the place might be stormed and taken by European troops. All the obstacles to easy troop movements or natural defensive positions where Maori warriors might lie in ambush were described. He thought that Parihaka might easily be reduced by

> mortars and rockets . . . without any attempt at a surprise. . . . Before exposing riflemen to the Maori fire the use of rockets would . . . quickly clear the cover of Maoris lying in ambush, who would . . . retreat upon Parihaka. Cooped up there, and with a few guns or mortars planted on the hill marked W in both sketches the reduction of the place would be comparatively easy.

He also took the opportunity to report on the arms situation as he perceived it. He estimated Parihaka sported 'quite a thousand guns'. He had seen no ammunition but suspected it was stored with other arms 'in two strongly-built whares, the doors of which were heavily padlocked'. There was also 'an enormous number of picks and shovels', most of which were obviously not in daily use. Croumbie-Brown offered Hall his opinions with 'great diffidence, and only from the sense that in a matter of this kind everyone is in duty bound to contribute as much information on the subject as he can'.[70]

After sending his report to Hall, he pestered to be accredited as special correspondent with the armed constabulary. Hall referred him to Bryce and at the same time told Rolleston it would be unwise to refuse to allow him to go to 'the front', and that he should be offered reasonable facilities such as were offered to correspondents of English newspapers.[71] Croumbie-Brown was quite at home around the armed constabulary camp by the time the West Coast Commission began its hearings. Fox was obviously not happy with this arrangement, but Hall insisted that as long as there was no interference with the work of the commission 'it would be a difficult and delicate matter to exclude him from the camp' and impossible to ban him from the district. His reports were picked up by newspapers throughout the country and so far they had been favourable to the government and the work of the commission. Hall was afraid to do anything that might 'give them a different tinge'.[72]

The favourable tinge did not last long and Hall was soon complaining of mischievous 'telegraphic effusions' which riled him greatly. However, Croumbie-Brown's presence around the camp was suffered for some months before Fox was able to report his pleasure that he had 'got his congé. He had axes of his own to grind which were of more consequence to him than the settlement of the West Coast difficulty'.[73] Fox also made a scathing attack on Croumbie-Brown in the House, saying he had done all in his power 'to throw difficulties and impediments in the way of the Government'; that his writing was full of sensational rumours and prophecies and was the laughing stock of the whole country; and that his principal informant was 'Kimball Bent, this deserter', who supposedly lived in the dark recesses of the forest, whereas in reality he 'had been living for months, if not for years, with some Maoris within a mile of Hawera'.[74] It is doubtful whether Croumbie-Brown was any worse than the other correspondents writing sensational copy about the west coast, but the *Lyttelton Times* was anti-government – and pro-Grey – so that paper and its 'precious correspondent' were anathema to many.

The roadmaking and surveying continued without interruption through April, and Parris reported that the seaward boundary of the continuous reserve would be cut by the end of the month. Te Whiti would not cooperate with the government but neither would he offer active opposition. Charles Brown thought he was 'at the pinnacle of his power' and that any day might see the collapse of his influence.[75] Bryce was so pleased with the success of his operations that he told the governor matters on the west coast were at last 'in a fair way of being peacefully and satisfactorily settled', and he too predicted that belief in Te Whiti's supernatural powers would be diminished by the government's having falsified all his prophecies. Bryce said the government was almost ready to assign reserves on the plains and would do so when the local people were 'prepared to tacitly acquiesce' in the arrangements; in any case he intended to recommence the sectional survey which had been 'so rudely interrupted 14 months ago, and sell land on the Plain for immediate European occupation'.[76] Bryce was determined to have his way and was already undercutting the work of the commission: the people would not simply be granted reserves, they must 'acquiesce', that is, they must submit. To him the European settlement of the plains, not the granting of reserves to the Ngatiruanui and Taranaki people, was 'the only certain way' to settle the problems on the west coast. He had not learned from the interruption to the survey or from the recommendations of the commissioners, but was continuing a policy which had failed before and was a sure invitation to further failure.

Thompson reported that at the Parihaka meeting in May Te Whiti seemed to express his despair at the continuing 'vexatious works' of the government: 'These are the days of darkness and the moon and stars give no light'. He counselled his people to be peaceful and to have faith, and he consoled them by telling them that the days of 1880 would not be like those of 1860. Then there was war and killing, now there was just a show of force to overawe them into giving up their tapu land. Thompson said he had heard Te Whiti addressing the people in his wharenui and he had told them 'there was a man between the Government and the Maories who had all things in his care and . . . if he saw that there was a sign of justice being done to the natives . . . he would step forward and bring matters to a conclusion'.[77] Te Whiti waited in vain for any sign of justice.

The commissioners had issued a very strong warning that it was 'dangerously absurd to let a question on which may hang the peace of the country be subordinated as it might be by surveyors to the question of the easiest point at which to ford a stream or make a road'.[78] Despite this, the constabulary's roadmakers advanced with scant regard for the sensibilities of the people whose land they were invading. They cut fences, crossed cultivations and looted Maori property. At the June hui, Te Whiti and Tohu again stressed forbearance: their people must restrain their feelings of vexation at the works of the constabulary and not 'by retaliation . . . cause a war'. The constabulary officers gave 'stringent' orders to their men, but this 'failed to restrain the looting propensities of some who . . . are sufficiently numerous to bring discredit on their more orderly comrades'. Thompson explained that he had difficulty convincing Maori that the looting was *against* the orders of the government and not a *result* of them.

But Thompson had scant sympathy for the people at Parihaka, 'not a tithe' of whom were of Parihaka. The place was 'full of Ngatiawa, Ngatitama, Ngatiruanui and Whanganui tribes' together with people from Patea, Waitotara and other places, while the numbers from Waikato increased from month to month. He thought it was ridiculous that the commission talked of giving the Parihaka block to Te Whiti so that aliens such as these could 'partake of the blessings to accrue when the Europeans are abased, the chieftainship has returned unto the Maories and Te Whiti's millennium is established in happy independence from British Rule'. But more than all this, it was the allocation of reserves on Taranaki land between the Oeo and the Wahamoko streams to Hone Pihama, 'a Ngatiruanui man . . . of the Tangahoe hapu', which really riled Thompson.[79] Certainly he had an axe to grind as no provision had yet been made to return land on the plains to his wife's hapu who 'had never been in rebellion', but he was right in questioning the favourable manner in which Pihama and Manaia were treated. Their people were 'to a man' followers of Te Whiti and that should have been enough to damn them in government eyes. Te Whiti, who had never been in rebellion, was held responsible for his followers whom, it was acknowledged, he was able to restrain; Pihama, an 'ex-rebel', was not held responsible for his and he was unable to restrain them. He could not even restrain his daughters and nephew who had moved to Parihaka, nor prevent his wife regularly appropriating his government salary to Parihaka funds.[80] The government's inconsistency did not escape Te Whiti, or anyone else on the coast, and must have called into question the impartiality of the findings of the commissioners whose hearings, after all, were conducted exclusively amongst those whose views were unfavourable to Te Whiti. Those who would talk knew nothing, and those who knew something had kept their counsel.

The new session of parliament had opened on 28 May and the question of the Maori prisoners was soon raised. An order in council dated 31 March had postponed the date of trial yet again from 5 April to 5 July 1880, and on 29 June the government bought more time by having a further order in council issued which postponed the trial till 26 July,[81] the day before the act under which these orders was issued was due to expire. When questions were raised on 17 June about the west coast situation, Whitaker, with Bell's backing, declined to discuss the question 'piecemeal', saying that 'within a few days' they would have the commissioners' report before them and they would then fully consider the whole matter.[82] But before the report was ever discussed in parliament and just two days after it was issued on 14 July, a new bill, the Maori Prisoners' Bill, was introduced as a 'temporary measure' to provide for the further detention without trial of the ploughmen protesters. Despite the commissioners' report which stated as clearly as it could be stated that the west coast tribes had legitimate grievances, all pretence of bringing the prisoners to trial was now dropped. It was not deemed necessary to try them 'with a view to infliction of punishment', but since their release 'would endanger the peace of the colony, and might lead to insurrection' they were to be kept safely out of the way while 'measures' were taken on the west coast. All the untried prisoners, and those who had been tried but were still held in prison because of their failure to find sureties to keep the peace and whose sentences were about to expire, were by this act (the Maori Prisoners Act 1880) deemed to have been lawfully arrested and to be in lawful custody: they could be lawfully detained but could not be discharged, bailed or liberated except by the governor in council 'any law or statute to the contrary notwithstanding'. There was provision in the act for the governor from time to time to release some of the prisoners, and this enabled Robinson to describe the act to the secretary of state as one designed to release rather than detain prisoners.[83] The act was to remain in force only until the end of October, but it could be extended at the governor's pleasure for three months at a time.

Bryce was anxious to hurry the bill through the House, but it occasioned fierce debate and was strongly opposed by those who were averse to the suspension of *habeas corpus* and who hoped by stonewalling to prevent the passage of new legislation before the old expired and the prisoners had to be freed. Bryce claimed that his government had made no mistakes on the coast and their actions had been an unqualified success. The telegraph line was almost completed, the roadmaking had been uninterrupted, they were about to erect a lighthouse at Cape Egmont, and before long he hoped to see a good deal of land sold and hundreds of Europeans settled on the Waimate plains, 'thus disposing of the Native difficulty on that coast for ever'. These were the government's 'measures' which were to be put in place before the ploughmen could safely be released. There was no mention of reserves and no mention of the recommendations of the West Coast Commission, whose report the House had awaited, but had then not discussed, before bringing in legislation. Te Whiti was dismissed as a chief who was not 'of the very highest rank',[84] his people were described as 'the most turbulent and courageous of the Natives upon the coast', and it was thought to be in the interests of the colony and of the natives themselves to keep the ploughmen in prison. Bryce maintained that Te Whiti was glad to have them there out of the way; because he was a man of peace and they were troublesome, he had sent them to plough to get rid of them.

At last Bryce openly admitted that it was 'a mere farce to talk of trying these prisoners for the offences with which they were charged'. All provision for trial had been dropped from this bill and its purpose was simply to enable the government to hold the men in prison for as long as was thought necessary. This admission drew indignant protests from many members. Even those who had not demurred at a farce of a bill which pretended prisoners would be tried in due course said they would not be party to a bill which transgressed Magna Carta and suspended *habeas corpus*; it was a disgrace to the colony and a blot on its escutcheon. But Hall, whose government had set up a commission that justice might be done, maintained with rare logic that a trial would be of no 'advantage whatever to the Natives', and that the government was actually making a concession to them 'in dispensing with a trial, and in asking for power to let them go . . . the moment we can safely do so, forgiving all that has been done'.

Fox scorned Grey's description of the act as a penal statute, a bill of attainder, by comparing it with an act Grey had signed in 1863 'with the advice of his Ministers – of whom I believe I was one'. Brandishing the Suppression of Rebellion Act, he declared that there was no trial by jury in that act, no liberty of the subject nor Magna Carta, but that such acts were necessary in times of rebellion when 'the lifeblood of the colony' was in peril.[85] Apparently he was trying to justify the wrong he was prepared to do in peacetime in 1880 by comparing it with that which he had done in wartime in 1863. As a commissioner, Fox admitted these men had legitimate grievances; as a politician, he was prepared to pass legislation which would hold them without trial for protesting their grievances. Fox's impartiality was questionable. Even Hall had chided him gently about the commissioners' interim report: 'At the first blush it sounds something like an attack upon the late Government. . . . I think it will be said the report breathes an animus against Grey. . . . [It] is in my drawer and if you would *like* to make any alteration in it I will have it returned to you.'[86]

Fox was now contending not only with the opposition, but also with his own native minister. Bryce had said the ploughmen's real offence, and that for which they were imprisoned, was 'provocation to war'. Fox defended Maori against any such charge, saying he did not think they had any intention to provoke hostilities: 'if they had hostile intentions, why did they not fight?' His apparent defence of Te Whiti, who, he said, had sent his men to plough 'solely for the purpose of bringing the Government back' to the natives and not with the idea of provoking hostilities, was in reality an attack on Sheehan, who had provoked and disappointed Te Whiti by making no 'communication whatever' with him after Mackay's visit. Fox could see the danger in Bryce's reasoning and hoped the government would not be influenced by it, but would aim to negotiate a settlement with Te Whiti. When Reader Wood advised giving the ploughmen the reserves recommended by the commissioners and letting them 'go back to Taranaki to their own peaceful avocations on the land', Atkinson was indignant. He declared that Te Whiti was 'in direct communication with heaven' and might at any time have a revelation that it was time to cut everyone's throat; like Bryce he threatened to resign if the bill was not passed and the prisoners were let loose.[87]

These scare tactics had rather a hollow ring in 1880, after almost 12 months in which the only sign of hostility on the coast came from the armed constabulary, and especially after the presentation of the commissioners' second report which gave not the merest hint that there was any danger of an outbreak. But there were enough members who favoured the bill, or who still perceived the 'Grey spectre' and were afraid that the government might fall if they did not favour the bill, or for whom the thought of the *expense* of war was too much, to pass it by a large majority after several divisions.

Before the bill had passed the House, the activities of the roadmakers in Taranaki had provoked a new challenge that brought about a further series of arrests. Undeterred by past experience and heedless of the commissioners' warnings, the roadmakers had once more carried the road through Maori cultivations. Charles Hursthouse, the surveyor and engineer in charge of road construction in Taranaki, had been told to 'lay out a first class trunk road' and to make it as straight as possible. He found that requirement difficult as it would mean cutting through 'a dense forest', so he took the road through the cultivations instead.[88] And in early June the armed constabulary, working on Bryce's orders, opened gaps in fences surrounding 'the Parihaka clearings'. Roberts telegraphed Bryce on 9 June to tell him the Parihaka people had repaired the damage, and a week later informed him that his roadmakers would be making gaps that day in three fences. Parris testified later that two of these fences enclosed a field in which the previous year's crops were stored. For the next fortnight, each time the Parihaka men repaired the three gaps, the armed constabulary broke the fences down again, till finally Te Whiti sent Te Whetu to ask Roberts to put a gate across the road. Roberts' helpful reply was that the Maori would have to fence the sides of the road, but he did agree 'not to let the pigs into the sown paddock' and asked Bryce if the armed constabulary might help with the fencing. Although he reported that the Parihaka men seemed to be in a 'very reasonable and talkative mood' and thought that with careful treatment they would 'be willing to come to reasonable terms', he obviously got no positive response from Bryce. Bell had warned 'from the first' that they ought to fence both sides of the road wherever it went through a cultivation, but more than two weeks later the stand-off still continued. Each day the constabulary broke down the fence and each day men from Parihaka repaired it. Roberts reported Maori were willing to put up a swing gate if Bryce would agree to that, but Bryce would only agree to a gate as a temporary measure and insisted that Maori fence the sides of the road. They refused and said they would re-erect the fences as often as they were taken down and that they were doing it only to protect their crops, not to stop the road.[89]

Even the local press found Bryce's intransigence hard to accept and asked if there was not a simpler solution than that of the native minister and his 'sagacious advisers', who were making war on an enemy which did not want to fight. Was it better, they asked, 'or cheaper or easier to take Maori fencers prisoners and keep them untried in gaol for a year or more than to set your 800 armed idlers to work putting up fences where the highway has cut through native plantations?'[90]

The arrests of the fencers began on 19 July as Te Whiti sent his men, usually four a day, 'to be taken prisoners, without the slightest violence, or even trace of rancour or vindictive feeling'. 'They . . . came down to the work knowing perfectly well that they would be taken prisoners, and that their attempt to re-erect the fence would prove a mere demonstration – a demonstration repeated some forty or fifty times at least.' They seemed to rejoice in arrest. 'Those last taken had prepared themselves for their arrest by washing themselves and putting on their best clothes and when taken they held out their arms to receive their manacles.' Robinson thought they were 'merely acting under the influence of fanaticism, but what Te Whiti's object was could only be conjectured'.[91] It should not have been too difficult to discern. Even Bryce noticed that no opposition had been made to the construction of the main road; nor had any obstruction been made to the erection of the telegraph line, the cutting of the Stratford–Opunake road, the cutting of the front line of the continuous reserve, or the 'picking up' of the old surveys on the Waimate plains. Yet he insisted that Te Whiti's infatuated followers were suffering 'a mental epidemic' which drove them to protest against European authority by blocking the coast road.[92] Robinson decided that maybe Te Whiti aimed at provoking hostilities, 'the Maoris having a superstitious aversion to drawing first blood', or perhaps it was

> simply an ingenious device on the part of Te Whiti . . . with the twofold object of disposing of some of his followers who were beginning to be troublesome, and of imposing on the Government the cost of maintaining them through the winter in greater comfort than they would have experienced in their own homes in Parihaka, where provisions were supposed to be running short.[93]

The government had been waiting for the final report of the west coast commissioners to enable them to bring in a 'measure dealing with the whole question', but suddenly they were faced with this new outburst of fanaticism, just when Bryce thought he had, with his roadmaking and surveying for sale, already solved the west coast problem without recourse to the commissioners and their report. He now asked the House to pass a purely temporary measure, forthwith and without discussion, as it had become necessary to arrest certain people whom he feared were 'part of an organisation which was hostile to the authority of the Queen'. The Maori Prisoners Detention Bill provided that 'all Natives' arrested between the White Cliffs and the Waitotara on or after 19 July should 'be deemed to have been and to be detained' under the provisions of the Maori Prisoners Act, excepting only that in no case should they be detained beyond the end of October. No offences were mentioned. It was enough that such Maori be arrested and this new act would then have the power of *ex post facto* legislation.

Bryce did not get his bill through the House without both discussion and division. The Maori members objected, and the Speaker 'regretted exceedingly' that once again there had been an infraction of standing orders in that the bill had not been translated into Maori. Bryce brought up all the old arguments: the people were 'in general opposition to the authority of the Government and of the Queen', and members had a duty to the country and should not make the vote a party matter lest these misguided people think they had 'friends in the House who would encourage them in their evil-doing'. But he had to admit that the 'technical offence' of those affected by the bill 'would scarcely subject them to arrest at all'. Grey labelled the bill a general warrant for the arrest of any Maori for any offence or for no offence at all – a highly unconstitutional step, at which Fox protested that 'that which the Parliament said was constitutional was no longer unconstitutional'. Downie Stewart reminded Fox that what was legal and what was constitutional were two different things. Reader Wood told Fox he was surprised that he would vote for such a bill when he had just issued a report showing that all these troubles were the fault of successive governments and could be laid at the feet of the Europeans who had failed to fulfil the promises they had made. He said men were dying in prison while parliament went on passing these bills to detain them, but Bryce assured him that only two had died, and only nine could be called old and feeble; the rest were really a fine robust lot of men.[94]

The Maori Prisoners Detention Act became law on 6 August, one day after the commissioners presented their final report to the government setting out their recommendations for putting an end to the troubles on the coast. The commissioners had two objectives: 'to do justice to the Natives' and to continue 'English settlement of the country'.[95] Bell, whose voice in parliament was much less strident than Fox's, had asked that parliament act 'in the spirit in which the Commissioners had made their recommendations' and that they accompany any steps taken to maintain the peace 'with mercy towards the Natives, and a desire to conciliate as far as possible the feelings of those who had been living so long in chronic insurrection'.[96] The commissioners believed that full justice would be done to Maori if the government now redeemed the promises made over the years by successive ministries, especially that those who lived in peace should not be dispossessed of their land. They said there was the clearest evidence of 'the good faith of the Crown being engaged by Sir George Grey's Government to the Parihaka people',[97] and their recommendations differed from the Grey government's intentions *only* in that they would retain for the Crown the section of the Parihaka block between the new road and the coast –

which just happened to be the area of best arable land – but return the rest of the block to Te Whiti and his people. They dismissed entirely the red herring often raised that Hiroki's presence at Parihaka would be a barrier to the settlement of the whole question. Hiroki, they said, had happened upon Parihaka, he had not been invited there, and if the sanctuary extended to him had not prevented government ministers and commissioners from visiting Parihaka, it could not now be raised as an excuse to deny consideration of Te Whiti's claims. Successive ministers had met with and enjoyed the hospitality of Tawhiao, Rewi, and other leading King movement chiefs who sheltered 'half a dozen men charged with murders and outrages more deliberate than that committed by Hiroki'. The commissioners were clearly of the view that no act of Te Whiti's between the ploughing in 1879 and the fencing in 1880 could 'fairly be called hostile', and that it was no less hopeless then than previously to suppose any settlement could be made except by resort to force, unless it was made with Te Whiti.[98]

Bryce's views on how to settle the west coast question were directly opposed to those of the commissioners. To him there was 'One means, and one means only, of settling for ever this vexed question' and that was to establish 'a close European population' on the coast, and the sooner the better. This would be his constant aim and he would keep it 'before the mind of the Government as the principal object to be attained'.[99] He obviously meant to push on with his policy of ignoring Te Whiti and the needs of his people; they must be induced to accept the position and concur in his arrangements and if that entailed resort to force, so be it. If Maori and European were not on a collision course, then clearly the commissioners and the native minister were.

Within two weeks of receipt of the commissioners' final report, Bryce introduced another of his repressive double-barrelled bills to the House. The aim of the West Coast Settlement (North Island) Act was ostensibly to enable the government to put into effect the recommendations of the west coast commissioners. However, the singular penal clauses enabled the government, at any time during the next three years, to arrest without warrant and imprison for up to two years, with or without hard labour, anyone committing, or 'reasonably suspected' of intending to commit such crimes as interfering with a survey, unlawfully ploughing or fencing or obstructing a road or assembling for such purpose, or assisting in or countenancing such acts. The act also provided that those who had been or who might yet be arrested under the Maori Prisoners Detention Act should be deemed to be arrested and imprisoned under the Maori Prisoners Act; that is, 'prisoners arrested under one Act, shall by virtue of the provisions of a second, be deemed to be arrested under a third, all passed in one session of Parliament'.[100] The fencers could now be held beyond 31 October 1880 since the governor had the power to extend the 'temporary' act under which the ploughmen were held. Robinson thought such remarkable legislation necessary in the Maori's own interests and that it was 'devised for the purpose of averting a Maori war'. Speaking as though out of Bryce's mouth, he said that Maori were victims of a delusion and beyond the reach of reason since they believed Te Whiti 'could, if he thought fit, release them from prison and raise them from the dead'. They needed saving from themselves since their reckless fanaticism would have led to their extermination had war broken out.[101] Once formulated, such statements were endlessly repeated and were a convenient means of justifying European insensitivity and high-handed government action.

Bryce's speech introducing the bill made it very clear (as indeed did the title of the bill itself) that justice to Maori was secondary. Settlement of the coast was to be the government's first priority: they intended to have 'that Coast settled by European settlers, and it is to that that they look for the healing of the sore which exists there'. But they would also make some 'concessions' – they would assign 'suitable reserves' and grant them to the natives as might be found 'expedient and necessary'. Bryce praised the commissioners, faintly, for their work on the coast, said they were not infallible and doubtless might be mistaken in some of their conclusions, and suggested that if he needed advice or assistance he could get it from his predecessor, Sheehan. There was no suggestion in his speech of an intention to implement the commissioners' findings. Grey insisted that the one thing above all others which would ensure peace on the coast was the adoption in total of those findings; he suggested they be 'presented to the Natives as a charter of rights' and not mixed up with Bryce's penal clauses. The penal clauses were almost overlooked in the discussion on the bill, most of which centred on the work of the commissioners: gratitude was expressed to them and to the government for its perceived intention to carry out the commissioners' recommendations.[102] Indeed Grey gave such fulsome praise to the work of his old adversary Fox that it might be wondered whether he had suffered a change of heart, or whether he was just taking the opportunity to help widen the split between Bryce and the commissioners in the hope of precipitating Bryce's resignation – which might lead to the 'dismemberment' of the Cabinet and the fall of the government.

Some who had objected to previous bills made no objection to this one because it at least supposedly provided for fair trial, but F. J. Moss (Parnell) and James Macandrew (Port Chalmers) were not so easily mollified. To them the bill was another 'disgrace to the Statute book of New Zealand' and 'utterly unworthy of Englishmen'. It was left to John Ballance, a west coast politician and future Liberal premier, to show his colours. He called on the government to make a display of power to intimidate those 'Natives under the control of Te Whiti' and so prevent another war. He believed that if negotiations were begun with Te Whiti they would inevitably fail and the government would just strengthen his hand by allowing him to rebuff and insult them. Te Whiti, he thought, was a 'clever, designing man' who would show his teeth the minute the government showed any weakness. He believed the commissioners' reports were based on 'arbitrary decisions', and that there was no basis for them except in the minds of the commissioners. He could not go along with their view that Te Whiti had benign intentions, nor could he agree to effect being given to the promises of successive governments as the commissioners recommended. The premier, Hall, heard this speech with pleasure and thought Ballance had stated the case very fairly. He believed that if they took *power* to do *justice* to the Maori people, within a year peace would be assured and the west coast difficulty would be a thing of the past.

Only the Maori members had thoughts for those still imprisoned without trial. They said it was the delay in returning confiscated land that had resulted in so many of their people being imprisoned. Now that it was at last decided to return the land to Maori, it was high time to return Maori to the land: 'just try them; put them on the land and see if this is what they have been wanting'.[103]

By the time the West Coast Settlement (North Island) Act became law on 1 September 1880, about 150 fencers had been detained under the Maori Prisoners Detention Act and sent to South Island gaols. The day after the act came into operation, copies of it were distributed at Parihaka by Thompson. Tohu gathered up the copies and threw them back at him, and to reinforce the message bigger groups than ever went to man the barricades. On 4 September, W. E. Gudgeon of the armed constabulary arrested 59 of them. They appeared in the District Court in New Plymouth on 23 September before one Judge Shaw and a jury of 12 settlers, charged with having unlawfully obstructed the free passage of a thoroughfare. After hearing the evidence and the judge's summing up, the jury retired and deliberated for three-quarters of an hour before announcing that they could not agree on their verdict. His Honour instructed them in their duty: although counsel for the prisoners had stated that requiring them 'to obtain sureties to keep the peace might practically mean to imprison them for life', he wished the jury to understand that the judge in his wisdom and mercy might sentence them 'to only one hour's imprisonment' and bind them over to keep the peace for 'only a nominal time'. He then impressed upon them 'the serious miscarriage of justice' that would arise if the jury could not reach a verdict and warned them that if they could not agree within an hour he should be 'compelled to perform the unpleasant duty' of locking them up for the night. Suitably enlightened and instructed, they brought down a verdict of guilty after 'a few minutes' deliberation'. His Honour pronounced sentence: two years' imprisonment with hard labour in the common gaol in Lyttelton and a requirement for each to find one surety of £50 to keep the peace for six months.[104]

This example of the government's power to do justice must have given even the Hall ministry pause, especially since that power seemed to have little effect on Te Whiti or his followers. The fence repairing went on unabated, but with 216 fencers held in South Island gaols and the cost of maintaining them in 'great comfort' bearing so heavily upon the government, there were no more arrests. Bryce claimed that this was because he (but not the Cabinet) was of the opinion that enough prisoners had been taken and no more should be apprehended. When the fencers appeared on the road as usual on 12 November, instead of making solid fences across the gaps they erected slip rails which would keep stock out of their wheat paddocks but which could easily be moved to allow free passage of the road. Perhaps at this Bryce finally discerned Te Whiti's object, for he allowed the slip rails to remain. The fencing emergency was over.

The responsibility for the whole episode ultimately lay not with Bryce, but with Hall. Bryce was something of an embarrassment to the Cabinet. He was exceedingly stubborn and did not have the sharpest intellect, but he was useful as a hatchet man to do the dirty work the gentlemen ministers eschewed. Atkinson approved Bryce's methods, but was content to have *him* carry them out. In putting up with Bryce, the Cabinet was in a sense accommodating Atkinson and his settler followers. Both Bryce and Atkinson continually threatened resignation if 'those fanatics' on the west coast got their way. Hall had contented himself with a gentle suggestion to Bryce: 'Would it not have good effect on Te Whiti and his followers if Government undertook to fence road through cultivations proposed?'[105] When Bryce remained stubborn, Hall allowed the colony's finances to be squandered on a standing army rather than insist it turn its hand to erecting a few chains of fencing or, simpler still, adopt the Maori solution and put up a couple of slip rails.

On 22 September 1880, Bryce informed Hall that he had determined to resign from the ministry because of the 'constant differences of opinion' which existed between himself and the Cabinet over west coast affairs. These differences, he said, had increased until they had become 'constant and uniform', and there were times when he had not been overruled only because he had 'ventured to disregard the wishes of Cabinet'. But he had been opposed over moving the armed constabulary across the Waingongoro and over removing the prisoners from Wellington, he had been overruled in many matters concerning the prisoners, and he could be no party to the Cabinet's wish to allocate reserves 'while the men who should receive the land and whose evidence must be necessary to a fair enquiry are in prison'. It had not appeared to concern him that they were in prison while an earlier inquiry was made before the west coast commissioners. But Bryce's main complaint was that he had been completely frustrated in his determination to arrest Hiroki; unlike the commissioners, he believed this to be the thing most likely 'to lead the Maoris to a frame of mind which would facilitate the settlement of the West Coast difficulty'. He had even 'indicated the means and the day on which it should be done', but Cabinet differed and again he was overruled. He had also suggested that 'under certain circumstances which might arise' Te Whiti and Tohu should be arrested too, but he had been advised of the 'desirability, if not necessity of getting evidence connecting these men with the depredations or offences of their followers – a thing obviously next to impossible of attainment beforehand'.[106]

The day Bryce had in mind for the arrest of Hiroki was that of the September hui at Parihaka, but Whitaker could see 'no advantage' in attempting an arrest because he was afraid Hiroki might be acquitted; he had never been sure they had 'sufficient evidence to ensure a conviction'. He thought taking Te Whiti would be a bold stroke, but if they failed it would be mischievous and if they succeeded it would probably lead to war. He said if Te Whiti meant peace they should not give him a cause for war; if he meant war they should 'drive him to take the initiative' so public opinion would be with them. Hall feared failure was 'more than probable and would raise Te Whiti's prestige'.[107]

Cabinet assured Bryce that no real differences existed between them, but only after 'repeated discussion' did they persuade him to withdraw his resignation. It was not so much their wish to keep Bryce in as their determination to keep Grey out. They feared Bryce's resignation *would* lead to a dismemberment of the Cabinet. Moreover, they knew the real reason behind his attempted resignation: 'the sore is not in anything mentioned in his letter. It is in the West Coast Commission. He has always been opposed to it, thinking . . . it was taking his work out of his hands. He talks of having been on his knees before the Commission and of now having to take orders from Bell'. Whitaker agreed that he had seen 'all through that Bryce was very jealous and dissatisfied with the proceedings of the Commissioners' and that Bryce would have been pleased if they had never been appointed. He thought if Cabinet ignored the commissioners altogether they would not hear 'much about anything else' from Bryce, but this could not be done because 'The Assembly and the country are with the Commissioners'.[108]

At the September hui at Parihaka, 2,000 men, women and children drank in the words of Te Whiti and Tohu. 'All the important men for many miles around' were there.[109] Hiroki, 'contrary to his usual custom', stayed close by Te Whiti's side and kept a fearful eye on the Europeans present. Word of Bryce's machinations must have reached Parihaka: rumours abounded that 'the Armed Constabulary force intended to make a raid on the pah on that day'. According to Thompson, Te Whiti told his audience that imprisonment had brought no mate to his people, it had not set them back, although the law had been made to throw them into distress. He had told them the 'quarrel must be burnt even unto ashes which can not be made again into cinders, which can never return to wood, and which can grow no more', and now he told them the fencers were the men he had 'appointed to blow the embers of the smouldering fire'. Tohu told them war was a thing suppressed for ever and ever. 'For whom is the olive branch? for you who have escaped. . . . The parliament have worked their work because they see you are small and poor, blind and ignorant but they shall not succeed.'[110]

While the fencing continued through October and Maori were 'carefully avoiding arrest', Bryce thought it a good opportunity to begin releasing some of the first ploughmen arrested, and announced to Hall that he proposed to do it 'by return of Hinemoa on Tuesday'. Hall's reply was a gentle reminder that in fact he and not Bryce was the premier: 'Think time good for experiment of return of few old prisoners. Might be well to let them see something of a large

European town before they leave'.[111] Wi Kingi Matakatea was among the prisoners selected for release. On 4 October 1880, his 'friend John Bryce' wrote him a letter of explanation about the government's motives and actions. It resembled a proclamation more than a friendly letter and Bryce took the trouble to send a copy to the editor of the *New Zealand Times* for publication. Matakatea, who was arrested on 14 July 1879, had been imprisoned in Dunedin since January 1880 and was now being released so he could see the truth of the governor's words: 'that he did not wish to . . . retain the prisoners longer than was necessary in the interests of both races'. Bryce went on to tell him the government had, as promised, appointed a commission to inquire into 'the discontent of the natives' and was now prepared to set aside 'Large and ample pieces of land . . . for those natives who desire that trouble should cease'. They also wished to release all the prisoners and would do so if, on the return of this first party, 'the natives accept the proposals now made to them'. Bryce sent Matakatea copies of laws and proclamations to do with the West Coast Commission and instructed him to assist the government 'to cause the confusion to cease, and to promote the real interests' of his people.[112]

Matakatea was free, but as a kind of hostage, and the government were now crediting him with the chiefly mana they believed they had destroyed by imprisoning him. The government thought they understood Maori custom with regard to prisoners: to be imprisoned was to lose one's mana, to suffer spiritual death. Daniel Pollen told the Council when the ploughmen were being imprisoned in 1879 that there was 'no greater disgrace which can, according to Native notions, be inflicted on a Maori than to make him a herehere – a prisoner. He is . . . in the eyes of his people, degraded for ever afterwards'.[113] It escaped the government entirely that the Maori custom referred not to imprisonment, willingly sought, but to a state of captivity – captivity through war. When the Confiscated Lands Inquiry and Maori Prisoners' Trials Bill was before the House, Tomoana said he could not agree with its title as there were no prisoners, since 'war between the Maoris and Europeans had ceased long ago. There had been no outbreak . . . to justify the taking of . . . prisoners. . . . They were not prisoners of war'.[114] Matakatea had suffered no mate through imprisonment[115] and the government tacitly acknowledged the fact by entrusting him with a mission to carry the government's word to the people of the coast. But while they would recognise the mana of Matakatea which they had thought to destroy, they would not recognise that of Te Whiti with whom they wished to communicate.

The publication of Bryce's letter to Matakatea had no effect on Te Whiti according to Thompson, and caused 'not the slightest alteration in his programme'. But just what Te Whiti's programme was Thompson could never be sure, since it was 'impossible to extract any particulars of Te Whiti's intentions from any of his followers'. In his speech at the October hui Te Whiti spoke of the hawk and the tui, meaning that the government released the prisoners not 'for their own good but that the Government may profit by it'. He said there would be no war because he would 'give no cause or reason for the Europeans to attack him'. But Tohu counselled the people 'to enjoy themselves while they could for the days of rest would not last for ever and . . . they would have to pay for their rest bye and bye'.[116]

This was Thompson's last report to the government. While he had been in their service as an interpreter he had kept an eye on his children's heritage – the land of his wife's hapu on the Waimate plains. He was obviously out of step with the west coast commissioners,[117] but claimed they promised him a separate reserve for his wife and children on condition that he did not make a formal appearance before the commission. When the commissioners' reports were issued and he found his claim totally neglected while 'reclaimed rebels had large reserves' allocated to them, he 'remonstrated' but to no avail.[118] Then in late October, when Bryce was about to achieve his goal – the sale of the plains, Thompson in great anguish begged 'to protest against the sale and occupation of that portion of the Waimate Plains belonging to the Kupanga hapu . . . until their rights . . . have been acknowledged as laid down in the act of confiscation'. He guaranteed to do nothing 'to bias the natives' but felt his duty as a parent called for 'some expression of opinion and protest at the present crisis'.[119] Bryce had to suffer the opposition of his colleagues and superiors, but he was not about to let his subordinates question his methods and motives. Thompson was summarily dismissed – and the government was to find it had increased Te Whiti's following by one.

While the government studiously avoided direct contact with Te Whiti, they always assumed he was kept fully informed of all that went on and that he knew what they wanted him to know. They published notices in the *Gazette* and kept the English language press supplied with information; their officers 'frequently met natives' to whom they explained policies or dropped hints they were sure 'would be reported to Parihaka'; and they met with or wrote to other chiefs, especially loyal ones like Pihama who was 'in touch with Te Whiti'.[120] It was an old ploy to have those chiefs whose mana the government did not care to recognise made aware 'indirectly, but not officially' of that which they wished them to know.[121] So it was frequently claimed that Te Whiti was 'aware'; aware of proclamations, aware of acts of parliament (even when they had not been translated for the Maori members), aware of proceedings in the House, aware of the contents of reports – and especially aware of the government's 'intentions' to make reserves. But in late September 1880, a friend of Fox's dropped in at Parihaka 'informally en passant and had a pretty free talk' with Te Whiti, who told him he would be interested to know about the commissioners and their work and would like to see a copy of their report. This surprised Fox as he had 'heard of at least three copies being sent through different channels by which it was believed they would reach Parihaka'; and it annoyed him because the commissioners had several times impressed on the government the importance of having an abstract of their report 'translated in Maori and circulated not only at Parihaka but everywhere'. He reminded Hall that even had English language copies been sent, Te Whiti did not speak a word of English and any translation made 'by any of the Pakeha-Maoris who have access to him will be of a very unreliable character' and likely to nullify the good effects he was sure the report would have on the Maori mind.[122] Hall assured Fox several attempts had been made 'to communicate to Te Whiti all that has been done and is proposed to be done towards a settlement of the West Coast question'; but as a consequence of Fox's letter they had now despatched Parris to Parihaka to explain everything. Hall was still assuming that Te Whiti was already 'aware' even before Parris could appear at the October hui at Parihaka, for he went on to tell Fox that: 'The impenitence of the returned prisoners and the persistent opposition of the Parihaka magnate and his deluded followers after they know what is intended is very embarrassing'.

Hall complained of the ruinous expense of maintaining a standing army on the coast 'to keep up our present farce' (but did not oblige Bryce to end it) and was happy that Bryce had hit on a means of saving money – he had 'retrenched' Charles Brown as civil commissioner and the Native Office staff was 'growing small by degrees and beautifully less'.[123] Hall repeated his sentiments to Bell: they had sent Parris to Parihaka so that 'Te Whiti and his followers might have no excuse (they have no good reason) for saying they did not know all about the Commissioners' report'. But it seemed that partly because of the 'inclemency of the weather' and partly because of Te Whiti's 'indisposition' Parris had not done his work thoroughly and would have to be sent again. Despite this, the government were determined on the immediate sale of 'another slice of the Plains and as much of the Forest behind them as is ready for sale'. They also proposed to commence surveying 'under Te Whiti's nose', at once. 'If we were not spending £600 a day on our armed force we could afford to go more gradually to work.'[124] For reasons of financial expediency, Hall was listening to Bryce and ignoring his commissioners' repeated warnings. Fox renewed the warnings: when the Parihaka block was surveyed, care must be taken to see that reserves were defined before any land was surveyed for sale and Maori must be informed exactly what their reserves were to be.[125]

Hall ignored another warning. Te Whiti had twice refused to deal with Parris as a government official, yet Hall sent him back to Parihaka for a third time to attend the November hui and explain the commissioners' work and their recommendations to the 1,200 or so people assembled there. Parris, with remarkable insensitivity, rose to his feet immediately Te Whiti finished speaking and, when Te Whiti told him 'Do not speak now, speak tomorrow', asked if he might speak after Tohu; 'Who could answer for tomorrow?' he asked, 'perhaps tomorrow may never come.' 'Ka pai,' Te Whiti replied, 'speak on the day that never comes.' Parris quickly told the people that he had addressed them many times and had never deceived them, but Te Whiti was leading them astray and was afraid he, Parris, would 'detach' his people from him if they heard what he had to say. Te Whiti told him whatever he had to say would not be his own words but his superior's; let his superior come himself and say the words. Then 'to prevent Mr Parris speaking, he said to his people "Me pakaru te hui" . . . whereupon they all rose as one man and left the meeting place'.[126]

Parris' insensitivity was but a mirror of government insensitivity. The great monthly meetings at Parihaka were not the time for calm rational discussion between the government and Te Whiti; and subordinates who had repeatedly failed to communicate with him were not acceptable as karere, or envoy. It takes a man of mana to fill that role successfully. If the government had been serious in their intention to communicate with Te Whiti they could have done it, but it would have involved acknowledging his mana and treating him as an adult and rational being. Instead they were content with window-dressing and play-acting, making a display so that they could maintain Te Whiti was 'fully informed'. Their aim was to 'make him give in, or resist', or make him overcome his 'aversion to shedding first blood' so that when they took the final step in forcing him to submit, public opinion would be on their side.

CHAPTER SIX

The Road to Parihaka

1881

It matters not whether you are among those who hit or among those who watch, among those who perform or among those who let it happen.
You are all guilty, actors and spectators.[1]

THE NEW GOVERNOR, SIR ARTHUR HAMILTON GORDON, ARRIVED IN New Zealand at the end of 1880 after concluding his term as the first governor of Fiji. His arrival had been anticipated with mixed feelings, for he came with something of a reputation as an expert in 'the native races' at a time when so called Maori experts, Maori doctors and philo Maoris were decried. He was a friend of Exeter Hall, a Christian humanitarian who was opposed to discrimination and the oppression of coloured races by their governing masters. He was seen to labour under a double handicap in that he was also a friend of Sir George Grey and was said to look up to him and be prepared to consult him. This was of especial concern to a ministry very jealous of its role as a responsible government and wary of a governor used to crown colony government, whose only experience of a constitutional colony was well dated. Gordon hoped his ministers would recognise his ability and experience and at least occasionally seek to profit by it; and that the native question was, as he was assured, as good as settled so he would not be embroiled in events he could neither control nor condone and, above all, so he could maintain his ties with Fiji and devote much of his time to the work of the Western Pacific High Commission.[2]

When Gordon arrived on 23 November, the ministers were congratulating themselves that the west coast difficulty was well on the way to being solved and they feared his obvious sympathy towards Maori would awaken their frustrated hopes. But they were in fact the least affected by Gordon's arrival and Te Whiti, told by Parris that a new governor was coming, replied, 'Although a new Governor comes, it is still the same Government'.[3] Te Whiti had seen a procession of governors come and go while the Foxs, Whitakers and Atkinsons still governed. He was no more hopeful than Gordon that a governor could do anything the government did not want him to do to alleviate the lot of his people.

Hall had faced the arrival of the new governor with some trepidation, believing him to be 'about the most unfit man the Colonial Office could have selected'. He was convinced Gordon would 'play into Sir George Grey's hands' and asked Julius Vogel, then New Zealand's agent-general in London, if he couldn't drop a hint to R. G. W. Herbert, the permanent under-secretary for colonies, that the appointment was 'considered a heavy blow and great discouragement to men in the Colony who are opposing reckless finance, wild democratic theories and real separation from the Empire'. But Hall apparently changed his mind when he actually met Gordon, and wrote again to Vogel saying he thought he would get on well with this 'straightforward and conscientious man' who declared his respect for responsible government as practised in New Zealand, and he felt the reputation which preceded Gordon to the colony had done him an injustice.[4]

One of Gordon's first duties was to appoint a commission to give effect to the West Coast Settlement Act. The government had offered the new commission to Fox and Bell but then decided to send Bell to London as agent-general to succeed Vogel. When Bell sailed from New Zealand in the middle of December 1880, Fox was left to go on with the work on the west coast as sole commissioner. He regretted Bell's loss and told Hall that because of his special knowledge of west coast affairs, his personal acquaintance with leading chiefs, and his knowledge of the language 'which he speaks fluently and I don't', there was 'no man living . . . capable of doing what Bell could in the matter'.[5] Brown had once said sourly that Bell 'liked to speak on both sides and vote in the middle',[6] but Bell had often spoken up for justice when others had remained silent, and he certainly helped oppose Bryce's violent views. Te Whiti himself regretted Bell's departure. He thought him stronger than Fox, who 'was not free to do as . . . Bell would have done'.[7] It was believed in some quarters that Bell's absence exacerbated the differences between Fox and Bryce, and the *Otago Daily Times* spoke of 'the impolicy of depriving the West Coast Commission of the moderating influence of . . . Bell'.[8] But it may have been a conscious act of policy on the part of the government to promote Bell out of the way in an attempt to placate Bryce, Atkinson and the west coast settlers. After Bell's departure the recommendations of the Fox-Bell commission were but partially and tardily implemented, and Fox's later recommendations were much less conciliatory than those of the earlier commissioners – although Bell's voice was certainly less conciliatory in England than it had been in New Zealand. As a good diplomat, he was loyal to his government and always prepared in public to defend the reputation of the colony against criticism of its handling of native affairs.[9]

The new commission issued on 23 December 1880 empowered Fox to allocate the long-delayed awards of the Compensation Court and to define reserves 'in satisfaction of all promises or engagements made by or on behalf of Her Majesty or the Government . . . which have formed the subject of inquiry' by the west coast commissioners.[10] Fox, with Bell's help, had drawn up a 'description . . . of the scope and extent of the powers' which should be given to the new commission. But Hall was still afraid it would not be plain sailing on the coast, and he told Bell on the eve of his departure that the ministry hoped what had already been done there would have 'brought matters to a *head*; that Te Whiti would have either given in or resisted. . . . But he is either too cunning or too well advised: he contents himself with a financial warfare. He can afford to wait any length of time while we cannot'.[11] Time was about the only weapon Te Whiti did have; time and patience and a certainty of the justice of his cause.

When Parris' November mission to Parihaka failed, Bryce continued to agitate for more 'active measures' to be taken against Te Whiti. There was some short-lived opposition to the survey about that time and Bryce declared he would stand no nonsense; the culprits, men women or children, would be arrested. He was also prepared 'to go one step further' and, although the Cabinet was not, the press was prepared for this move which 'unquestionably means a march to Parihaka . . . where we may lay hands on the prophet himself and certainly will, if we can, apprehend Hiroki for murder'.[12]

In December, the ministry received a letter from the Colonial Office enclosing a request to that office from Charles Bradlaugh, a member of the British parliament, for some action on behalf of the Maori prisoners 'unjustly detained . . . without trial'. Secretary of State Kimberley thought he had not been informed so fully as he would have wished of the circumstances which had led to the passing of the Maori Prisoners Act, and asked that he be furnished with 'a full report respecting the Native disturbances of 1879 and 1880, and the measures taken by the Government of New Zealand in consequence of them'. Gordon did not feel that the plethora of documents, acts, memos and letters which his responsible advisers produced in answer to Kimberley's request in any way absolved *him* from furnishing a full report on the subject, and he promised Kimberley he would do this as soon as he could procure the requisite data which was not in some cases 'altogether easy to obtain'.[13]

The government reacted swiftly and very self-righteously to the question of their handling of west coast affairs being raised in the British parliament. Most of the papers they supplied for Kimberley's edification were simply duplicates of ones previously sent. Rolleston, on Hall's behalf, wrote an accompanying memo which argued that Bradlaugh was calumniating the colonial government without revealing the name of his New Zealand informant, and since both Bradlaugh and his 'supposed informant' had doubtful reputations, the government felt itself able to dismiss the question by equating the justice of the cause with those who espoused it.[14] Bryce's 'Memorandum on the Causes which Justify the Detention of the West Coast Maori Prisoners' was a travesty of the truth and a statement of Bryce's racial prejudice and ignorance. He admitted Te Whiti had never 'taken any personal part in active warfare' but had always preached peace, and that his influence over the Maori community was largely due to this, yet he attempted to justify his own high-handedness and the repressive legislation by portraying Te Whiti as a madman who convinced his followers to have faith in him as a great prophet or god. He claimed that when the surveyors were removed from the plains

> the Maoris regarded the whole operation as a miraculous exhibition of Te Whiti's powers, and felt that his gods or spirits were pressing on and subduing the heart of the white man. . . . The mental epidemic among the Maoris of the West Coast . . . then attained an intensity and force . . . which has enabled the faith of the Maoris in their prophet and lord to withstand the effect of all the falsified predictions, and all the sufferings he has brought upon them. Clearly at that time his own dreams of power became unbounded. . . . He was to recover the whole of the confiscated lands in New Zealand. . . .

> Te Whiti was to become the supreme ruler of the West Coast, of the whole of New Zealand, indeed of the whole world: nay, not only the ruler, but a prophet, a king, a god.

Lest he had not yet convinced his readers Bryce introduced a new theme, saying Te Whiti's followers not only had faith in him, they *feared* him and his 'associate' Tohu, with a fear 'far exceeding in its intensity the ordinary fear of death'. This 'horrible dread of being *makutued*', or bedevilled, was an ever-present fear and caused them to 'adhere to Te Whiti and obey him'. They dared not do otherwise because of 'what we should call the "evil eye" of their chief'. Instances had occurred, he said, where the disapproval of Te Whiti and Tohu had apparently, and Bryce thought really, 'caused the death of individuals, probably by force of imagination, possibly by more tangible means'.[15]

This last was pure fantasy and it might well be asked who was the fanatic, who was the victim of his own delusions. Gordon knew what he was doing when he decided to prepare his own report for the Colonial Office. He was not another Governor Robinson to parrot Bryce's phrases[16] and he knew the proclivity of white settlers to oppress indigenous races. If he needed alerting to the local situation, Bryce's extravagant phraseology would have been sufficient warning. In a confidential despatch to Kimberley, he said he could not 'wholly concur' in Bryce's conclusions and thought 'some of the facts . . . not altogether accurately stated'.[17]

The Cabinet, wary of Bryce's fanaticism, and with an eye to Kimberley's expressed interest in their doings, decided suddenly on a move quite contrary to their habitual policy of avoiding any high level contact with Te Whiti. On 22 December 1880, they sent Gordon a draft of a letter they wished him to write to Te Whiti. They explained that they had previously communicated with him by talking to Hone Pihama, writing to Matakatea and sending Parris to Parihaka, even though Te Whiti had often said he would only discuss his troubles with the governor. But now, surprisingly, they were willing to try any 'reasonable means for arriving at a satisfactory settlement' of the west coast difficulties (except actually making the promised reserves), and they suggested Gordon invite Te Whiti to meet him and 'discuss these matters'.[18]

Whatever their intentions, they ensured the failure of the mission before it began. First, the letter was to be delivered to Te Whiti by the friendly chief Hone Pihama; should he fail to deliver it they would go one worse and send 'the

Government interpreter'. Then they decreed that the governor should invite Te Whiti to go to Wellington to meet him; or if that was too far he could go to New Plymouth; or he could even meet him on his upcoming journey round the colony 'at any other place' on the *inland* road between New Plymouth and Hawera. Any other place, that is, but Parihaka. And finally, they suggested that Te Whiti write out his complaints and send them to the governor in advance.[19] The government had always considered itself well-informed on Te Whiti's grievances. Now, instead of telling him straight out that the governor was prepared to share the land with him, they simply asked him to enunciate the grievances they had never been prepared to entertain. It may be wondered what they hoped to achieve by an approach like this to a Maori chief who knowingly, consciously and by free choice repudiated such European ways. But they had salved their consciences: they had now 'completely carried out the recommendations' of the west coast commissioners.[20] This was a strange claim when they had not yet attempted to mark on the ground the all-important reserves for the Parihaka people.

There was at least one trap the governor did not fall into: he entrusted his letter to his aide-de-camp, Captain L. F. Knollys. But unfortunately he agreed to his being accompanied by Hone Pihama and by Charles Hursthouse, the 'engineer in charge of road construction on the confiscated land' – he who had taken the road through the Parihaka cultivations and sparked the fencing dispute. On Christmas Day 1880 they went to Parihaka where Pihama proffered the governor's letter and Hursthouse attempted to explain it. Te Whiti was not interested. It was simply one more piece of Pakeha paper delivered by government functionaries. The governor had not come to Parihaka but had just sent a subordinate 'in stripes, like a soldier'.[21] And anyway, it was too late: kua maoa te taewa, and the cooked potato could not discuss.[22] When asked if there was any message for the governor, the reply was that there was nothing 'unless the Governor is able to bring to its raw state the cooked potato'.[23] The government party withdrew; they could still discuss, if the cooked potato could not, but there was disagreement as to Te Whiti's meaning.

Knollys sent his companions back to Parihaka next day and then determined to return himself – perhaps on the advice of Atkinson and Rolleston who were operating 'in the wings', giving Hursthouse and Pihama directions in the evenings between their visits to Parihaka.[24] Pihama had the grace to be whakama about these visits in his capacity as messenger for the government and required a great deal of persuading to make them at all. On the first visit,

Knollys had noticed that in presenting the governor's letter to Te Whiti Pihama 'was nervous, and his hand shook'. He would not go alone on the second day, and on the third visit to Parihaka he would not go near Te Whiti. It was this 'fear', this acute embarrassment of a 'loyal' chief, the only one of his people who had gone over to the government, that was the source of Bryce's myth of the people living in mortal fear of Te Whiti. Pihama had excused his wife's practice of taking his government salary to Parihaka by explaining to Bryce that 'all the Maoris, including himself and his wife, were afraid of offending' Te Whiti. When pressed for an explanation, Pihama was so distressed that Bryce, and Parris who was interpreting, concluded he was afraid of Te Whiti's power of makutu. Bryce 'knew from that time forth' that what he was up against on the west coast was not a question of reserves, but of 'mental conditions'.[25] The government might have seen Pihama as loyal and friendly; to Te Whiti he represented te hunga he – those who had erred. On Knollys' second visit, Te Whiti was civil and hospitable but he would say only that the governor had heard about the cooking of the potato from others, and he knew how it was done. 'He spoke again about Mr Hursthouse being concerned in the wrong, and so being a man he could not talk to about it.' If the governor wished to know more, 'he must come to the pot where the potato was cooked'. In the end this governor was like other governors: 'a Governor for the white man'.[26]

Unhappily this was true; it seems Te Whiti was well-informed on the realities of responsible government. With the best of intentions the governor could not do a lot, but he did what he could to inform himself of the situation on the west coast and to inform the Colonial Office of the true picture. On some points Knollys was refreshingly perceptive, but he did not see that it was Hursthouse who had torpedoed the mission, or that Pihama was the source of some of the old clichés he repeated in his report. But he could see that Te Whiti had been 'so often interviewed, questioned, examined – it may be, promised something – by different emissaries of the Government, without any satisfactory result, that he is weary and sick of the sight of such emissaries', and that as long as Te Whiti was at Parihaka he was 'certainly of value in keeping the peace'.[27]

Although Knollys' mission was a failure,[28] his report was valuable and it strengthened Gordon's hand, or at least stayed the Cabinet's. It highlighted the positive things about Parihaka – the extensive acreage of well-tended crops, the comfortably housed and well-nourished people, the total lack of fortifications – and suggested that it would be better to spend time coming to an agreement with Te Whiti rather than money on fighting him. This information put the governor in a stronger position than before Knollys' visit to Parihaka, but he was not 'without apprehension' that an idea was entertained of arresting Te Whiti.[29]

That idea was entertained very strongly by Bryce, who had first urged it in September 1880 in the interregnum between Robinson's departure and Gordon's arrival while the pliant chief justice, James Prendergast, was administrator. Knollys' mission to Te Whiti was the last straw for Bryce, who believed 'the idea of negotiating with Te Whiti to be perfectly preposterous',[30] and he now urged a 'vigorous course' on the Cabinet again, before Knollys' mission was even complete. He was told there was still some hope for negotiations and it would be unwise to interfere, but a week later the stresses and strains in Cabinet became public when Bryce once more tendered his resignation. He had in fact written his letter a month before, but at Atkinson's request held it back until Cabinet could discuss his proposal 'in reference to the capture of Hiroki and possibly of Te Whiti and Tohu'. He told Hall he had understood then that if the issue had not been resolved by other means within a month he would be free to go ahead with his plan, but now Cabinet had 'completely broken faith' with him and he had 'been placed in a false position'; and he correctly surmised that no further objection would now be made to his resignation.[31]

The government was more anxious for the moment about defending its good name in the British parliament than it was about marching on Parihaka. Bradlaugh was expected to 'raise the question' early in the session and ministers were busy ensuring accord between their respective reports. Bell was to be 'posted on all that happens' so that he could report to the Colonial Office on the Maori prisoners soon after his arrival in Britain.[32] It would actually strengthen Cabinet's hand now to let Bryce resign, and they carefully drafted a press release saying Bryce had resigned because of the 'refusal of Cabinet to agree to the immediate adoption of active measures with regard to Parihaka'. Gordon thought that although Bryce had not succeeded in his 'attempt to engage the Government in hostilities' he had in fact come close to succeeding, that his views had 'narrowly escaped acceptance' and that 'a renewal of similar proposals at a future day' was not improbable.[33]

These were prophetic words, although in fact Bryce had strong opposition in Cabinet – but for a variety of reasons. Richard Oliver, the rather ineffectual public works minister, was glad Bryce's bellicose proposal had been rejected and said Bryce got too much of his own way, more than any of the other ministers. Whitaker thought Bryce's proposal to take Hiroki was a sham as his real object was to 'join issue with Te Whiti' and take him and Tohu as well; he felt 'the attempt to take any one of them was as objectionable as the lot', especially as parliament had adjourned under the impression that effect would be given to the commissioners' views, not Bryce's.[34] Public opinion seemed to be in favour of moderation: if the ploughing had not called for Bryce's vigorous policy, the present situation when provocation was lacking was certainly not the time for it. Just the day before Bryce's resignation, the *Lyttelton Times* had commented in an editorial that a 'weak and nervous Parliament was terrified into maintaining an incompetent ministry'; surely, it went on, we are 'not reduced to such straits that we must have Hall to save us from Grey'. It thought Bryce unfit for the office of native minister because he was narrow-minded, opinionated and obstinate, and had no sympathy with the Maori race nor understanding of Maori values, although he was useful in that he could be 'made a tool of by designing men of higher social standing and greater mental capacity'.[35] This included their dispensing with Bryce and replacing him with an educated gentleman, the reasonable and much more moderate William Rolleston, at a time when it was important to the Cabinet to appear in British eyes as conciliatory towards the colony's native population.

Gordon sent Kimberley a despatch containing a cutting from the *New Zealand Herald* on 12 January which was said to be Bryce's own explanation of his resignation. It was very close to the official explanation but also surmised that 'in the influence of Sir William Fox in native affairs Mr Bryce has seen a shadow behind the throne'.[36] When the governor's despatch was laid on the table of the House, Bryce complained that in sending the newspaper reports to Britain Gordon had endorsed those reports, and that this was treatment to which he 'ought not to have been subjected' by the governor. He held the government partly to blame in view of the constitutional rule which made the government responsible for the governor's actions; and he decreed that 'no public man ought to have motives attributed to him upon the authority of unverified statements found in newspapers'.[37] Bryce's reservations did not extend to the motives which newspapers attributed to Te Whiti. The press was credited with accuracy when it came to judging a most public Maori man, but not a government minister. Bryce meanwhile delivered his own explanation for his retirement in a speech given at Wanganui on 23 March 1881, in which he prophesied that the plan he had devised for dealing with Te Whiti would still have to be carried out. He could justify all he had done on the coast and claimed success for all his plans: 'I moved the armed constabulary across the Waingongoro. . . . I made roads . . . I completed the telegraph line . . . I caused the lighthouse to be begun . . . I falsified all his predictions and put the camp within two miles of Parihaka, and the law was vindicated'. But then he was frustrated by Cabinet:

> I ought to have been permitted . . . to have paid a visit to Te Whiti. I ought to have gone and seen him with such a force at my back as would have commanded respect . . . and I ought to have said then to Te Whiti . . . "Either the Queen or you must prevail, and I must see the authority of law shall from this time forth prevail at Parihaka". . . . I would have told him that he could no longer be permitted to harbour criminals . . . that there was one murderer there who must be arrested, and that I had come to arrest him. . . . There would have been no necessity for the arrest of Te Whiti himself, except . . . that it would have been the one thing necessary to destroy his prestige among the Maoris. . . . If he had resisted . . . I should have arrested him, and that, I believe, would have been the best thing which could have happened for the solution of the West Coast difficulty.[38]

Bryce had delusions of grandeur. He, not the west coast commissioners, had the answer to the native problem. Just as Fox began his work of giving effect to the commissioners' views, Bryce was ready to destroy Parihaka. By persecuting Te Whiti, he meant to make his name as the saviour of the west coast tribes and of the colony in general. He admitted it: 'I have some personal ambition in this matter. I did strongly desire to associate my name with the settlement of the West Coast difficulty which had baffled successive governments for years'.[39] But, as he could not get his own way with a Cabinet backed by public opinion and committed to its commissioners and to an attempt at negotiation, he resigned.

Hall was sorry to see Bryce go as he found him 'very honourable and very thorough', but also 'very reticent and not ready enough to share his powers and his responsibility in Native matters with his colleagues'. It was no secret, Hall told Bell, 'that Bryce was always jealous of the West Coast Commission, and although I managed to keep the peace, it was a devil of a job'. Hall denied the truth of Bryce's statement that Te Whiti would only be arrested if he resisted Hiroki's arrest. 'When Bryce in cabinet was asked what he would do if he found

Hiroki flown (which he would have done) he replied that he would "not have come back empty handed". . . . Nor would he. . . . His object was to break up Parihaka by taking Te Whiti and Tohu.'[40]

Gordon meanwhile was continuing his search for information which would enable him to write the report he had promised the Colonial Office. The new native minister, Rolleston, who had been under-secretary for native affairs from 1865 until he entered parliament in 1868, was helpful to the governor and placed all the Native Office papers at his disposal, but Gordon found them 'too imperfect' for his purposes. A great deal of important information had been passed orally or by telegraph, and 'no official record remains of the information received, agreements made, or orders given'. Long after Gordon had sent his report to England, the under-secretary for the Native Department discovered an additional 86 telegrams which he handed to Gordon. Gordon altered parts of his report and sent an amended version to Kimberley.[41] It was that amended version (still dated 26 February) which was finally presented to the New Zealand and British parliaments. The Cabinet thought they had satisfactorily answered the Colonial Office's request for information to supply to Bradlaugh and did not suppose that Gordon himself would write so detailed and sensitive a report. When they learned of its existence a storm of controversy erupted and they managed to delay its presentation in England as well as New Zealand for more than a year.

Through the summer Hall still found Gordon 'perfectly easy to work with', although many in New Zealand believed he had been 'meddling in native matters so much that Bryce would not stand it and resigned'. Hall declared that this was not so, that the governor had acted 'as well as he possibly could have done' and if he continued in like vein there could be no possible reason to complain. By April he was less enthusiastic. He had just toured the South Island with Sir Arthur and 'was very glad when it was over'. The governor was not, he said, a genial man, and while prepared to accept his role as a constitutional governor he evidently did not relish it. 'His Excellency also has a "hankering" after dealing direct with the Natives which will have to be watched.'[42] The government's wariness of Colonial Office interference in colonial affairs extended to its representative in New Zealand. Since responsibility for native affairs lay with the colonial government, so, they felt, must the power and control, for it would be unjust to the settlers and a misfortune to Maori if outside interference were allowed: it might lead Maori to look beyond the colonial government for 'redress of possible grievances'. But Hall was prepared, in public, to defend the governor against newspaper reports in New Zealand and Britain which claimed that he had 'interfered unconstitutionally in the matters of the mission to Te Whiti and the release of the Maori prisoners'.[43]

The government had continued to make a token release of prisoners. By the end of February, 56 ploughmen and 23 fencers were free.[44] They had all been due for release at the end of January, but on 7 January Gordon had issued a proclamation to extend for a further three months the Maori Prisoners Act under which the ploughmen were held and the fencers were 'deemed to be held'. He told Kimberley he was prepared to extend the act once more so that it remained in effect until parliament met, but that he would 'experience considerable reluctance in prolonging its operation after that time'.[45] The government may have sensed this reluctance; in April, when they formally advised him to extend the act yet again, they also informed him that 86 prisoners had already been released – five or six of them on account of sickness, and that they hoped soon to be able to release 'a considerable number' of those still imprisoned. Gordon extended the act for another three months, but this time told Hall of his reluctance to extend it once parliament was in session 'without previously learning in some manner the opinion and wishes of the Legislature on this subject'.[46]

Before Fox had even begun work on his new commission, the survey for sale of the seaward Parihaka block had been commenced under Te Whiti's nose, and a block of about 5,000 acres on the coast between Cape Egmont and the Warea river was to go on the market before the end of January 1881.[47] It was only two months since Fox had reminded Hall that this was a situation which must be avoided at all costs, and one month since Bell had sailed for England, yet when Fox began work early in the new year he started not with the Parihaka reserves, but with those at the opposite end of the confiscated block. Fox had made an abrupt change of course, and far from continuing to press for the immediate carrying out of his and Bell's recommendations, he apparently acquiesced in the government's intentions to put an end to an embarrassing financial situation by provoking Te Whiti till he either gave in or resisted.[48] It was in the government's interests to ignore Te Whiti, who was a nuisance financially, but not Titokowaru, who was still deemed to be dangerous. The report Fox submitted about his work on the coast stressed that 'the cardinal point of the case', the marking out of the continuous reserve and other smaller reserves on the

'Fox himself delighted in over 3,500 acres of choice land between Marton and the Rangitikei River.'
'Westoe, Rangitikei County', watercolour by William Fox. *Alexander Turnbull Library*

'Parihaka and Mt Taranaki 1881'. Watercolour by G.C. Beale. *Taranaki Museum*

'Finnerty, a particularly stubborn man, was told his work was that of a robber and a thief.' Finnerty's Survey Camp, Waimate Plains.
Best Collection, Alexander Turnbull Library

'While Maori fought a new kind of war, the settlers prepared for such a one as they remembered.'
'Maoris ploughing settler's land at Tikorangi'. Pencil sketch by Ph. Walsh, 1879. *Alexander Turnbull Library*

Above: 'Survey Camp, Waimate Plains'. Chromolithograph from E.S. Brookes, *Frontier Life: Taranaki, New Zealand* (H. Brett, Auckland, 1892).
Below: 'The village presented a most melancholy appearance.' Parihaka, November 1881, occupied by constabulary and volunteers.
Parihaka Album, Alexander Turnbull Library

Above: 'The armed constabulary were well prepared for a struggle against their doughty foe armed with sticks.' Rahotu Redoubt.
Parihaka Album, Alexander Turnbull Library
Below: Officers' Quarters, Pungarehu. *Parihaka Album, Alexander Turnbull Library*

'There was no doubt that nine-tenths of the colony were behind the ministers.' Volunteers in Camp at Parihaka. *Parihaka Album*, *Alexander Turnbull Library*

'The patriotic rush to arms of the Taranaki Mounted Rifles.' Taranaki Rifles in Camp at Parihaka.
Parihaka Album, Alexander Turnbull Library

Waimate plains, had been accomplished to the satisfaction of 'the chief Titokowaru' with whom Fox had maintained close contact. But there was no mention of the Parihaka block which he had earlier considered inseparable from the question of the plains.

With Titokowaru appeased, Fox turned his attention southwards, away from Parihaka, and undertook subdivisional surveys south of the Waingongoro, where the people were 'more desirous of having their reserves defined'.[49] In March, he circulated a panui, a notice, among all the people from Waitotara to Paraninihi, explaining the work in which he was engaged. The reserves were to be divided among the constituent hapu, and each hapu was to name its members so that a crown grant could be issued in those names. Even at this stage, when reserves were at last to be assigned, the government had European not Maori settlement in mind. Once a hapu had its crown grant it could lease its land; rent money was the bait dangled before Maori eyes. The people were told that when the Waimate plains had been dealt with the work could continue south of the Waingongoro – but the Taranaki lands were to be left until last. When the Patukai, Upokomutu and Puketoretore hapu chose to give the names of their people, their crown grants would be issued to them.[50]

This was one more ultimatum to Te Whiti, delivered second hand. Fox and Bell had said that 'definite intimation can and should be given to Te Whiti on the manner in which it is proposed to deal with the disputed districts: and he should be invited to concur in that "sharing" of them' with the governor in which he had seemed ready to acquiesce when Mackay visited him. But instead of intimation, Te Whiti had been offered intimidation. The time had arrived when the 'offers and promises of the Crown must be either accepted or refused once for all'.[51] News could filter through to him; he could listen to Parris trying to detach his people from him; he could send the names of his people to Fox's Hawera office; but no one was prepared simply to go to Te Whiti with plans, maps and clear words – as had even been done with Titokowaru, with positive results. Sheehan had at first decided that returning the Parihaka block to Te Whiti would be paying too heavily for his having kept the peace; then he decided that the whole block down to the sea should be returned if Te Whiti continued to keep the peace. Then the commissioners in their wisdom decided to cut the Parihaka people off from their mountain and from the sea, but to return about 25,000 acres to them *at once*, for they would never get the plains in peace without Te Whiti having an assurance that he was safe at Parihaka. Twelve months later, the government had got the plains in peace but Te Whiti had still not got his assurance. The government had overlooked *that* recommendation of the commissioners while accepting the one that said 15,000 acres between Parihaka and the sea, Te Whiti's best arable land, should at once be made available for settlement: 'at the very doors of Parihaka, the establishment of English homesteads, and the fencing and cultivation of the land, will be the surest guarantee of peace'.[52] It seemed that Te Whiti was to be intimidated to the point where he could no longer keep the peace. The minimal portion of the Parihaka block 'intended to be reserved for him' could then be further whittled away.

There had been little to report about the monthly meetings at Parihaka through the summer except that Te Whiti and Tohu continued to counsel patience, forbearance and peace, and urged their people to set a good example to the Europeans and not to follow the bad example set by them. In January about 1,200 people were present and Te Whiti 'spoke with soreness about the land being surveyed and sold' but reminded his people that land had always been a source of trouble. In February he was reported to have likened the government to a cannibal who would destroy his people, yet he assured his listeners, Europeans among them, that the government could invade Parihaka and take him and Tohu prisoner and still their people would make no resistance.[53] Things were so quiet on the coast that the most the normally strident *Taranaki News* had to say about the March meeting, 'the annual gathering', was that it was well supplied with food, and 'nothing worthy of record transpired'.[54]

Hall too responded to Te Whiti's peace-keeping and to Gordon's obvious misgivings – not with the return of land, but with the return of prisoners. Early in April 1881 he reported to Rolleston that he was 'favourable to the release of a further batch of prisoners', but he had received an unfortunate report from Lyttelton that some of them had 'lately become very insubordinate'. However, if Parris could be spared from his work with Fox he should go south 'and make a selection'.[55] This was odd justice. The fate of several hundred political prisoners – imprisoned for months without trial for protesting against government injustice, and the only protest left to them a spot of insubordination – was to be determined by some sort of selection ballot. Some would be released and some would be detained – at the Cabinet's and Parris' pleasure. A month later, 161 prisoners, 47 of them ploughmen and 114 fencers, were landed from the *Hinemoa* at Opunake, after being discharged from prisons in Dunedin, Hokitika and Lyttelton. This left a mere 156 still in custody.[56] War did not break out on the coast with the return of these 'turbulent and dangerous men', but communications seemed to have broken down. On 3 June, Gordon was required to telegraph to the Colonial Office that all the remaining prisoners were released, but when he opened parliament on 9 June he was obliged to admit that all the prisoners were not yet free; those few remaining would be freed 'in a few days'.[57] The *Taranaki News* of 11 June 1881 reported that 'Another batch of Natives, released political prisoners, were brought up from the South by the Government steamer "Hinemoa" on Saturday and landed at Opunake'; and a week later the same paper reported 'The remnant of the Maori prisoners – 37 – were brought up from Hokitika gaol by "Stella" on Wednesday' (15 June). It had taken almost two weeks for theoretical release to become practical freedom, but the government did manage to release all the prisoners before the last extension to the Maori Prisoners Act expired – and they ensured the British government was prematurely informed of the fact.

The press had so little to report about Maori affairs on the coast that they found something to report on the reporters instead. Bryce had complained about 'misrepresentation by a section of the press' and had publicly attacked Croumbie-Brown, accusing him of 'attempting to levy black mail from the Government, and telling falsehoods about the Government out of revenge at his failure'. Croumbie-Brown was very outspoken in refuting the charge, and the controversy raged in print for some days.[58] The pro-government press was delighted. They had always said the *Lyttelton Times*' reports from the west coast were 'a series of audacious fabrications, conceived in the worst spirit of personal prejudice and calculated to mislead public opinion',[59] but the *Lyttelton Times* vigorously defended its stand, and its correspondent. Hall, from his Canterbury home, thoughtfully sent the cuttings to Bryce who exulted that what he had said about *that* paper and its precious correspondent 'was said deliberately and with the full knowledge that it would produce the kind of abuse which it has done'.[60] Bryce was later to rue his outburst; the press was a powerful opponent to tangle with.

The June hui at Parihaka was a very large one, with about 3,000 Maori and a number of Europeans present, including the interpreters Wellington Carrington, Charles Messenger and R. S. Thompson. The released prisoners, conspicuous by the raukura, the albatross plumes they proudly wore in their hair, were singled out for special attention by Te Whiti. The press gave an official résumé of Te Whiti's speech, which 'was better understood and more pacific than usual'. He had said the night had passed and morning had come;

there would be no more arrests; the men were safely back on the land where they belonged, under the protection of their atua; and those who had faith in the atua, the god of the Maori, would be great in the land.[61]

But while all was peaceful on the coast, a war of words was beginning in Wellington between Gordon and his responsible advisers which rivalled that of 1864 between Grey and his. When Gordon sent the amended version of his 26 February report to Kimberley, he also released it to the premier. The ministers were not pleased, feeling it would 'convey a wrong impression', and they regretted they could not write an explanatory memo in time to catch the mail by which the report was sent. They gave Gordon their memo just before the closing of the next mail – so that the secretary of state would have a month to mull over it before Gordon in his turn could make any detailed comment on their views.[62] But it was, Gordon said, 'feeble and querulous' and for the most part 'little more than an expression of difference of opinion as to the appreciation of admitted facts'.[63] Gordon was too kind; Hall's memo was misleading and quite at variance in many vital details with written reports presented over the years, printed and published and long since sent to the Colonial Office, and indeed at variance with many facts presented in the reports of the west coast commissioners.

Gordon assured Hall that he did not intend to enter into controversy with his ministers, but he felt his report was 'judiciously impartial' and could see no reason to alter or modify his conclusions. Before sending it to the Colonial Office, he had shown the whole report to Fox who thought it was 'a fair and impartial summary of events which ought not to have excited any susceptibility' on the part of the ministers; and he had shown the 'narrative portion' of it to the under-secretary of native affairs who, he said, examined it carefully and pronounced it correct.[64] Gordon's ministers were afraid the publication of his view of events would 'injuriously interfere' with the settlement of the west coast difficulties. They had no intention of laying the despatch before the New Zealand parliament and they had Gordon telegraph the Colonial Office to ask that its publication in England be delayed as long as possible. The Colonial Office was not surprised at the controversy, and on 9 August Herbert minuted that it had been expected that Gordon 'would not be long in New Zealand without forming and expressing views on native questions opposed to those of the Legislature and of the people generally'.[65] Hall complained to Bell that the governor was giving 'quite a good deal of trouble'. He had heard on good authority that Knollys had been up the west coast again 'cross-questioning Charles Brown on matters referred to in the despatch' and he did not think it right that a governor should 'collect materials for criticising the conduct of his ministers without telling them of it. . . . Already the Natives have somehow got it in their heads that the Governor is on their side'.[66]

While Gordon and his ministers were busy declining to enter into controversy with each other, Fox had allowed the survey of the seaward side of the Parihaka block to be continued. He had forgotten all the warnings from the past; he had forgotten that it was not offers and promises that were needed, but reserves marked out on the ground. This was the ultimate provocation, knowingly perpetrated by a government intent on ending the financial warfare which Te Whiti had time to wage, and they did not. Fox later sought to exculpate the government from this latest act of injustice by saying that they had, 'in a spirit of wise forbearance', given Te Whiti 'full time to consider his position and . . . avail himself of the opening afforded by the Governor's invitation'. But once more Te Whiti was required to accept or reject words, not reserves, and lest he reject their words yet again, the government had prepared the way for a full-scale invasion of Parihaka by completing 'several miles of road'.[67]

But still Te Whiti and his allegedly warlike followers had remained peaceful, and the survey for sale had gone ahead unopposed. Then in July he sent his men once more to assert their mana whenua. They began enclosing various old cultivations on their ancestral land seaward of the road and prepared the ground for planting. Parris was sent to tell them that this land was 'not set aside for Native occupation', and they were acting illegally and must desist[68] – although the people were only peacefully working their land as they had done for generations. It was also hard to concoct a Maori scare out of the preparations they were making for the August hui. The press reported the 'Te Whiti craze' still continued; between 30 and 40 carts had passed through Manaia on the way to Parihaka loaded with offerings – 'flour, sugar, dried lampreys and eels, pigs, geese, pigeons, parrots and other delicacies . . . and mutton birds in kelp bags that must have come from the extreme south'.[69] If proof were needed of the feelings of Maori from many parts of the country towards a chief who gave them pride in their identity and hope for the future, these tokens of aroha were that proof.

As the spring advanced, more cultivators appeared. They were warned they were 'trespassing in an illegal manner' and when they failed to take down their fences a massive force was brought in to deal with this new uprising. The armed constabulary men on leave were called back to assist their 150 comrades at Pungarehu and 50 at Cape Egmont to pull down the fences, and Hursthouse was moved to Pungarehu to assist Colonel Roberts in preventing the traditional owners of the soil from 'taking possession of Government land'.[70] The constabulary were ordered to avoid violence, but on 12 September 'an act of aggression' occurred when the cultivators found the constables loading up drays of firewood on the disputed land. The cultivators unloaded the wood, told the constables to go away and not come back, and returned to their work. This was indication enough that they were determined on 'more active and serious obstruction', and Roberts soon found further proof of it when on 15 September a big group of men, stripped and armed with ko, or digging sticks,[71] followed his party at a distance of about 150 yards when they rode over the surveyed land. Asked the meaning of this threatening behaviour, the leader of the Maori party who approached them said he was 'very angry, and that they were not to cut his fence'. Roberts was satisfied that a critical period had arrived and that there would be a serious disturbance next time a fence was removed.[72]

The armed constabulary were well prepared for a struggle against their doughty foe armed with sticks. They had four main camps within ten miles of Parihaka: Pungarehu, one and a half miles away, was on a strong natural site, had a temporary breast-work and was 'about to be strengthened by the addition of a blockhouse'; Rahotu, five miles away, was on 'the site of an old Native fortification'; Egmont, five miles away, was 'a small stone Redoubt . . . and a main camp, enclosed in a substantial palisading'; Opunake, the district headquarters, had 'a Redoubt capable of accommodating 100 men . . . with a bullet-proof, loop-holed Blockhouse'.[73] In the nine months to 31 December 1880, the armed constabulary in the Patea–Taranaki district had cost the country £69,000. The cost had diminished from £9,000 in the month of May 1880 to £5,000 in November 1880, but could 'be said to be at the rate of £75,000 p.a.'. It is not surprising that Te Wheoro (Western Maori) should remark in the House that he thought Europeans in Taranaki with an eye to trade caused rumours of Maori scares to circulate 'for the purpose of getting additional numbers of constabulary up there'.[74]

Hall reported to Bell that west coast affairs were 'rather mixed'. They had explained, remonstrated and pulled down fences to no avail, but as yet had stopped short of taking prisoners. Te Whiti was supposed to have said that if they did so he would retaliate; then the order must be 'to Parihaka, quick march', but Hall hoped this might not come before the session was over.[75] The more restricted the audience, the better the European actors liked the situation.

There can be no mistaking government intentions. Despite the promises of the act of confiscation; despite McLean's injunction to the west coast tribes to be strong in cultivating the land and to let their future fighting be with the soil; despite the Grey government's intention to return the Parihaka block; and despite the solemn promises over the years that old cultivations would be reserved, the Hall government was determined to divide Te Whiti's blanket. The west coast commissioners had changed their ideas about reserving from sale the seaward part of the Parihaka block because that would have meant allowing the people to maintain their 'present isolation'. In the government's view there was much more at stake than just this strip of land. Maintenance of isolation signified maintenance of mana, and it was the mana the government was intent on destroying. Despite all their earlier protestations of good intentions, the seaward Parihaka block was surveyed and sold under Te Whiti's nose, and no reserves were yet marked out on the ground. It was not to be wondered at that the people were out there engaged in their age-old pursuit of spring planting on land hallowed by association with the ancestors. But their persistence in 'flouting the law' provided an excuse for the government to bring the west coast situation to a head; it would be easy then to claim what their intentions had been, when, through failure to put any of them into practice, the people had finally been forced into a situation which could be labelled rebellion and put down with a firm hand. The road to Parihaka was paved with the government's good intentions.

Another obstacle was removed from the government's path in mid September when Gordon left for Fiji for an important land court hearing.[76] As the parliamentary session had been unexpectedly prolonged, Gordon had asked his ministers whether he might leave as planned 'without injury to the public service'. The ministry thought no inconvenience would result since, as soon as the ship taking him to Fiji had 'got out of New Zealand waters', the dormant commission would come into force and the chief justice, James Prendergast, could 'at once be sworn as Administrator of the Government'.[77] However, when questions were raised several times in the House as to whether the dormant commission would cease on the governor's return, the government consulted first Whitaker, the attorney-general, and then the secretary of state. The reply of 30 September from the Colonial Office was simply that 'Temporary

Administrator's commission ceases to have effect on return of Governor'.[78]

Gordon sailed from Auckland on 13 September and was expected to be absent for six or eight weeks. The ministry was not sorry to see him go. Hall wrote to Bell that there had been some grumbling in the press and in the House about the governor's absence, but 'No inconvenience will arise (*tout au contraire*) from the Chief Justice stepping into the Governor's shoes'.[79] Prendergast was chief justice for 24 years from 1875 to 1899 and on six occasions administered the government in the absence of a governor; his most notorious act was his legal ruling that declared the Treaty of Waitangi 'a simple nullity'.[80] The ministers could see their critical audience being further depleted and one more obstruction removed from the road to Parihaka.

After Gordon had left Wellington, the government introduced a new bill to the House 'to provide for the Administration of Reserves made for Natives within the Confiscated Territory' on the west coast. Under the West Coast Settlement Reserves Act, the reserves 'for the natives' were to be vested in the Public Trustee who would sell the alienable reserves and lease the inalienable ones, but retain complete control of their administration; this included the right to alter the rules governing their management and leasing and the application and expenditure of the lease money due to the beneficial owners.[81] From the rent money that remained when the Public Trustee had made the appropriate deductions, the beneficiaries would be required to pay a sum towards the support and maintenance of native schools in the neighbourhood of their reserves. The trustee was empowered to lease these just and ample reserves in lots of 40 suburban or 640 urban acres to any one European, on 42 or 21-year leases. The vaunted continuous reserve, which was to make the Waimate plains people the richest natives on the coast, was part of this scheme.

When the bill came before the House, there was once more a chorus of complaints that important bills regarding native affairs were being rushed through the House in the last days of the session. Asked if the bill had been translated, Rolleston 'presumed' it had since it had already passed through the Council and he was certain the natives were 'aware' that such a bill was under consideration. He explained that since the introduction of the West Coast Settlement Act both inalienable and alienable reserves had been set aside 'for the benefit of the Natives', and this act would provide for the survey and division of the alienable reserves 'so as to promote the interest of settlement'.[82] The government knew very well that the money the tribes received for their land would rapidly be lost to storekeepers and grog-sellers, but as usual the welfare of the tribes came a poor second to settlement of the country by Europeans. Whether their land was sold or leased, the making of these long promised reserves meant that Maori would still be crowded off their ancestral lands by European settlers. If they were lucky, in time they would be left a few settlements, cultivations and fishing stations, but the promise that loyal natives and returned rebels would be left in 'possession' of their lands was indeed a hollow one.

There were still a few who would raise their voices against the government, but more because they were in opposition to it than because they really espoused the Maori cause. As one member said, they had had 'a series of reports, and a large expenditure of public money', but they had not yet attained any good results for it. The Maori members objected to the fact that control of the reserves would be in the hands of Europeans and Maori would have no say in the matter, and a European member suggested leases be made 'with the consent of the Natives entitled', as recommended by the commissioners.[83] But the government did not mean to relinquish even the slightest control of those west coast lands. Their window-dressing performance of fulfilling the promises of successive governments was complete.

The governor was hardly out of New Zealand's territorial waters before the government increased the strength of the armed constabulary on the coast. Opunake was reinforced by the addition of 50 men, and on 14 September the House agreed to a vote of £84,000 for contingent defence.[84] The governor's private secretary, F. P. Murray, who also acted as secretary to the administrator, was to keep Gordon informed about events on the west coast during his absence, so as soon as he sent off the first news of this sudden change in the government's attitude, Prendergast hastened to communicate with Gordon himself. He wrote an 'intentionally unofficial' but reassuring note on 16 September, the day *before* the important half-yearly meeting at Parihaka, although he knew it would not leave Wellington until 23 September to catch the monthly mail to Fiji. He kept no copy of it, but later remembered he had 'briefly informed' Gordon of the 'state of affairs' on the coast. Fortunately Gordon kept his copy:

> Mr Murray tells me that Mr Rolleston has permitted him to copy a telegram the Government have received as to the state of things at Parihaka, and as you will see from that all the information there is on the subject, I need do no more

> than say that Mr Hall and Mr Rolleston agree in thinking the appearances do not indicate serious mischief. I have nothing else to inform you of.[85]

Despite Prendergast's opinion that an absent governor 'ought to be kept generally informed of any matter of extraordinary importance' with the object of 'enabling him to determine his course of action as to expediting or not his return to his government', Prendergast did not write to Gordon again either before the mail left or afterwards,[86] in spite of the immediate development of a situation which the government claimed was so threatening they could use it as an excuse for a complete turn around and a justification for adopting Bryce's 'vigorous policy'.

On 17 September, the half-yearly meeting was held at Parihaka. There are several accounts of it; practically every newspaper in New Zealand reported it, and no two reports are the same. They did not agree on how many were there – estimates ranged from 2,000 to 3,000, on whether or not there was beer in great abundance or only tea to drink, and especially on what was said and, even more importantly, what was meant. Certainly there were Europeans present and they were as welcome as usual, and the released prisoners, proudly wearing their raukura, again came in for special notice from Te Whiti. The speech, particularly as reported by Hursthouse to Bryce,[87] might not have attracted great attention had there not been those who were looking for trouble. Te Whiti had been provoked by the increase in the armed constabulary and was expected to react. The speech was more ambiguous than usual and was interpreted to fit existing preconceptions. The most inflammatory account of the hui and the speech was given by the *New Zealand Times* of 20 September without the least suggestion that the words may have been ambiguous or could have been misinterpreted or misunderstood: 'Pakanga, pakanga, pakanga. . . . All our talk today is of fighting, and nothing is now left but to fight. . . . If when pakeha goes on the land they strike you with a stone, strike them with a stone. . . . If they bring guns, take your guns . . . fight and kill; don't save anyone; destroy all before you'. The account in the *Taranaki News* of 24 September was much more subdued: 'Their trouble had been the land, and it was still the land that was the trouble. It did not matter now who was originally right or wrong . . . the time for peace and forbearance was past'. This paper admitted that while there were some 'expressions that might be taken to mean an immediate antagonistic action' they were qualified by other remarks and also by Tohu who, the next day, 'called a meeting of the Natives, to explain to them the meaning of Te Whiti's speech'. He insisted they must not be the ones to break the peace; that they should continue fencing their own land but should not allow any of their number to be taken prisoner and indeed should resist arrest, meeting force with force. The *New Zealand Herald*'s special correspondent reported that official telegrams transmitting the speeches placed a 'less formidable construction upon them, while the context of the speeches tends in a large degree to lessen their apparently menacing nature'; and that Te Whiti had said 'both sides take up your weapons', but then said 'goodness was the only weapon which would be victorious, and good would rule the world'. The speeches were in fact 'thoroughly ambiguous and might mean anything', but the main fear seemed to be that Te Whiti's influence over his people was waning and he might give them more freedom to act than before. While one paper said Maori had been told that if rifles were fired they must fire back, another said they might use fists but not guns; while one said the returned prisoners were spoiling for a fight, another said there would be no fighting on the part of Maori; while one said Te Whiti was threatening war, another said Te Whiti's speech was not warlike, that there would be fencing, planting and talking, but no guns would be used, there would be no fighting.[88]

A day or two later Croumbie-Brown reported that while persistent efforts were being made in certain quarters 'to work up a Maori scare' there was nothing in it. In the meeting house at night Te Whiti had 'explained the real meaning' of his speech: he did not mean to fight and his people must be careful not to bring the anger of the government on them. He warned them not to give his speeches a literal meaning but to wait until they were explained to them.[89] It was this later explanation that the reporters and official interpreters seldom heard. Hursthouse, for one, recognised the importance of the night meetings but was rarely present, and he merely 'arranged to get news' of what took place at the crucial evening meeting of 17 September 1881.[90] A few days later, when there was nothing new to report, the *Herald*'s special correspondent was pleased to note that his report of Te Whiti's speech had been the correct one. 'The original alarming versions emanated simply from one source'; someone interpreted the speeches in his own way and 'communicated his free translation of Te Whiti's mystic and allegorical verbiage to various Europeans present. These took alarm and telegraphed in all directions'.[91]

The House was still in session when reports of the 17 September speeches reached Wellington, and the Maori members were obviously disturbed at this new Maori scare the press was creating. Te Wheoro told the government not to place too much faith in the newspaper reports; he did not think they were justified in believing they had any foundation. Tomoana suggested, very perceptively, that there were 'several office seekers in that part of the country' who needed a cause to campaign on in the coming election. Tawhai went further, saying it was likely the newspapers circulated these reports so that the Maori race might be quickly exterminated. For once Hall sought information of the Maori members and asked if they had heard anything which gave them grounds for telling the government there was no cause for alarm. Te Wheoro assured him that if war was a possibility news of it would long since have been passed through the Maori kin network, and anyway there were Europeans living there and how was it they had not 'run away and left the district?' Hall hastily thanked the Maori members for their good intentions and assured them the government was not alarmed, and that they knew perfectly well what was being said and done at Parihaka. If the government knew that, they had no possible excuse for the policy they were embarking on. The very next day, with only a handful of members left in the House, the government asked for and got a further contingent defence vote of £100,000 'in order that they should be in a position to deal with any difficulty that might arise'.[92]

Fencing and cultivating on 'European' land in the Parihaka block continued unabated. Te Whiti's pakanga, the spring planting, was in full swing on land they had had in cultivation the previous year but which had now been sold under their feet, and immediately the House rose on 22 September the native minister, Rolleston, hastened to the west coast to assess the state of affairs for himself. He decided there would be no cause for alarm until the government took 'active measures', as all was quiet around Parihaka; New Plymouth, however, was in a ferment, expecting Te Whiti to invade and burn the town. He wired Atkinson, confidentially, that Charles Hursthouse and W. J. Butler had been at Parihaka 'chatting with the natives in a most friendly way (don't publish this)'. According to his official report he had, on arrival on the coast, 'at once placed himself in communication with many of the leading Natives in the district' and told them of the government's intentions to meet their wishes 'in respect of particular lands for which they might have any predilection'; and, in typical fashion, he explained 'the general proposals of the Government and the Commission, to such Natives as would be sure to convey a statement of them to Parihaka'.[93] Hall told Bell he was thankful the governor was away as he would give 'no end of trouble without doing the Natives one bit of good'. He added that although Rolleston had assured him the natives did not wish to fight, the government had recruited 200 men for the constabulary and any more they required they would get from the various volunteer corps.[94]

The Maori scare in Taranaki was illusory, but the government was facing an election. They had satisfied the settlers' clamour for land by selling the plains and the seaward Parihaka block; they now had to satisfy the settlers' clamour for protection. Atkinson was satisfied there was 'no reasonable probability of natives making immediate hostile movement', yet he approved the increases in the constabulary and volunteers while insisting it was 'Very important not to give our enemies an opportunity of saying that Taranaki people are creating a scare or fermenting a disturbance for the sake of expenditure'.[95] But the rest of the colony was saying just that. Either there was a Maori scare and the huge additional expenditure on the armed constabulary was justified and they should 'make an aggressive move' immediately, or the west coast Maori had no warlike intentions and the armed constabulary force should be reduced. But the ministry wanted it both ways. The Taranaki settlers wanted action, a 'powerful display of force'; they could not 'consent to be continually living under the will of Te Whiti and in slavish submission to his caprice'. What they needed was someone 'at the head of native affairs . . . who understands the native character and habits'. In their view, Major Atkinson was the '*only* member of the Ministry' capable of dealing with the matter.[96] Major Atkinson apparently thought so too. He criticised Rolleston for increasing the armed constabulary *on the plains*, where the settlers were scattered, rather than nearer New Plymouth. Rolleston was very put out. 'Surely some confidence must be placed in me here with better means of knowing than can be in Wellington . . . if you share the want of confidence you say Atkinson feels you only have to say the word.'[97] Rolleston was facing an imaginary threat from Titokowaru; Atkinson was facing an election.

The Press Association continued to send back alarming reports from 'the front', but Rolleston sent long telegrams commenting pointedly on the 'total absence of any warlike preparations on the part of the Natives'. Neither at Parihaka nor elsewhere was there 'the slightest indication of any intention to fight'. The attitude of the people was 'thoroughly pacific and good tempered'; they were unusually busy 'sowing and planting extensively and engrossed in agriculture'. The Reverend Mr Luxford visited Parihaka and reported that even Te Whiti was away planting crops, but he saw Tohu who said that native grievances had not been addressed and the people were complaining bitterly of their good arable land being sold.[98] Rolleston talked to a couple working on a surveyed section and asked if they did not realise their illegal fence had been removed and that section sold. They only knew 'it was a melon clearing for March on their land' and the woman asked why they could not work together 'instead of playing round the fences'.[99]

There was clearly bewilderment but no hostility among these people and this was becoming very apparent to Rolleston. Hall thought it was time some 'misunderstandings were cleared up', so he and Atkinson went to the coast to talk to Rolleston and Roberts 'to obtain information as to the exact position of affairs'. There was nothing new, he told Whitaker; statements as to 'the warlike intentions of the natives' were incorrect. They did not want to fight, but persevered in a course which would make it 'difficult to avoid'. He was convinced that 'Thompson, the Interpreter, and other blackguard Europeans' had done much harm and this had encouraged the natives to become 'insolent and aggressive in a variety of ways'. But Rolleston was anxious to go into Parihaka and see Te Whiti and although Hall thought nothing would come of the visit except 'proof of our desire for pacific settlement', he was prepared to agree to the visit 'on the understanding it would be done very quietly'.[100] Nothing could be done quietly on the coast. The press speculated wildly about this ministerial meeting: 'Premier and Treasurer Gone to the Front'; something serious had happened; shots had been fired, blood had been shed and a rising of the natives was imminent. The *New Zealand Herald*'s intrepid correspondent once more calmed the situation. The ministers simply wished to confer, he said, and he had their 'distinct assurance' that there was no change in the position of native affairs. However, there were many theories abroad to account for this conference and one of them connected 'the Ministerial movement with the absence of the Governor and with some impending change'.[101]

As a preliminary to visiting Te Whiti himself, Rolleston sent his interpreter, William Riemenschneider, a son of the early missionary at Warea. Te Whiti had known this young man since he was a child and talked to him very freely. The conversation as reported back to Rolleston and recorded in his diary is one of the very few occasions when we hear Te Whiti's own words,[102] spoken in normal conversation to a person whom he knew well and who really understood the language. It is as though we hear his very voice. Te Whiti's first concern was the garbled versions of his 17 September speech that had appeared in the newspapers. He was sorry that such stories had been circulated and had alarmed the settlers unnecessarily, and he thought it was in everyone's interests that newspaper correspondents be kept away from his meetings since they caused mischief by misrepresenting what he said. His pakanga was not a fight, but a dispute with his only weapon, the tongue, over the ancestral cultivations to the seaward of the Pungarehu road. He again indicated his willingness to share his blanket, saying that on the Waimate plains and north of Pungarehu 'the land was occupied by the pakeha who had built houses and erected fences and there they would remain'. He had heard many rumours that had got abroad – that the settlers on the plains were to be disturbed; that Titokowaru was coming with 200 fighting men; that hostilities were about to break out at any moment – but all were lies and he was pouri about them and would take care no such outrages took place. He asked about the governor and why 'he had rushed off to Fiji and forsaken his sucklings, caring more for those who are better able to look after themselves'. He asked where Fox was and wanted to know when the government intended giving effect to the commissioners' recommendations. He had Tohu take Riemenschneider around the cultivations near Parihaka and when he returned asked him 'if the work of the hoe and the spade' looked as though they meant mischief.

> Now you have seen with your own eyes and I hope these exaggerated reports will be contradicted. . . . As to fighting it is absurd. You ought to know me better . . . we are but a small people, merely a handful, is it likely . . . after all these years of peace that we should again take up arms. Be assured if there was likely to be trouble you would know it, but there is no such thing.[103]

This was no new stand of Te Whiti's. His words of 1881 were those of 1871. He had always preached peace, he had always said there was room for Maori and European to live side by side. The government had always chosen to interpret his claim to land north of the Waingongoro as a claim to all the confiscated land on the coast. But Te Whiti had been prepared to 'share his blanket' to the extent of giving up land from Waitotara to Waingongoro and, once reserves had been made for Ngatiruanui on the Waimate plains, his concern had been for the seaward Parihaka block. He would not stand by now and see the rest of his blanket torn from him, his ancestral lands invaded, when he had only ever been offered vague promises and never definite reserves. From the time he stopped the survey, he had been treated as a fanatic and a fool, and no man of mana had ever sat down to negotiate with him and agree to let him remain undisturbed on those lands hallowed by association with the ancestors.

Now that the government had decided to take 'strong and decisive steps', they agreed on one last gesture designed to forestall criticism at home and abroad. The native minister was to be permitted to visit Parihaka himself, to discuss the 'lands still unsold' in the seaward Parihaka block. Rolleston could hardly expect to have a very amicable discussion on such a sensitive matter, but the official report of his interview with Te Whiti reflects a very different attitude from that expressed earlier in his diary.[104] There was no suggestion then that Rolleston believed the situation to be other than that described by Riemenschneider, and just four days after the interview, Hall told Whitaker that Rolleston seemed to shrink from the responsibility of the position of native minister 'and the action which has to be taken'.[105] It took two weeks and 'a long talk with Hall' for him to face his 'responsibility' and to write a report stating that Te Whiti's concern over his ancestral cultivations was in fact intransigence and proof of his refusal to share his blanket; he did not mention that Te Whiti was willing to see Europeans settled on those parts of the coast to the north and south of the Parihaka block which he 'did not care so much for'. Rolleston, obliged in an official document to portray the government in the right and Te Whiti in the wrong, concluded that Te Whiti's intransigence stemmed from his *amour propre* and from an ill-founded idea that the imperial government would interfere in his favour.[106] Almost a century later, Rolleston's granddaughter offered quite a convincing explanation for this *volte face*. She suggested that Rolleston's frustrations grew when he could persuade neither government nor settlers that the west coast people had no warlike intentions, until his wife took a hand and began to persuade him that he had a greater duty to his colleagues than he had to the truth. She believed that these 'curtain lectures' delivered by Mrs Rolleston, who admired Bryce and approved of his policies and who despaired of her husband's liberal leanings, finally drove him to support a policy he had never advocated.[107]

Rolleston's interview with Te Whiti was considered to have been 'unsatisfactory' as it had produced nothing in the way of a settlement, and the native minister dutifully followed it up with a threatening letter, another ultimatum. He told Te Whiti this was his last chance, that the government had wished to treat him as a friend but as he would not listen to their word the blame would lie with him, not with Rolleston and the government, if no good came of the meeting. Meanwhile, he warned Te Whiti that the illegal fencing which he had sanctioned was wrong, could not be permitted and must be stopped, and that his fencers were breaking the law and were liable to punishment.[108]

As the time of the October hui approached, the military build up intensified. After Hall's visit to the coast he told Whitaker the government had to stay its hand because they were not yet strong enough to take any 'decisive measures', but as soon as they had built up the force on the coast they would start pulling down fences. He added that Atkinson was 'strongly inclined' to have Te Whiti arrested at once but Hall, unsure what charge they could bring against him, preferred to wait till the local Maori gave them a good *casus belli* in the resistance which he was sure would be offered to their pulling down fences. Meanwhile, Hall had called Bryce to Wellington and thought he would accept an offer to rejoin the Cabinet as native minister, since circumstances might now 'justify the adoption of strong measures such as he proposed at a time when they were not justifiable'. Whitaker saw objections to Bryce being native minister and would have much preferred that Rolleston retain the position, but he agreed that if there was any fear of his 'shirking the responsibility' then control would have to pass to someone who would not flinch. In any case, he advised Hall that the government's object should now be to satisfy public opinion in both New Zealand and England that they had no 'reasonable alternative' to the use of force. The only question in his mind was that of 'the best way of bringing about the inevitable collision', and he opted not for the arrest of Te Whiti and Hiroki, but for the removal of 'everything and everybody that stood in the way of . . . complete and sole possession of the country without interference'. This would necessitate the prior organisation of an overwhelming military force which would ensure the government's success in any conflict. He assumed that Maori would offer resistance 'either armed or only obstructive' which would 'constitute a riot', so they should then read the Riot Act and 'proceed at once to arrest and disperse the rioters'.[109]

For all Rolleston's public show of belligerence, privately he was still not convinced of the justice of the government's stance. He knew there was no warlike intention on the coast and absolutely no preparation for fighting: no defences, no build up of arms, no sign of hostility. Even the *Taranaki News* reported reassuringly that 14 gentlemen from New Plymouth had just paid a Sunday visit to Parihaka. The place was so quiet it seemed deserted but then the village turned out *en masse* to greet the visitors. The chief Tahana who showed them around was 'particularly friendly' and introduced them to Te Whiti, who shook hands with each of them as they entered his whare. They returned to New Plymouth satisfied of the Maori's peaceful intentions. But the Auckland press thought Te Whiti's intentions immaterial, that as he was a 'living threat and a nuisance' it was 'lawful and just to suppress him', and since the government had sold the land and taken the settlers' money they now had no option but to heed the settlers' demands for protection, 'not only from danger, but from the constant dread of it'.[110]

Hall knew that Maori had no warlike intentions, but it was not a message that he or Whitaker or Atkinson wanted to hear. As long as the settlers continued to talk about the danger, and the colony to believe it existed, then ministers could justify their actions. Bryce was disturbed by Rolleston's views which, he said, were totally at variance with those expressed publicly by Atkinson and would have 'a disastrous effect on his election'.[111] Re-election, and the cost of 'maintaining the peace' were the burning issues, not justice over Maori land claims. The government needed an excuse for action in Taranaki and they hoped the October hui would give it to them, so they sent Hursthouse, Wellington Carrington and Riemenschneider to Parihaka and had them make out declarations 'as to the correct translation of Te Whiti's speech as far as they could note it'. The government could note nothing belligerent in the speech, but neither could they find any reason for believing that Te Whiti was taking 'a more reasonable view'. Moreover they had heard, on good authority, that Te Whiti's people were becoming very dissatisfied with the constant waiting for the fulfilment of his promises, and that if the government took him prisoner they would have to protect him from his own people.[112] But 2,000 Maori and 50 or 60 Europeans were on the marae at the October hui to witness to the peacefulness of it all.

The government had not found its excuse for action but it suddenly found an urgent need for it two days later. Ministers were subsequently to deny all prior knowledge of Gordon's unexpected return from Fiji and of his imminent arrival in New Zealand, and while they could certainly claim to have received no official communication, his departure from Fiji was known in Australia several days before he arrived in New Zealand.[113] There is little doubt that they knew what they had not been officially told, and their actions between 17 and 19 October confirm what they tried to deny.

Bryce had returned to Wellington late on Saturday 15 October; on the 17th, Hall telegraphed Whitaker in Auckland asking whether he would be agreeable to Bryce's rejoining the ministry, on the understanding that 'if hostilities do break out they should be pursued very promptly and very vigorously' so that the whole matter would be settled quickly. It was time, he said, to end the suspense and the expense of the west coast situation and as public opinion was with the ministry they proposed to bring matters to a head. They intended to draw up a proclamation pointing out that while the offer of reserves had been 'conditional on acceptance by the natives and their peaceful conduct' the Parihaka natives had not accepted the government's offer; instead Te Whiti had made a threatening and rebellious speech and his people had fenced European land and resisted the armed constabulary. If within fourteen days of the issue of the proclamation they agreed to accept 'reserves on the conditions attached to them', the commission would 'sit at or near Parihaka to enquire into their claims and grievances', but if they did not accept them the government would withdraw its offers and take what land they thought proper.[114]

The proclamation was one more rhetorical flourish. Chiefs and tribes were obliged to entreat government indulgence in the question of reserves, but it was the government that decided what entreaties it would indulge. It was not a question of the government's recognising Te Whiti's right to reserves, but of Te Whiti's recognising the government's right to grant or withhold them. As usual, it was a question of mana. Had Te Whiti's claims and grievances been inquired into eighteen months earlier, or had he simply been granted the reserves which were his due, a settlement may well have been reached, but 16 years after an unjust confiscation Te Whiti was now to be given 14 days in which to agree to the government's ultimatum or face further confiscation.

The government obviously had no time to lose in implementing its plan. Within hours, Hall followed his telegram to Whitaker with another marked 'Strictly Private and Confidential': 'It is of importance Government should be committed one way or the other before Sir Arthur Gordon's return or we shall have great difficulties'.[115] Hall did not expect Te Whiti to accept the government's ultimatum and told Fox the government would, as soon as it had assembled a sufficient force, proceed to pull down the fences and arrest the fencers, as well as Te Whiti and Tohu if they could 'see a good excuse', and then 'make roads straight through the inland Parihaka block and probably sell portions of it'. Fox agreed the time had come 'when offers made to Te Whiti must be accepted or refused', but added that since Te Whiti in his meeting with Rolleston had 'affected not to know what reserves had been intended to be made for him', they should attach a map to the proclamation showing the reserves 'so that he may not pretend ignorance'.[116]

This was the first and only time it was ever suggested the reserves 'intended' for Te Whiti be marked on a map and shown to him. He had continually asked what reserves he was to have and continually believed he would get none, since none was ever shown him and the land all about him was being surveyed and sold. The government continually said he must point out the reserves he wanted, but it knew quite well it would be the government's intentions, not Te Whiti's wishes, that would be crucial in determining what reserves would be given to him.[117] Intentions were never good enough; they were certainly no better than the long series of unfulfilled promises made over the years by a succession of governments and ministers. As a final act of intimidation, the government would now define the reserves in an ultimatum which they did not expect would be accepted and which, 'for humanity's sake', would be backed 'with such a display of force as will convince these poor infatuated people of the utter hopelessness of resistance and so avert a collision'.[118]

The following day the draft proclamation was drawn up and agreed to by Whitaker, who hoped that Maori could be brought within English law 'instead of using our venial acts to try them'. At least the government would then 'stand better in public opinion in England'.[119] On 18 October, there was a convenient Maori outrage when some of the cultivators near Cape Egmont interfered with a new settler fencing his land and carried off his fencing materials. The district could be seen to be in a 'very unsettled state' and the government had its excuse for action. Their forces were not yet ready, but the proclamation was. Hall asked Whitaker to wire immediately if he had any further suggestions, as the proclamation was to be issued that night in a special *Gazette* and given to the Press Association. Bryce would then be sworn in as native minister and he and Rolleston, who were 'anxious to leave', would set off immediately for the west coast.[120] The government was displaying almost indecent haste after years of indecision.

Everything went according to schedule. A meeting of the Executive Council was held at 8 p.m. on 19 October, the proclamation was signed by Rolleston as his last act as native minister, Bryce was sworn in, and at 4 a.m. he was on the road. Rolleston was 'detained' in Wellington, but in any case Bryce was only getting out of town. He went as far as Wanganui; the proclamation did not reach Parihaka for another three days. But the ministers had won their race against time. At 10.30 p.m., just an hour or so after the Executive Council meeting ended, the *Emerald* bringing Gordon home 'post haste' from Fiji dropped anchor in Wellington harbour after a maddeningly slow passage. When he appeared in their midst next morning, ministers expressed great surprise to Gordon, but not to each other. Hall simply wired to Whitaker: ' "Emerald" arrived at 10.30 last night. Proclamation signed at 8.15 . . . and published all over the colony'; and wrote to Bryce: 'Sir Arthur Gordon came into harbour last night at half past ten'; and cabled to Bell in England: 'Gordon returned Fiji two hours after Proclamation signed. . . . Fear serious differences with Governor'.[121] Indeed Gordon was furious at the ministry's moves; he did not agree with Bryce's reappointment or with the proclamation, and asked that it be recalled. There was an 'unpleasant scene' at a hastily called Executive Council meeting and Prendergast, the erstwhile administrator, emerged from an interview with the governor 'ashen and fuming'.[122] His anguish soon passed; his knighthood, arranged for him by his grateful ministers, was announced on 1 November.

The governor demanded to know what changed circumstances had impelled the government to issue 'under the temporary government of an Administrator' so important a proclamation, and to appoint a new native minister 'when his own return within twenty-four hours was known to be at least probable, if not well nigh certain'.[123] He then raised the question of the validity of the administrator's actions when he was himself already within New Zealand's territorial waters. Ministers disclaimed all knowledge of the governor's impending return, and Hall requested Whitaker's opinion on the validity of the administrator's acts.[124] Whitaker replied that those acts 'were not invalidated by the presence of His Excellency . . . within the territorial limits of the Colony', although the dormant commission had, according to their earlier opinion, only come into effect when the governor *left* territorial waters. Gordon promptly cabled the Colonial Office to 'ascertain the effect on the Dormant Commission to the Chief Justice of His Excellency's return within the territorial limits of the Colony', and received the reply that the administrator's acts were valid 'up to the time of His Excellency's actual landing in the colony'.[125] The Colonial Office may have been purposely distancing itself from the fray. Herbert minuted on Gordon's telegram:

> The Governor when within the territorial waters had technically returned to the Colony, and it was a weak piece of sharp practice for the ministers (having heard that the ship was coming in) to induce the Acting Governor to re-appoint a minister to whose views the Governor was known to be decidedly opposed.[126]

Gordon had been presented with a *fait accompli*. He could get neither Bryce nor the proclamation recalled as it 'had fortunately been brought out in a *Gazette Extraordinary* on the night of the 19th',[127] and since it was obvious to him that his ministers had the confidence of parliament and would be 'supported in their "vigorous" action by nine-tenths of the white population of the colony', he felt he must comply with such advice as they gave him, or resign. The latter course appealed to him but he considered such a move would create 'false hope on the part of the Maoris' and embarrass both the imperial government and his successor. Hall assured him that in the absence of 'fresh cause' there would be no active military operations before the expiry of the fourteen-day period named in the proclamation, and the governor repeated his intention, in the event of a serious collision with the Maori population, to resign at once and leave on the *Emerald* without any appearance of an 'open breach'.[128]

The question of whether or not ministers knew of the governor's return was another matter,[129] but it would be remarkable, after a ten-year build-up of the situation and two years of heightened tension, for ministers to issue a proclamation in the middle of the night, appoint a 'vigorous' native minister and send him off with the proclamation before dawn, if they did not suspect Gordon was on the doorstep. Even had he arrived in time, Gordon could only with difficulty have rejected his ministers' advice, but his presence would at least have given them pause. Hall could rightly claim he had no official knowledge, but he realised Gordon would cut short his Fijian visit when he received the news sent to him by Murray. He knew the *Emerald* was on her way back with Gordon on board, and by the morning of 19 October he knew that the governor 'might be looked for at any moment'. At 5.30 that evening, Murray told Prendergast he was surprised, 'allowing eight or nine days for the passage', the governor had not already arrived; he had 'practically expected the "Emerald" during the last two or three days' and it was his strong belief she was 'within a few hours of Wellington'. Both Hall and Prendergast had expressed special interest that day in the governor's movements, but Murray did not feel he should tell them directly that Lady Gordon had received a cable from the commodore of the Australian station in Sydney three or four days earlier telling her Gordon was returning home immediately.[130] Many months later, they both contradicted Murray's version of the conversations held that day and written down by him the very next day and fell back on their assertions that they had no *official* knowledge of the facts; Prendergast even went so far as to say they had 'no information from which they could know or suspect' the governor's return was imminent, and that Murray's statement was 'an utter misrepresentation' of what had taken place.[131]

The ministers' memories a year or two later were as convenient as their consciences at the time. They not only acted while an unaccommodating governor was out of the country, they then tried to suppress all official documents relating to the events of the latter part of 1881 and the early part of 1882, and indeed succeeded in delaying their publication in New Zealand until after the 1882 imperial Blue Book containing them was received in January 1883.[132]

The proclamation which Bryce carried out of Wellington at 4 a.m. on 20 October did not reach Parihaka until the afternoon of 22 October in the hands of Carrington and W. J. Butler, a Maori speaker and secretary to Bryce. In its final form, the proclamation of 19 October 1881 berated the people for the crimes of 'making themselves poor by contributing to useless expenditure upon feasts'; for neglecting the cultivation of their own lands; for listening to the sound of Te Whiti's voice which unsettled their minds; for assuming 'a threatening attitude' which caused apprehension among the settlers; and for compelling the government to incur great expense on the armed constabulary. It exhorted them to leave Te Whiti, and ordered the visitors to go to their homes. The people were threatened that if they did not, within fourteen days, accept the 'large and ample reserves' it was intended to set aside for them and willingly submit to the law of the Queen, which must be supreme at Parihaka, the lands 'proffered' them would pass away from them for ever and they alone would be responsible for this and for 'the great evil which must fall on them'.[133] Carrington and Butler were received by Te Whiti in his usual friendly manner and he suffered most of the proclamation to be read in silence, then said: 'read no more. . . . These are not new words; they were uttered some time ago in the House by Sir William Fox, who said the Maoris were to be deprived of all their land this year. Do not now attribute any blame to Te Whiti for this: it is the doing of the pakehas entirely'. He was calm and temperate but looked 'weary and careworn'.[134] He had 14 days of peace left after his 14 years of effort to keep the peace and obtain justice for his people.

The sound of marching feet could already be heard on the road to Parihaka. There was no doubt, as Gordon said, that 'nine-tenths' of the colony were behind the ministers. Indeed they had 'the entire colony at their back' and would be supported 'even should the result of their present action be a native outbreak'. The period for action had now arrived; a blow must be struck. The chairman of the Patea County Council telegraphed Atkinson to say the government's actions 'met with the unanimous approval of the settlers', and Bryce 'was heartily cheered' when he passed through the town. The *Timaru Herald* proclaimed that the country was 'at one with the Ministry, barring perhaps the *Lyttelton Times* and most probably Sir Arthur Gordon'.[135] The *Lyttelton Times* was certainly not at one with the ministry. They feared the proclamation would end all hope of a peaceful settlement of the west coast difficulty and that any war that followed must be 'an unjust war, involving this country in the crime of bloodguiltiness'. They hoped, in vain, that the country would protest 'in the strongest manner' against the 'carrying out of the threats of that nefarious document' which created a new crime: 'refusal to accept an offer of the government', punishment for which would be 'further confiscation'.[136] 'Telegrams came pouring in,' Hall told Bell, 'thoroughly approving of our conduct, and protesting against Sir Arthur Gordon objecting to our proceeding or daring to obstruct it. He did object very strenuously, but he did not obstruct.'[137]

The proclamation appeared to Gordon to give expression to a policy which he deemed 'injudicious'; to contain statements which were 'at least disputable'; and to intimate an intention which was 'inequitable'. He told Hall that had he been in the colony he would have 'experienced great difficulty' in complying with a recommendation to sign it. Since what was done could not be undone, and since he could see no prospect of calling 'other Advisers to his counsels', he felt 'constitutionally bound to give effect to the recommendations of those already in office, whatever his own opinion as to the morality or justice of the measures suggested by them'. So, as volunteers enrolled all over the country, he reluctantly signed a warrant to bring under military law corps from New Plymouth, Patea, Wanganui, Rangitikei, Nelson, Thames, Wellington and Wairarapa.[138] The government obviously did not expect Te Whiti to submit quietly to their final ultimatum and they began moving the volunteers to the west coast. As offers came 'pouring in from all parts . . . in little more than a week, at very little expense', they were able to place 1,000 trained and well-armed volunteers on the Parihaka block. In fact they were soon 'suffering from an *embarras de richesses*' as regards volunteers and were 'giving offence all round at being compelled to refuse further offers'.[139]

At the same time, Hall was seeking legal opinions in Wellington and of Whitaker in Auckland as to what charges could be brought against Te Whiti and Tohu when they were finally arrested. He was advised that the Press Association report of their 17 September speeches contained 'sufficient to justify charges against both of them, of uttering seditious words and that on information charging use of those words . . . warrants would issue' for their arrest.[140] This was truly trial by the media and Whitaker at least recognised the fact; he told Hall that one difficulty he could see about a charge of sedition was 'the language being Maori the case may break down in translating'. He also objected to the fact that the speeches pre-dated the proclamation, they were open to more than one interpretation – indeed he had seen two versions of the one speech in one newspaper, and they appeared to him 'rather the ravings of a madman than of men deliberately talking sedition'.

Hall had no time for legal niceties. The huge armed constabulary force on the coast was costing a fortune, it had been 'brought together to put an end to the chronic state of disturbance', and its presence probably meant that Maori would inconveniently 'suspend any further acts of provocation'. If the ministry did not secure an 'effective solution' of the difficulty there would be 'general public dissatisfaction'. In other words, Whitaker should remember there was an election in the offing. These circumstances rendered the earliest possible solution desirable, so if no solution offered itself they 'should seek one'. The arrest of Te Whiti and Tohu 'would make more impression on all sides . . . than anything else'. And finally, Bryce was in a position to say there was an implied understanding that 'he should be allowed to take very energetic measures', so Hall trusted Whitaker would see his way to concurring in, or at least not objecting to the government's proposals. Whitaker was not in fact objecting: he only wanted to be sure that those who arrested Te Whiti were armed with arrest warrants so that the ministry would carry public opinion with them, 'especially in England which I think we risk by any measures that may be considered hasty or precipitate'.[141]

As Te Whiti's days of grace slipped by, he and Tohu gathered their people on the marae at Parihaka and exhorted them to patience and moderation. According to the government interpreters, they said land had been a cause of strife from time immemorial, but they would not carry on the quarrel, they would not use carnal weapons. The south wind was bringing men from all parts and the big guns were approaching, but there was no cause for apprehension: forbearance would be their canoe of safety, stout-heartedness and patience their salvation. 'Let us all remain here at Parihaka, which came from heaven, and none shall be taken. . . . Let us rest quietly upon the land . . . let the booted feet come when they like, the land shall remain firm for ever'.[142] The press did not agree with this official translation but thought the speech an admission on Te Whiti's part that he was only forswearing violence now because the government happened to be too strong for him. The monthly meetings at Parihaka, those 'schools of fanaticism and sedition', would have to be put down with a firm hand, the 'multitude of loafers' expelled and sent home to their own tribes, and Te Whiti and Tohu 'taught the lesson of submission and obedience' lest the power of the European be dragged through the dust.[143] It was a question of mana.

Meanwhile, the government was arranging for warrants for the arrest of Te Whiti and Tohu 'if they do not give us their submission'. Hall thought it probable they would allow themselves to be arrested, and hoped their 'infatuated followers' would not interfere. Bryce actually declared that if Te Whiti submitted and his people became angry with him, he, Bryce, would 'offer him protection in good faith' – but he thought most Maori were 'heartily tired of Te Whiti and would be glad to see him a prisoner'.[144] The *Taranaki News* agreed. They noted that government interpreters and reporters were allowed to be present at the big hui on 31 October and obviously thought them some sort of security to Te Whiti, since it was 'not at all improbable' that he might be in 'considerable danger from his own deluded followers'. But 'those well versed in Maori ways' believed that Maori had decided on 'a novel and ingenious mode of defence'. They would all 'strip naked, cover their bodies from head to foot with grease and then surround Te Whiti in a closely packed mass'.[145]

Gordon had asked what instructions Bryce had received to regulate his actions on the coast and was told it had 'not been considered necessary to furnish written instructions' to him, that he must be given 'a large amount of discretion', and would in special circumstances, act 'on his own responsibility'.[146] He was, in effect, given *carte 'noire'* to do what he thought necessary. Hall later 'jotted down' a few ideas for Bryce, 'for what they are worth': he should not leave Parihaka once he got there; he should establish a camp, a redoubt if necessary; he should take possession of all arms and ammunition; he should order all strangers to their homes and warn them 'that *all* Natives found out of certain defined localities after a certain date' would be considered as in arms against the government and treated accordingly; he should 'clear the whole forest and crop to the Railway and destroy the cultivations at Parihaka'. And if actual hostilities commenced, Bryce would know better than Hall 'how to carry them on'.[147]

On 3 November, with a military escort and Butler as his interpreter, Bryce reconnoitred the district towards Parihaka to plan the route for their invasion. They saw that the Parihaka people had taken down a fence to facilitate the armed constabulary's approach and they observed all the inhabitants of the village peacefully assembled on the marae. When the Europeans were seen nearby, the 'policeman' of Parihaka was sent to invite them into the village. Bryce thanked him and declined the invitation 'but promised to pay them an informal visit on Saturday'. All was quiet on 4 November and the people sat patiently on the marae where Tohu addressed them in the evening, 'calling on them to be patient and unresisting when the time came'. By 10 p.m. the village was quiet, but the people were astir again at midnight when it was reported mistakenly that the troops were surrounding Parihaka. By 1 a.m. they were all assembled on the marae; at 2 a.m. they all ate together, then quietly faced their long vigil awaiting the arrival of the troops.[148]

The official reports of the events of the infamous 5 November 1881 were exceedingly brief, and not published for another two years: 'Parihaka occupied by colonial forces this morning. They met with no resistance, nor was any offered to the arrest of Te Whiti and others'. This cable was followed a month later by a brief despatch stating that about 1,500 men, women and children had been arrested, Parihaka 'completely broken up', the Maori population over the whole district deprived of firearms, Te Whiti and Tohu 'committed for trial on a charge of sedition', and the old warrior Titokowaru, unable to find sureties to keep the peace, 'imprisoned in default of procuring them'. It was also noted that 'the action taken by the Government undoubtedly meets with the entire approval of the great majority of the people of the colony'.[149] Gordon sent this information with 'bulky' enclosures comprised of official telegrams, and cuttings from the pro-government *New Zealand Times* and from the *Lyttelton Times* which, reprinted, occupied 73 pages in the imperial Blue Book of 1882.[150]

Bryce had fully intended that no news of his 'aggressive Napoleonic' actions should reach the outside world. The evening before he marched his 1,500 men up the hill to Parihaka, he ordered that none of the special correspondents or any civilians be allowed to accompany the troops and if any were seen on the field of action they were to be arrested and held for 24 hours. There was nothing like a news black-out to enrage the pressmen who had gathered from all over New Zealand, and in particular Bryce's old adversary Croumbie-Brown.

He had gone to Parihaka as a 'friend' of Te Whiti, he had gone as a government spy, and now as a triple agent he meant to go 'to defeat the common enemy' and get his own back on Bryce by reporting every detail of the day of shame to a news-hungry world. At daybreak, accompanied by two other pressmen and a former British army officer and with a government surveyor as guide, he set off by rough bush tracks, swamps and 'square miles' of cultivations, and after two hours the party was behind and overlooking Parihaka. Croumbie-Brown and Humphries of the Press Association had decided 'to enter Parihaka and take the risk of arrest'. The other three stayed on the hill and heard the 'band playing the force out of Pungarehu'; they saw Bryce looking 'exceedingly anxious' riding a white charger, accompanied by three of his Wanganui electors and followed by Rolleston on foot;[151] they watched the booted feet of the armed constabulary and volunteers advance on Parihaka, to be greeted 'with loud cheers by the children, who afterwards kept up the haka and skipping with great vigour', and by the women who had baked 500 loaves of bread to feed their visitors. The enterprising special correspondents were well received when they entered the village, and were told the people could understand why the government was 'ashamed that the country should know' what it was doing. They wanted the specials to sit amongst them but, realising they must remain hidden, allotted them a whare from where 'full observations could be made', and their own interpreter – none other than R. S. Thompson.

The government had assembled an impressive military force to subdue the Queen's rebellious subjects at Parihaka. There were 945 volunteers and 644 armed constabulary, of whom the 109 in A Company were men specially selected 'on account of their size and strength'. In addition, sufficient armed constabulary men were left behind to garrison the posts at Rahotu and Pungarehu. The two columns which marched on Parihaka, the volunteers under Major Pitt, and the armed constabulary under Major Tuke, each carried two days' rations and 40 rounds of extra ammunition and were accompanied by pack-horses carrying a further supply of ammunition. Guards were posted at points where 'the enemy' might threaten communications and a chain of sentries was posted. Major Pitt's 'skirmishers' hastened to occupy the hilltops on the northern side of Parihaka while the constabulary moved onto the high ground to the west. But before these formidable military manoeuvres were completed, it had become 'apparent that no armed resistance was intended'.[152]

As the military surrounded the village, the 2,200 people on the marae sat silent and unmoving. Te Whiti and Tohu had several times addressed them, enjoining 'peace and forbearance under any insults or oppression'. At 9.35 a.m. Major Tuke, with Butler interpreting, asked for an answer to the proclamation. None was forthcoming, so the Riot Act was read and translated to an impassive audience who had eyes and ears only for their chiefs. The bugle sounded 'Advance', the cordon of troops left their high ground and 'occupied the outskirts of the settlement', and Captains Gudgeon and Newall moved up with an arresting party consisting of the formidable A Company, armed with revolvers and handcuffs. Tuke cautioned them 'against excitement' but told them that 'if any Maori flashed a tomahawk' they were to 'shoot him down instantly'.[153] Tohu again spoke to the assembled people: 'Let the man who has raised the war finish his work this day. . . . Let none of us stir lest any of us be absent. . . . Even if the bayonet comes to your breast do not resist'. When the hour required by law had passed, Te Whiti was called on to go and 'stand in Mr Bryce's presence'. Naturally Te Whiti replied that if Bryce wished to speak to him he was welcome to come and do so. But Bryce, like an antipodean emperor, could not descend from his high horse to converse with a native, so he ordered Roberts who ordered Tuke who ordered Newall to have Te Whiti arrested. The fanatical and deluded followers of Te Whiti, who were expected to fall on their chief or on the armed constabulary or both, quietly made a passage for the arresting party, who at the last moment were ordered to use no violence. Te Whiti, his mana dominating everyone present, quietly stood and told his people: 'Be of good heart and patient. Today's work is not my doing; it comes from the hearts of the pakehas'. As Tohu was arrested, he told the people: 'We looked for peace and we find war. Be steadfast; keep to peaceful works; be not dismayed; have no fear.' The 'common criminal' Hiroki was then arrested, searched, handcuffed and taken away under guard. The 'state prisoners' Te Whiti and Tohu were led away, Te Whiti's wife following close. At the edge of the marae Te Whiti stopped and called to his people: 'Let your dwelling be good in this place, oh my tribe'.

When they had gone, 'an aged Taranaki chief' spoke, advising the people to continue to follow the teaching of Te Whiti and Tohu, 'even if they were all arrested on the land of their ancestors'.[154]

In the days following the government's bloodless victory at Parihaka, attempts were made to disperse the strangers, first by tacking up a panui and then by calling out to the individual tribes to depart. Parihaka was to be cleared, surprisingly, 'for the people who own it by ancestral title'.[155] No one paid any attention; the marae was still packed with a silent, impassive crowd. Fox told Hall he must be firm and 'send the aliens home', but he advised him to disarm them all first because there was considerable feeling among the settlers on the coast, 'perhaps not uninformed', that if the strangers were forced to leave Parihaka 'they might scatter and attack country settlers'.[156] As a result of this warning, Bryce ordered Parihaka to be searched for arms and ammunition and about 210 guns, 'principally double-barrelled fowling pieces', were found, together with powder, caps, cutlasses, tomahawks – and two constabulary wheelbarrows. Then, when it seemed the troops would be ordered to start destroying Parihaka, they were suddenly withdrawn under orders from Wellington and 60 of them from the Alexander Cavalry, accompanied by Bryce, Rolleston and Atkinson, set off to search the villages in the surrounding countryside.[157]

The search did not turn up a great cache of arms. Only another 339 guns, about two-thirds of them serviceable, were found along the length and breadth of the coast.[158] This search of friendly and rebel villages alike, accompanied by pillage and destruction, in which everyone was deprived of the guns on which they relied for food supply, caused much adverse comment in the press, but it appeased the settlers and Bryce turned his attention once again to dispersing the strangers. Fox advised appealing to them 'on the utter failure of Te Whiti's prophecies'. He said he had been told 'repeatedly' that if Te Whiti was arrested despite his predictions his people would 'denounce him as an impostor' and maybe kill him, so now Rolleston or 'someone familiar with the details' should persuade them that the prophecies *had* failed.[159] The government had never questioned the accuracy of the reports they received about Te Whiti's prophecies, but since their failure was only apparent to Europeans their very existence needs questioning. It is possible that the only prophecies that had failed were the government's, for they were based on the reports of interpreters, loyal natives like Katene and others with an axe to grind, and the fringe of Te Whiti's followers, some of whom may have believed what they said while others enjoyed inventing myths for Europeans anxious to hear them. As Thompson said, those who would talk knew nothing and Te Whiti's confidants would not betray his counsels. Government thinking had for so long been coloured by settlers' memories of earlier conflicts and by a belief in their own prophecies that they found it impossible to accept the peaceful intentions of the west coast tribes. They had captured the fanatic Te Whiti, who had all this time somehow maintained the peace, but they did not know how they would cope with his infatuated followers. If they admitted now that there was no danger, they would have to admit there never had been any and that they, not Te Whiti's followers, had been misled.

The press was ambivalent about the government's actions. The pro-government *New Zealand Times* on one page lauded the native minister whose success could 'scarcely be overrated', and on the next accused him of assuming the powers of an autocrat: he had affected 'an air of mystery . . . and provoked ridicule and grave apprehension where he might have maintained the most profound confidence and respect'.[160] Other newspapers which normally supported the government began to find reason for criticism. For one thing, their reporters had been threatened and some had even been arrested, and they had all been banned from the field of operations. The *Evening Post* of 7 November was very bitter 'on the action of the West Coast dictator', and the *New Zealand Herald* of the same date spoke of his 'gratuitously and uselessly tyrannical conduct'. The Taranaki papers reserved their criticism for the niggardly treatment and pay of the volunteers. Voices were raised too about the treatment of the prisoners, who six days after their arrest were still confined in the blockhouse at Pungarehu while no effort had been made to arraign them on any charge.

Meanwhile, efforts to identify and arrest the immovable inhabitants of Parihaka were spectacularly unsuccessful. It was impossible to use 'severely coercive measures with people who assume the characteristics of dumb driven cattle'.[161] Bryce could not identify chiefs of note, let alone 'the 2000 men, women and children who are nobodies'. They did not have the name of their tribe written on their foreheads, he lamented, and as for calling on the people to disperse, he might as well have called 'from the vasty deep'. He warned Hall to remember these difficulties if he was 'forced into a choice of objectionable courses'. On 13 November, he sent Mete Kingi and Hone Pihama to try to reason with the few chiefs of various tribes he had managed to identify and arrest, and to persuade the people on the marae to disperse. His loyal chiefs 'entirely failed' in their mission and had to admit that Te Whiti's mana was paramount even among the people of their own tribes. Their sole achievement was to identify some Wanganui and Ngatiruanui men, and as they were arrested Bryce had their quarters destroyed. He then tried to identify their women by calling on them to claim their belongings piled in front of their destroyed whare, but that tactic did not work either.

Bryce's failed prophecies were painfully apparent to all. He was going to get no assistance from Te Whiti's 'disillusioned' followers, not one of whom would voluntarily abandon Parihaka, even now that the chief of whom they were supposed to be in mortal dread had been removed from their midst. 'We must do the best we can,' he wired to Rolleston, 'this is not a very pleasant process we are going through, but we must just plod on with it.'[162] One of his easier jobs was to arrest the guards who were watching over the gaps in fences by the armed constabulary camp at Pungarehu. No slip rails had ever been erected there and Maori had guarded the gaps night and day for months to keep stock out of the cultivations. As soon as it was known at Parihaka that these guards had been removed, others were sent to take their place, in a clear demonstration which even Bryce would have been hard pressed to misunderstand as obstruction. On 23 November there was no one on guard at the fences and 'several horses strayed onto the potato cultivations'.[163]

The arrests and the destruction of the village went on over a period of several weeks. By 21 November, 1,507 people had been removed from Parihaka under escort. They did not leave passively and dispiritedly or even sullenly. Nor did they actively resist their dispersal. When they were recognised and drafted out of the mob and finally gathered into their tribal groups for departure, they paid little attention to the Europeans but, spirits unbowed, performed a rousing farewell haka to their friends still in the village. A grand total of 43 had left voluntarily and only six remained in custody: Te Whiti, Tohu, Hiroki, Titokowaru, who was to be charged with uttering threats, Rangi Puahoahoa,[164] who was to be charged with obstruction under the West Coast Settlement Act, and 'Pioti, the thief'. The others had all been released when they reached their home villages.[165] Titokowaru had been arrested on 10 November and was kept in custody in a whare on 'Fort Rolleston', the hill overlooking the village where the armed constabulary had installed their six-pounder Armstrong gun. He was still there a week later, handcuffed and in solitary confinement 'owing to his threatening manner'; he had compared the rather puny Nelson volunteers who were guarding him with his own warriors and asked if the Europeans had forgotten his fighting prowess of past years. Bryce had made up his mind that Titokowaru and 'many of his particular hapu wished to fight but circumstances were against them'; and that 'if bloodshed occurred it would be at Titokowaru's place, near Manaia'.[166] He could see good political capital in Titokowaru's arrest and kept him confined as he was sure the west coast settlers would be 'very glad to hear of his being under arrest'. Titokowaru's response to the insult of manacles was to go on a hunger-strike. This alarmed Rolleston: 'That starvation business would be rather ugly and I don't like the idea of his dying with you. He ought to die in gaol with charge pending'. Rolleston hoped they might be able to bring a charge of murder, 'which would involve endless remands', rather than a mere 'charge of threatening'; he suggested Bryce contact Whitaker about it since the lawyers in Wellington gave 'very dry law, untempered with any other considerations'.[167] Titokowaru did not oblige Rolleston by dying. In fact he could not maintain his hunger-strike and Dr O'Carroll 'found him in tears, evidently annoyed at his endurance not lasting so long as he expected'.[168]

As the people were removed from the village, their houses were destroyed to discourage their return. Croumbie-Brown described the village as presenting 'a most melancholy appearance'. Half of it had been torn down and homeless Maori could be seen 'searching among the ruins for such of their household goods as have not been ruthlessly destroyed or stolen'. Those arrested had 'made no secret of their intention to return to Parihaka at the earliest opportunity',[169] although Bryce confidently predicted that there was very little danger of those who had been dispersed attempting to return. Bryce showed he knew little of the Maori mind when he remarked that even those who would be permitted to remain at Parihaka – those presumably to whom it belonged by ancestral title – would not continue to reside there as it would be 'contrary to all traditional feeling to do so'. Bryce's scorched earth policy extended to the surrounding cultivations to ensure there would be no attraction for alien tribes at Parihaka, although it was clear to the government that those returning to half-abandoned kainga, or settlements, would be short of food. Bryce said he would deal with this problem by offering the dispersed men 'road work at low wages' but he would 'carefully avoid all pampering'. He also intended to institute pass laws, by which people whose bullock drays or horses were still at Parihaka would be issued a pass to enable them to return and collect their property and cart back some potatoes 'under strict supervision'.[170] In the event, many of those whose crops were at Parihaka suffered 'great privation'. According to Parris they gathered fungus and sold it to buy food, and during the autumn fell back on 'indigenous food'; but their prospects through the winter and until the next harvest might have been desperate had they not been allowed to return for their crops at Parihaka.[171]

When almost no one but the iwi kainga, those who belonged, were left at Parihaka, Bryce prepared to 'pull down a number of whares around the marae . . . and put them into the marae so as to deprive it of its sacred character, and break the magic spell'. He followed this up with his most inexcusable act of vandalism and vindictiveness. He pulled down 'the sacred medicine-house, where people had to take their shoes off before entering. It was a great job to get it demolished, as it was very substantially built'. The pro-government press, as uncomprehending as Bryce, lauded his efforts: all traces of Parihaka would be destroyed, the tribes would not again gather at the 'scene of their surrender', and there would be 'no shepherd permitted to call together the dispersed flocks'. It was 'in dealing with such matters that practical knowledge of the Maoris and of Maori customs [stood] the Honourable John Bryce in good stead'.[172]

Bryce's paranoia was tinged with shades of Black Africa and the Zulu wars. To him Maori were incomprehensible savages who practised mystical rites and whose property was to be desecrated in the cause of civilisation and with the aim of teaching submission to the Queen's law. His colleagues supported him for their various reasons: Atkinson with a view to re-election; Rolleston to show he was not shirking; Hall to tidy things up, reduce expenditure and eliminate an impediment to smooth government; and Whitaker, who, with an eye to business, wanted an end to native difficulties but was anxious not to alienate British opinion and jeopardise future loans. Even Sheehan added his voice of approval: Bryce was doing the necessary work of breaking up Parihaka in a 'resolute, humane and effective way', and he was satisfied that the colony's native troubles were now at an end.[173]

The road to Parihaka had been a long one. It had begun with a failure to allot reserves and was continued in a determination to teach Maori who was master. But Te Whiti would not oblige the ministry by either giving in or resisting. Baffled and uncomprehending, the government carried on their injustice to the point of violence, and justified it by portraying their opponents as madmen and fanatics who had to be saved from their infatuation. They set up a much publicised commission to inquire into Maori grievances, then failed to implement the commission's findings. They trumpeted their good intentions, but at the time of Te Whiti's arrest they had still not defined his reserves. They proclaimed, especially to the British public, that they had the Maori's own welfare at heart, but in breaking up Parihaka and depriving the people of their leaders they destroyed a thriving Maori settlement, perhaps the most stable in the country, and exposed the people to all the negative factors of European civilisation from which they had insulated themselves for years. Parihaka was not a centre of passive resistance to European encroachment; it was a centre of active resistance to social disintegration.[174] It was not a centre of negative prohibitions; it was a centre of positive teaching, a fount of aroha, something the government could not recognise and would not accept. The government acted not in Maori interests, but in the interests of colonisation and more immediately, through financial and political expediency, in their own interests. And since the wisdom of the time held that the spread of European colonisation was in the interests of native races, the end was widely accepted as justifying the means. Only a minority of people in the colony at the time, and few enough since, have questioned both means and end.

CHAPTER SEVEN

Aftermath

1882–1884

We shall live; this generation will not be lost sight of.[1]

THE GOVERNMENT HAD ACHIEVED ITS GOAL OF BREAKING UP THE 'NEST of fanaticism' at Parihaka but it soon found it had not solved the native problem. It had forced the people to submit to removal from where it decreed they had no business to be, to those parts of the country where they were deemed to belong. But it had not cowed them, it had not taught them the lesson of submission and obedience or forced them to admit to European supremacy. It forced them into hunger and hardship, but it did not succeed in breaking their spirit, and above all it did not succeed in lowering their leaders in their eyes. It was European prophecies, not Maori ones, that were confounded when Parihaka was physically destroyed and its people dispersed.

The government may have achieved a political and economic victory at Parihaka but Maori had achieved a moral one. These subtleties were not lost on all of New Zealand, and criticism arose on many sides when the imminent native uprising was revealed as a myth and an illusion, and the Parihaka people shown to be unarmed, unresisting and imbued with aroha for their leaders. Bryce's demeanour suffered in comparison with Te Whiti's dignified bearing and, perhaps still smarting from the restrictions imposed on them by Bryce, the press reflected a widespread feeling that the Maori people had been unjustly treated and unfairly maligned. In Taranaki it was different. There they were ready to occupy the land that Maori had 'so long and so unprofitably encumbered', and they hoped to see Parihaka 'merged into a road' and all trace of it destroyed. As a topic, Parihaka soon disappeared from the news in Taranaki and it scarcely became an issue in the 1881 election campaign there; it was already past history.[2]

With the native difficulty safely out of the way, Hall and most of his ministers could concentrate on the coming election. On the very day Parihaka was invaded, Hall wrote an eight-page letter to Bell in which there was not a mention of west coast affairs. 'Atkinson is away on the stump,' he reported, and 'I *ought* to be so as they are going to oppose me.' The opposition he expected was not over the government's native policy but over Grey's influence on the electorate. He believed Grey would go back to the House with diminished strength but, as he told Bell, 'the seed he has sown is bearing fruit. In towns ultra radicalism is rampant'. He was soon on the stump himself and, for all his protestations, was not above using the 'Parihaka affair' as an election issue.[3] Bryce, having at last associated his name with the settlement of the native difficulty, commuted between Parihaka and his electorate, destroying the one and receiving the adulation of the other. Rolleston's image had suffered from his participation in a discreditable affair, but not enough to prevent his re-election to the Christchurch electorate of Avon – and he protested with righteous indignation at the suggestion that the march on Parihaka had been made with an eye to the elections. Hall too protested that the 'more unscrupulous' of their enemies, including the bishop of Nelson, had charged them with 'rushing into the business for electioneering purposes. The absurdity as well as the wickedness of the charge,' he plaintively told Bell after the election, 'will be evident on the slightest examination of facts' – although he had to admit that 'the success of the West Coast proceedings' had told in their favour.[4] But if Parihaka was nowhere a very strong election issue, it was because the majority of the colony supported the government's policies if not its methods.

On 12 November 1881, the government's prize prisoners were removed from Pungarehu at 4 a.m. and escorted by the Taranaki Mounted Rifles were driven to New Plymouth gaol. A little later in the morning, they appeared at the Resident Magistrate's Court before a magistrate and several justices of the peace. There were two counsel for the Crown, but none for the prisoners. Hiroki was charged with murder and remanded until witnesses were available. Te Whiti, on the information of the government interpreter Hursthouse, was charged with being 'a wicked, malicious, seditious and evil-disposed person' and with

> wickedly, maliciously and seditiously contriving and intending to disturb the peace of Her Majesty's subjects, and to incite and move to hatred and dislike of the persons of Her Majesty and the Government, and by inciting numbers of Her Majesty's subjects to insurrections, riots, tumults, and breaches of the peace, and to prevent by force and arms the execution of the laws of this realm, and the preservation of the public peace and on 17 September . . . did wickedly, unlawfully, and maliciously declare . . . the false, wicked, seditious, and inflammatory words following . . . 'Naku te whenua. Naku nga tangata. Ko te tino pakanga tenei o tenei whakatupuranga. . . .'[5]

The case continued for four days and Charles Hursthouse, Wellington Carrington and Charles Messenger were called to testify as to their knowledge of Te Whiti and his malicious actions and seditious words. Hursthouse had known Te Whiti for 25 years, Carrington for 35 and Messenger for nine or ten: surely long enough to understand the man – if they understood the language. All three gave different versions of the 17 September speech and all three admitted they had not been present in the evening when the speeches were explained. Carrington also admitted Tohu had warned the interpreters who took notes at the meetings that they should not write the speeches down as they did not understand the subtleties of the language. Te Whiti had told Rolleston his quarrel was about the lands of his ancestors and that he was not concerned about the parts of the coast to the north and south, but Hursthouse rendered 'naku te whenua', mine is the land, as meaning 'the whole of the confiscated lands on the West coast'. He gave two different versions of the one phrase 'we quarrel with all now', saying first that *we* meant 'all the persons of the Maori race', then that it meant 'all the Natives present'.[6] The 'interpretations' are full of such inconsistencies.

Te Whiti had only one question for Hursthouse: had 'the 25,000 acres reserved by the Government for the use of the Natives ever been shown to them?' Not, replied Hursthouse, that he knew of. And when Tohu asked him if he knew 'the division that was made of the land between the Europeans and the Natives', he affirmed that he did, but that he had not told them of it. Carrington informed the court that only about six months previously he had been given the map 'showing the boundaries of the reserves and the land temporarily reserved from sale',[7] but he had not been asked to explain it to the natives and had not done so. Parris, who was sitting on the bench that day, said 'a little excitedly' that the witness seemed to have forgotten he was on his oath as he, Parris, remembered giving such instructions. At this his fellow justices 'whispered to him that this was not a question, but that he was giving evidence himself'.[8] Rolleston too was 'disturbed' by the interpreters' assertions and said it was 'clearly impossible' the natives did not know of the reserves, as Kahu and others had 'made claims in respect of timber on the North side of the road' and on the south side they had 'practical knowledge by warning given over many weeks'.[9] This would seem to mean that if Maori were *not* ordered off they could presume it was land 'intended' for them.

On the third day of the trial, Te Whiti addressed the court and explained that he and his people thought there was no land for them, that after the confiscation it all belonged to the government and that since that time they had lived on government land. (Kua kiia katoa te whenua ma te Kawanatanga. Ka noho matou ko nga Maori i runga i te whenua o te Kawanatanga. Ka noho mai matou i runga i te wahi i rahuitia i te mutunga o te patu.) But they had cultivated that land, not in order to cause strife, but for their wellbeing. It was not his wish that evil should come to the two peoples. He had never wished that anyone be killed; his wish was that they should all live happily on the land (engari kia ora katoa tatou ki runga ki te whenua), and this was the way he had always addressed his Maori people.[10]

Nothing could be clearer than that Te Whiti had obeyed McLean's injunction to be peaceful and cultivate the land, believing that in this lay prosperity for European and Maori alike, but that never having been shown the land intended for his people, and seeing the government selling off 'its' land all around him, he came to the only possible conclusion: that the promise of 25,000 acres, like all the other promises before it, would never be translated into reality. In a desperate effort to obtain justice for his people he had resisted, pacifically, to the end.

Asked to sign their statements, Te Whiti and Tohu were reported to have said they *could* not write. It is much more likely that they *would* not write. Such was the fraud perpetrated over the years in regard to land deals that many Maori who had been taught to read and write refused to put pen to paper.[11] When they were asked to touch the pen while a cross was made on their behalf, Tohu was reluctant to do even that. Justice having now been dispensed to Her Majesty's subjects, the prisoners were 'committed to the common gaol of New Plymouth, there to be safely kept until . . . delivered by due course of law'.[12]

On 23 November 1881, Titokowaru and two other prisoners were taken by the regular coach from Pungarehu to New Plymouth, with an escort of two armed constabulary men. Titokowaru was 'perfectly well behaved throughout', but despite his guard he remained manacled with 'exceptionally heavy handcuffs'. Two days later he appeared before the court charged with using threatening language. He was of course undefended, and he admitted he had chaffed a few Europeans who had offended him, but it was 'all gammon'. However, one witness who had not heard the threatening language and thought it probably was all gammon was cross-examined until he 'swore that he had reason to think' that Titokowaru might carry out his threats. An armed constabulary captain giving evidence said Titokowaru's threats were 'mere bounce' and although there *may* have been an intention to do some harm, he did not think so. This was taken by the court to mean that Titokowaru *would* take some lawless revenge. Having considered the evidence, the magistrates ordered him to find two sureties of £500 each to keep the peace for 12 months and to be kept in the common gaol in New Plymouth in the meantime.[13]

The idea that the due course of law might deliver Te Whiti and Tohu from the government's clutches gave the ministers pause. The trial was set for 1 May 1882 and the crown prosecutor, Arthur Standish, had told them that their case for sedition was weak, that the prosecution might fail and that Te Whiti and Tohu had 'carefully kept themselves out of the reach' of the West Coast Settlement Act so could not be brought on an alternative charge of obstruction. Hall hoped Bryce might know of something that would bring them 'within reach of the law'. He was determined they must be detained, but hoped the government could do it *legally* as it would be a 'great crow for Gordon, Stout, Nelson and Co' if they could not.[14]

Hall was not prepared for Bell's disapproval of the government's actions for he looked to him, on the spot in England, to counter the 'curious stories' Gordon was sending to the Colonial Office. But Bell did not approve either the government's treatment of Te Whiti or the 'dispersion' of Parihaka. According to Hall, he should have termed the latter 'the removal of strangers who had no business there', and he begged Fox to 'find time for a few lines to Bell to turn his head in the right direction'. He lectured Bell himself about the propriety of the government's actions and hoped to convince him that, with Te Whiti in prison or out, there would have been no peace at Parihaka as long as the 'discontented and fanatical spirits' had been allowed to remain there; that 'some other Te Whiti would have been forthcoming, perhaps less careful and less able to control the excitement which he aroused'. Hall followed up this admission that it was Te Whiti's followers and not Te Whiti who needed to be kept from

Parihaka by confessing, in strictest confidence, that they feared they had no case against Te Whiti 'with Gillies as judge', so they planned to have the trial adjourned and then ask parliament 'for authority to assign the Prophet a "residence" for a limited term in some part of the Colony where he will be harmless'.[15]

The government was also carefully considering how it should punish the Parihaka people for failing to heed the warnings in the 19 October proclamation, and concluded that the continuous reserve on the Waimate plains, the Parihaka reserve and possibly the Opunake reserve, should each be reduced by 5,000 acres – *not* for the sake of the land, which would not repay their expenses, but for the sake of 'not letting the proclamation be a dead letter'. Hall hoped it would thus be 'shown to the Colonial Office and the enlightened British public that confidence in our moderation has not been misplaced'. Fox 'entirely concurred' with the reduction of the first two blocks, but on the question of the Opunake block was less accommodating. He insisted that while the official papers did not exactly *authorise* its return to Matakatea's people, Ngatihaumiti, they did *recognise* it 'very distinctly'. Hall 'rather pressed on him the desirability of inflicting some punishment' on those people, but could not exactly point out how this might be done without exposing the government to a charge of breach of faith. It seemed to him that they would need special legislation to enable them to 're-confiscate' 5,000 acres, but he was afraid they could not find any facts to put before the House which would 'induce it to agree to such a course'.[16]

Despite mere technicalities of the law, the government considered the Taranaki question sufficiently resolved for them to turn their attention back to the opening up of the King Country. Bryce was anxious to make his name there too. When the tension was building over events at Parihaka, concern was expressed that Tawhiao might join Te Whiti in an island-wide native rising. Nothing was further from the mind of either chief; they did not acknowledge each other's mana. Te Whiti had publicly expressed his disdain of Tawhiao and his people and Tawhiao kept aloof from all Taranaki concerns. In 1880 Major W. G. Mair, government agent in the Waikato, confirmed that Tawhiao wished to live in peace and that Taranaki would get no help from Waikato.[17] A year later Tawhiao made his famous gesture of crossing the aukati, the Maori frontier, and laying his gun at Mair's feet. In January 1882, in the euphoria following the great bloodless victory over Taranaki, the European population of Auckland prepared to extend a civic welcome to 'that great chief Tawhiao, the Maori King', whom so short a time before they had reviled as 'that drunken upstart the so-called Maori king'. Bryce saw great danger in this about-face. He was concerned lest another Maori chief question the supremacy of the European, but this time his heavy-handed approach was too much for Hall. Certain that the Cabinet was with him, Bryce told Rolleston that his difference with Hall over 'the course to be adopted in Waikato and Tawhiao matters' was so radical that he could not follow Hall's advice without suppressing his own views and committing the Cabinet 'to a doctrine of which it does not approve'. Rolleston had to admit he had not thought the Tawhiao question through, but despite that he was prepared to defer to Bryce's judgement in the matter. He told him that while 'the West Coast difficulty was pending it paid to tacitly admit a lot of folly', but there was no longer any need to turn a blind eye to Tawhiao's pretensions; Te Whiti would have just cause to complain if Tawhiao 'with Mair for Prime Minister' were to assume 'another kind of sovereignty equally mischievous if less dangerous'.[18]

Auckland had other concerns: the land beyond the aukati. Millions of fertile acres were lying waste while 'a most profitable and necessary' railway route was blocked. The press decided that Aucklanders should not get 'ecstatic' but they ought to entertain Tawhiao as 'a most distinguished and important visitor'. The mayor and the citizens set up reception committees, collected funds, decided the royal route, organised the children with banners, and planned a luncheon, garden party, torchlight procession and fireworks. The civic banquet was attended by the leading citizens, the mayor and city councillors and representatives of local bodies, and 'all sat mixed up' with the natives who accompanied Tawhiao and who were cheered by the Europeans as they entered the hall. There were more cheers when the mayor declared that the people of Auckland wished to 'manifest their friendly feeling towards Tawhiao and his friends and the whole of the native race of New Zealand'. The visit lasted more than two weeks and Tawhiao 'was the recipient of more congratulations and honours than ever fell to the lot of any man in Auckland'.[19]

This display of goodwill and brotherhood, just two months after the sacking of Parihaka and the dispersal of its people, culminated in a meeting between the premier and the king at which Tawhiao, when asked by Hall what he thought of the conduct of Te Whiti, gratified his listeners by declaring that he 'kept himself aloof from the action of the natives on the West Coast and did not recognise Te Whiti and his people in any way'. He was in fact 'very contemptuous' of them and said the longer Te Whiti was kept in prison the better.[20] Hall saw this not as a Maori response to rival mana, but as an expression of approval of the government and its policy.

A Wellington paper had been markedly unenthusiastic about the visit and hoped 'the good people of Auckland' would not overdo their hospitality to Tawhiao and give him an inflated sense of his own importance or the idea that his 'spurious kingship' was recognised by Europeans.[21] But Hall was pleased with the whole affair and declared the visit had 'done good' – and what was more, it had cost the government only 'about £20 and railway passes'.[22] Bryce, however, was totally opposed, and went to pay a visit to Rewi as a 'first step towards the correction of the excessive hospitality of the Auckland folk'. He had just destroyed one threat to European supremacy and was not about to countenance the emergence of another. He told Rolleston he was trying, at Hall's insistence, to come to grips with this 'Waikato business'. If he could do it with Tawhiao's assistance well and good, but if not Tawhiao 'must be broken to pieces' and Bryce was not at all sure this would not be the easiest course.[23] Bryce's attitude towards Taranaki Maori is sometimes justified on the grounds that he had fought against them in 1868–69, but it was not just Taranaki who were the target of Bryce's prejudice but the whole Maori race. He conducted himself as minister for settler affairs, rather than native affairs.

But once more Bryce was out of step with his premier, a fact which undoubtedly contributed to Hall's rather precarious state of health. For some time Hall had wished to resign the premiership on the grounds of ill health but had agreed to stay on first until the elections, then for some time longer 'as there was no knowing what Sir Arthur Gordon would do', and finally till Whitaker could reach Wellington about a month before the opening of parliament; but in any case on the understanding that there should be no dissension in the Cabinet at that time. Rolleston, Bryce and Atkinson were obliged to go to Auckland to confer with 'the constantly absent' Whitaker, too busy with his speculations and land deals to attend to Cabinet business in Wellington,[24] and were able to persuade themselves that no important differences would arise between them. Hall was less easily persuaded because 'very recently Bryce had, in several instances taken actions in important questions without . . . consultation with his colleagues'. He telegraphed Whitaker privately that he 'feared serious differences might arise if Bryce did not turn over a new leaf'. The telegram fell into the hands of Bryce who immediately took umbrage and sent Hall his resignation, and 'followed it up by another telegram, couched in terms which deeply wounded Mr Hall'. This was too much and Hall took ill, although, as he told Bell, had he been well enough and able to cope, he would simply have allowed Bryce to resign as he had done 'on a previous occasion'. But his doctor insisted he retire at once, and his ministers again allowed Bryce to get away with his tantrums and all resigned in a body, 'making a great effort' to represent Hall's illness as 'the real and only cause' for their action.[25]

Gordon received the ministerial resignations on 8 April 1882 in Christchurch where he was happily domiciled, as far as he could decently get from his antipathetic ministers. After the elections, in which the Hall government did not appear to Gordon to have obtained a clear majority, the governor had urged an early sitting of parliament. As this had not taken place and he now found himself without responsible advisers, he felt free to turn where he would for 'accurate information as to the state of the different political parties in Parliament'. When it was reported he had sent for Grey, 'a violent and unscrupulous partisan, whose administration has been odious to the Colony', the news was 'considered to be a hoax' and the people were 'astounded and furious'. However, Grey gave the same advice as Hall, and Whitaker was sent for and took office on 21 April. Hall had to admit that Gordon had 'a legal right' to do as he had done, but he was righteously indignant about the whole affair and told Bell he had done his best 'to keep Sir Arthur Gordon out of rows and get him out of them' but now he had 'done with him'.[26] The ministerial crisis only served to widen the gulf that already existed between the governor and his ministers, and it delayed Gordon's departure for four months' home leave granted him by Kimberley in September 1881, and later extended to six months to allow for a visit to Tonga on his way to England.[27] Gordon's last weeks in the country were marked by a new paper war between governor and ministers. Gordon's criticism of the government in public and confidential despatches was both trenchant and reasoned, but neither Hall nor Whitaker was prepared to have a constitutional governor express the least criticism of their policies.

Whatever matters had divided the Cabinet before its resignation, the justice to be accorded Te Whiti and Tohu was not one of them. On 8 April, a few weeks before the Supreme Court was due to sit in New Plymouth, Parris, in his capacity as resident magistrate, swore an affidavit applying for a change of venue for their trial to Christchurch, on the grounds that it was 'expedient that the trial . . . take place at some other Circuit Court'. The local jury list would almost certainly include a number of volunteers who had served at Parihaka, whereas in Christchurch 'no prejudice could be said to exist'. Such reasoning would indicate that the government could expect a conviction from a local jury, but the affidavit went on to say it was 'absolutely necessary' that Te Whiti 'should at all risks continue in the custody of the Government for some time to come and that his release at this present time would be a grave public calamity'.[28] The government could not count on a conviction in New Plymouth with their *bête noire* Gillies on the bench, but as the quarterly court sitting in Christchurch was safely past Te Whiti and Tohu were sent there, ostensibly to await the next sitting.

The west coast people responded immediately to the latest injustice to their chiefs and demonstrated that they were far from cowed and beaten by loading up their drays with supplies, arming themselves with the prescribed passes from government agents and setting off to stage an April hui at Parihaka. Roberts, on Bryce's orders, would not allow them to take supplies *to* Parihaka, but would allow them to go there with the object of bringing food back. That was not the Maori way, they explained. If they could not take their pork to Parihaka they would not go there to cart potatoes away. A hui took place anyway, and Roberts telegraphed Bryce that natives were assembling in the marae and distributing food, and that he had sent for reinforcements 'in case they should be required'. Bryce's answer to this 'act of antagonism to the expressed orders of the Government' was the ordering of further destruction, and another 'dozen whares round the old marae' were pulled down to teach the lesson of submission to the law. He also ordered the arrest of any adult male strangers who were present, but when Roberts found a dozen 'strangers' from neighbouring kainga in the Parihaka block who were equipped with signed passes, he stayed his hand and suggested to Bryce that it 'would be well not to allow passes about the 17th' of the month.[29]

Hall demonstrated his understanding of the Maori mind by writing to Bell that this attempt to revive the monthly meeting was significant in that it was a result of the ministerial convulsions in Wellington. Maori had heard, he said, that the ministry had resigned and Grey had been sent for – but 'Grey had returned to Auckland (*instead of to office*) and their attempt to hold a meeting was speedily put down'.[30] It might be wondered why Maori should prefer Grey and the perfidious Sheehan to Hall and the paranoid Bryce, but Messenger, with his imperfect understanding of Maori, had reported the natives had held a meeting because they had heard Bryce was not in office – and ministers were never easily persuaded that Maori did not dance to a European tune, but to a Maori one.[31]

When the court did sit in New Plymouth at the beginning of May, it was to hear charges against the prisoners arrested under the West Coast Settlement Act. The judge instructed the jury that for obstruction to be considered a crime under the act it was necessary that 'the order to remove should be given by a person authorised by the Governor. It would not be sufficient for some Minister verbally to give such authority'. And since Bryce had given the order, and he was simply 'some minister', the provisions of the act had not been strictly complied with. Enmeshed in their own toils, the government ordered the crown prosecutor to enter a *nolle prosequi* and the judge, discharging the prisoners, expressed his surprise at this 'extraordinary proceeding'.[32] Hall told Bell that the case had been dropped because 'Gillies, always anxious to show that he knows everything better than everybody else, declared that some special authority from the Govr for something should have been obtained'.[33] The government did not relish being foiled by some mere technicality of the law which they had written into their own act.

At the same sitting of the court, Hiroki faced a charge of murder. He pleaded not guilty and evidence was given that there was much disaffection in the district at the time over the confiscation, the survey, and the surveyors' killing the Maori's pigs. Hiroki, particularly, had complained about his pigs being killed.[34] It was no surprise that he was found guilty; he had been known as Hiroki the murderer for over three years. He was hanged on 8 June 1882 at New Plymouth gaol, the government 'having seen no reason to advise His Excellency to restrain the law from taking its ordinary course'.[35]

The eighth parliament of New Zealand finally met on 18 May. In his opening speech, the governor announced the government's intention to impose a further act of injustice on Te Whiti and Tohu. Since they did not wish to inflict punishment on them, 'to put them in a felon's gaol, or in felons' clothes, or in any respect in the position of persons who have been convicted of crime' as Whitaker put it, they would introduce a bill which would both render trial 'unnecessary' and prevent the two chiefs from returning to Parihaka – until settlement was so far advanced as to make their continued resistance to it futile. Te Whiti and Tohu would not be punished; they would simply be lawfully imprisoned without trial, at the governor's pleasure, and if once released would be liable for rearrest and imprisonment at any time, also at the governor's pleasure. Their detention in 'honourable restraint' in the South Island far from all that was basic to their identity and their wellbeing would, according to Grey, constitute 'but a slight inconvenience' for them and should not be construed as punishment.[36]

Bryce introduced two bills to the House: the West Coast Peace Preservation Bill and the Indemnity Bill. The former would have been better entitled the Te Whiti and Tohu Detention Bill, though the government later described it as an act empowering the governor to *release* 'certain native Chiefs' awaiting trial for sedition. It also contained a clause which made any group of more than 50 Maori assembling together in public on west coast confiscated lands, which did not disperse when commanded to do so, liable to arrest and to imprisonment for twelve months. Bryce moved the second reading of the bill on 26 May, with what Hall described as 'a long speech giving a good history of West Coast Affairs but no very strong reasons for passing such a Bill'.[37] His ploy in fact was to lose the question of the fate of Te Whiti and Tohu in a wide-ranging discussion, a vote of confidence almost, on the Hall government's west coast policy. That discussion rightly belonged with the Indemnity Bill but Bryce made light of the need for such a bill, as though his conduct had been quite within the law and needed no indemnification, and he invited the House to confine the debate to the one bill.

Since Bryce was not given to viewing west coast affairs through any but west coast settler's eyes, his speech was far from a good history. His prejudices got a new airing as he spoke of Te Whiti's prophecies, his witchcraft and evil eye, the fear he engendered in his followers, and all the other extravagant ideas suggested to him by friendly chiefs and the reports of government interpreters. Bryce once more expressed his antagonism to the west coast commissioners by ridiculing their suggestion that Maori had any reason to believe the confiscation had been abandoned, that the non-definition of reserves had anything to do with the troubles on the west coast or that Te Whiti had ever shown the slightest inclination to share the land with the Europeans. He did acknowledge that there was 'some doubt' as to whether or not Te Whiti had actually borne arms against the Europeans and admitted he was 'inclined to think he did not', even though his followers 'almost to a man had been in rebellion'. So although he believed Te Whiti to be 'essentially a man of peace', he still thought him a menace to the colony because his followers might at any time show themselves to be of warlike character, as they had done 'not long before' in the 1860s.[38]

This sort of logic could not allow that Te Whiti's very pacifism could have been an attraction to his followers. The fact that they had had ample opportunity for violent resistance yet even after Te Whiti's removal from amongst them had still opted for peaceful resistance was as immaterial to Bryce as if his own prophecies had actually come to pass. It was not so immaterial to some in the House, and later in the debate Bryce triumphantly countered their criticism by retracting his statement as to Te Whiti's pacifism and claiming he now had ample evidence to show that if Te Whiti 'did not take an active part in hostilities he was at any rate engaged in the rebellion'. Bryce's 'proof' consisted of two letters written in November and December 1862, each 'signed' by several chiefs, one of which he said was in Tohu's handwriting, the other in Te Whiti's – although according to Atkinson the letters and signatures were 'as usual in one hand writing', and one of the signatures may have read 'Tehu'.[39] Bryce conveniently overlooked the fact that even if Te Whiti and Tohu had signed the letters in question their action would not have come within the provisions of the New Zealand Settlements Act, which referred to acts of rebellion committed *after* 1 January 1863.

Grey surprised many in the House, Bryce included, by devoting his speech largely to praise of Bryce and extenuation of his actions. He declared they owed Bryce an indemnity 'with thanks', and they owed the colony the security of keeping Te Whiti in confinement since that 'impostor or the dupe of his own imagination' might be unable to continue to restrain his followers. Sheehan, warning against 'sham and highly absurd sentimentalism about the Maoris', whole-heartedly supported the bill. But one who was conspicuously silent in the House was Rolleston. He voted with Bryce at every division, but would not support him in debate, despite Bryce's suggestion that as minister of lands he should speak on the question of land settlement on the coast.[40]

Bryce came in for some sharp criticism as autocratic, overbearing and injudicious; and for 'a mede of praise' from those who approved his actions and hoped his efforts to restore law and order would be recognised by the Queen.[41] He could hardly express his gratification and obligation to Grey for his 'most generous and handsome remarks' and he paid tribute to Sheehan for supporting his native policy. He then told the House how, but a few months previously, he had seen 'in his mind's eye . . . slaughtered Maoris lying in their blood'. He had seen 'the ruined settler standing beside his burning house . . . the helpless wife weeping over her helpless children' and he knew it was his responsibility to avoid such an outcome.[42] The House did not need Bryce's fertile imagination, nor Grey's plea that they put aside party feeling and act like 'patriotic statesmen', to induce it to pass Bryce's shameful bill. Its ultimate fate was never in doubt, even though the opposition came from members on both sides of the House who strongly attacked the government for ignoring the commissioners' reports, denying the Maori community justice, and now proposing to imprison Te Whiti and Tohu without trial because they feared they could not bring a successful charge against them. It was a case of standing up to be counted; the critics could not turn a minority into a majority, but they would not sit by and watch Bryce and Grey 'fall upon each other's necks' and weep out their 'mutual love, admiration and undying esteem', or the native ministers past and present develop their 'marvellous unanimity' while the strong trampled on the rights of the weak and every principle of British justice was cast aside.[43]

The West Coast Peace Preservation Act was signed into law on 1 July 1882 by Prendergast who was again administering the government; it was followed on 7 August by the Indemnity Act which indemnified those who, in preserving the peace on the west coast, may have adopted measures 'in excess of legal powers'. The act made it quite clear that while it was illegal for a Maori to plough disputed land, it was legal for a European to destroy a Maori village. The only discussion of the bill came at the third reading, when it was suggested that some provision be made to compensate those Maori whose property had been destroyed. Bryce advised the House that this would be impossible since the lands on which property had been destroyed were 'lands of the Crown'.[44] This was the clearest possible statement that at the time of the sacking of Parihaka no land had been returned to the Parihaka people.

While their fate was being decided in parliament, Te Whiti and Tohu were undergoing a form of honourable restraint in Christchurch which raised some eyebrows. They had been transferred to Addington gaol on 26 April and assigned as 'warder and interpreter' John P. Ward, an Irish–Australian who had been in New Zealand since his youth, had served with Chute, McDonnell and Whitmore on the west coast and had lived long enough in the North Island to gain an acquaintance with the Maori language.[45] The government had sent its two prisoners to 'await trial' in Christchurch since that city would be free from prejudice, but when it showed itself to be so free from prejudice that it had their prison garb changed for tweed suits and the magnanimous Mr Beetham, a visiting magistrate and Maori speaker, took them sightseeing to the exhibition, cathedral and museum, and arranged a train journey to the far south, the minister of justice, Thomas Dick, was far from enthusiastic. He tartly told the offending magistrate that so far as the law went he had no more power to take them visiting such places than he had to arrange a visit to Dunedin for them. However, Dick was obliged to relent since the object of the exercise was supposedly to 'inform the Prophet of the power and accomplishment of the Pakeha', and he 'duly instructed the gaoler' to hand over the two chiefs – in exchange for a receipt – to W. J. Butler, sent by Bryce so that he rather than the minister of justice should have control of his two prize prisoners.[46]

On every visit the two chiefs made, and at each stage of their journey, they were lionised by a curious and admiring crowd, sometimes hundreds strong, attention which they did not relish. But they received great kindness, hospitality and civilised treatment from many individuals, including a former North Island resident magistrate and other good Maori linguists, a far more salutary experience than gazing on the might and power of Pakeha technology and an antidote to the uncivilised treatment they had received at the hands of many government ministers and officials. The government intended the tour to be an education for those who had lived for so many years insulated from the outside world, and, they thought, ignorant of it. Bryce hoped their South Island sightseeing would disabuse their minds 'of the ideas of greatness as regards their district and themselves, which their long isolation at Parihaka had encouraged'.[47] Certainly many sights and experiences were new to Te Whiti and Tohu, and some occasioned wonder and delight, some alarm and consternation, but they were not all entirely unexpected. They had always exhibited an interest in the affairs of the world beyond their village and were kept remarkably well-informed on international affairs and the progress of technology. European visitors were always welcome at Parihaka and there had been an endless stream over the years. It was European government and officials and European 'civilisation', not European people, that Te Whiti objected to. The ploughmen and fencers had spent months in Dunedin, Christchurch and Hokitika, and Te Whiti at least demonstrated some prior knowledge of those places. What the two chiefs learned and concluded from their educational tour was not necessarily quite what the government intended. After a particularly intensive visit to Christchurch, Timaru, Oamaru, Dunedin, Invercargill and the Bluff, Te Whiti was asked what was the best thing he had seen and he answered simply: the river Avon. That was God's work and would outlast all the works of man.[48]

Te Whiti and Tohu had expected to be tried in Christchurch on 6 June 1882, but at that date they were suffering the winter chill in Queenstown. Ward and Butler, a good Maori linguist according to Ward, were travelling with their two prisoners and were doing their best to keep them uninformed about the events which most concerned them. But finally on 14 June, in Oamaru, when the West Coast Peace Preservation Bill had already passed the House, Butler told the two chiefs of the government's intentions regarding them. Ward was not present at the time, but he maintained that they were told they would not be tried, that they would be given 'ample reserves', and that if they agreed not to hold meetings they would be taken back to Parihaka.[49] Ward, who was an unreliable chronicler with a colourful imagination, added a seat in the Legislative Council 'and other benefits' to the terms offered Te Whiti by the government. This may or may not have been part of the offer, but buying the cooperation of chiefs was an old government ploy; Rewi, Tawhiao, Wahanui and any number of chiefs had been offered pensions and seats in the Legislative Council or other inducements.

But Te Whiti could not be bought. As it was in 1872, when his scorn for European civilisation and his total lack of desire for money or anything else the Europeans had to offer made it 'difficult, if not hopeless' to enlist his aid in furthering the work of colonisation,[50] so it was in 1882, and Butler's proposals fell on deaf ears. The subject was reopened in Christchurch on 26 June when Butler, in Ward's presence, asked for a definite answer to the government's terms. If they were accepted, the chiefs would be returned to Parihaka; if not, they would be taken to Nelson and held there as prisoners. Neither the government's kindness in rewarding the chiefs for keeping the peace by giving them a paid holiday in honourable restraint in the frozen south, nor the threat to confine them for months in Nelson had the least effect.[51] Butler tried a third time on 17 July, after a voyage on the government steamer *Stella* from Bluff to Nelson via Fiordland and the West Coast, but with no greater success. Te Whiti did not want to hear of the commissioners' and the government's 'love' for him. He said the government had stolen his land and driven his people away, and it was too late now to come with 'the government food' after all the wrong had been done. Holding up his hands, he told Butler: 'See . . . I have no money, no riches; never had. I only want my land'. Both he and Tohu expected the justice of a trial, and when told the government did not wish to treat them as ordinary men but as gentlemen and chiefs Te Whiti said, 'My ears hear a different talk today to what they did in the past'.[52]

Te Whiti was held to blame for all that had happened to him, but he would not compromise his principles. If the government had loved him as a chief ten years earlier when he restrained his people from offering any obstruction, instead of condemning him as a fanatic and consistently denying him justice, they might have won the cooperation they now sought to buy. Butler left the two chiefs in Ward's custody in Nelson and returned to Wellington to tell the government there was nothing Te Whiti would ask of them or accept from them. On 24 July, Prendergast issued an order in council under the West Coast Peace Preservation Act which directed 'that John Patrick Ward . . . shall keep each of the persons named Te Whiti and Tohu . . . in custody within the Provincial District of Nelson until further or other order shall be made . . . under the said Act'.[53] Bryce intended that no other order should be made until the chiefs could safely be returned to Parihaka – sometime after the 'superabundant' food supplies there had dwindled and would no longer support large monthly meetings.[54] In the event, they remained in Nelson until the following March and only on one occasion, on 23 September, did they rebel against their honourable restraint in the care of their 'attendant'. They had promised to visit the local pa that day, but Ward told them he had too much work to do and could not take them. Tohu decided to go regardless and Te Whiti agreed to accompany him against Ward's orders. When Ward followed and grappled with Tohu, 'Te Whiti advised peace, and they all returned to the house'. Ward called in reinforcements and the local armed constabulary inspector made it clear the two chiefs were indeed prisoners and must obey orders.[55]

Late in August 1882, the Maori translations of the reports of the West Coast Commission, which in September 1880 and again in July 1881 were to be 'translated and circulated without delay', were sent to Ward for the edification of Te Whiti and Tohu. It was too late. They would not look at them.[56] It was claimed 'the whole object of the West Coast Commission inquiry was to show the Natives that we were going to inquire into unfulfilled promises, and to do them justice in respect of those promises'.[57] Those who had been held responsible for all that had happened on the coast and who were now kept in custody without trial at the administrator's pleasure, had never been given the chance to read in their own language the reports the government held up as models of their justice and goodwill towards the Maori people.[58]

On many occasions Te Whiti had been derided as a false prophet and a fanatic, but with the Parihaka question 'settled' and Te Whiti safely in exile the public could afford to be magnanimous and remember his positive qualities. In the spirit perhaps of smoothing the Maori's dying pillow, or perhaps in an effort to soothe consciences, it was not long before Te Whiti's virtues began to be extolled in print. Parris, who had recently condemned Te Whiti, now wrote a surprisingly frank and unbiased account of the man:

> To many . . . Te Whiti's . . . career will appear to have been one of mere folly, delusion, and unreasonableness. . . . But those who . . . can admit the full right of the Maori to strive by all fair means to retain his old free mode of life . . . will find in Te Whiti's conduct as the leader of his people in a trying period, much that is worthy of their sympathy and respect. Te Whiti was . . . the representative in this part of New Zealand, of the love of the Maori people for their ancient customs and ways of living, and of their dread of being hustled off the scene by a swarm of strangers. . . . Regarding Te Whiti's position and career from this point of view, all feeling of irritation against the man for his steady opposition to the progress of colonization must disappear; and we can properly estimate the firmness, combined with total absence of any recourse to violent measures, with which he maintained the unequal contest for so many years.[59]

While the Peace Preservation Bill was before parliament, it was noted that the only evidence available to the House to justify the legislation that was being brought down consisted of reports from 'certain Native interpreters . . . made to order', and 'garbled reports of the Press emanating from New Plymouth and Taranaki'. In the Legislative Council on 20 June, W. B. D. Mantell objected that the preamble to the bill asserted a number of facts that the legislators were unable to verify, as no information had yet been laid on the table of the House referring to any government action on the west coast since the issuing of the proclamation of 19 October.[60]

The documents Mantell sought had been the subject of controversy between Gordon and his ministers for some weeks. Gordon had urged publication, while his ministers felt that publication at that time of 'the whole of the despatches would be prejudicial to the public interest'. By 31 May 1882, they had agreed to the publication of Gordon's report of 26 February 1881 and certain ministerial minutes, but a week later the ministers decided that even these papers, which were already in print, should not be published, and they tried to return to the governor the order for publication which he had already signed. With more tact than truth, he told them that he had no difficulty in acceding to their recommendation to withhold further papers from parliament, although he deeply regretted it, but when it came to the papers already in print it was a different matter. It was more than a week since he had issued his order, and he believed he now had 'neither the power nor the right to recall it' and indeed would not do so.[61]

Thus Gordon at last managed to get his very able report into print, but by the time it went before the House on 9 June at the end of the second reading of the West Coast Peace Preservation Bill, its relevance was greatly diminished. Hall's memo of 15 June 1881 which was strongly critical of the 26 February report was printed with it, but the ministers were able to withhold Gordon's reply of 28 December 1881, and a crucial despatch of 3 December 1881 which was far too objective a statement about west coast affairs to be acceptable to the ministers; they were determined to prevent the expression of any view which did not support the case they had so carefully built up over the years. Among other things, the despatch summarised the crimes of Te Whiti and his followers which, according to Rolleston, had necessitated the issuing of the proclamation of 19 October. These were: interference with the armed constabulary's woodcutting parties, fencing on disputed land, Te Whiti's 17 September speech which 'conveyed an impression' that he would encourage and condone violence, Titokowaru's drunken threats, and the termination of Rolleston's unsuccessful interview with Te Whiti, none of which appeared to Gordon to be very 'novel' occurrences.[62]

The argument Hall advanced for the suppression of despatches[63] was based on the reasoning that any view contrary to that put forward by the ministers must necessarily involve a political opinion, rather than simply a more accurate or a more objective one. He claimed to be concerned that the publication of the governor's despatches on matters presently under discussion in parliament would bring the Crown into politics and lay the governor open to political attack. But he was not averse to the publication of those despatches which dealt with matters *not* currently in dispute in parliament.[64] In other words, it was their timing rather than their content that Hall was really concerned about. He was not concerned about the governor being attacked for his views as long as they were expressed *after* ministers had persuaded parliament to pass their venial acts.

Gordon believed the government had 'given in' over the publication of the papers already in print because they felt he stood on strong ground and knew he had determined not to give way. In an effort to get further despatches into print, he turned to Mantell and told him he thought it 'almost impossible for any government to resist a demand for papers explanatory of the measures they felt themselves compelled to take during the recess and for which they have to demand indemnity'. But Gordon knew his ministers, and added that 'what is *almost* impossible is very often not *quite* so'.[65] Mantell agreed to ask for the papers in the Council, and on 14 June moved that there be laid on the table copies of all public despatches between the governor and the Colonial Office not yet presented to the House. Whitaker declared that it would be 'inconvenient to the public service' to produce any further despatches and asked the Council not to pass Mantell's motion. Whitmore admitted the governor's 26 February despatch was 'fair, impartial, and clear', but was ready to vote against the motion for the rather curious reason that such documents, if translated badly to the 'uneducated portion of Her Majesty's subjects on the West Coast', might be productive of danger to the public safety. Thomas Fraser declared Gordon's despatch to be 'a most able paper . . . the only true account we have of the transactions that have taken place on the West Coast', and he felt they should not be asked to legislate without seeing further despatches that bore on the West Coast Peace Preservation Bill.[66]

Fraser and Mantell were voices in the wilderness. Mantell's motion was lost, parliament legislated 'in the dark', and all Gordon could do was point out to the secretary of state the colonial government's selective policy with regard to the publication of his despatches, and ask that if any documents be presented to the British parliament they include those suppressed in New Zealand.[67] Kimberley had until then been no more accommodating than Hall and Whitaker. Despite persistent requests in the House of Commons, he had managed for 15 months not to present Gordon's 26 February report, although he told the Hall government that it 'must be published if pressed for'. Sir Michael Hicks-Beach, the previous secretary of state, did press for it in July 1882, and in August a mass of papers, including Gordon's despatches of 3 and 28 December 1881, were finally laid on the table of the British parliament and published as the 1882 Blue Book (*c*.3382) at the beginning of November, almost a year before they appeared in print in New Zealand.[68]

Gordon had delayed his departure from New Zealand as long as seemed necessary to him, and as long as he could bear to stay. He was anxious to sever his connection with a ministry he found at best uncongenial, at worst unscrupulous. He did not think highly of the calibre of colonial politicians and regretted that each new election reduced the number of members 'of good education and fair social position'.[69] Despite his marked disapproval of Hall's native policy, he still regarded Hall as an educated gentleman and was not averse to recommending him for the knighthood which was announced a few weeks after his resignation.

Gordon was aware that the majority of the colonists who backed the government in its native policies were anything but educated thinkers. Higher education was not valued in a country preoccupied with taming the land by attacking both the bush and the indigenous people. Even educated settlers often lacked the means or the will to give their children higher education, and the emerging universities were criticised as unnecessary luxuries. The settler press reflected rather than moulded public opinion and was intolerant of criticism of the government's native policies, equating such criticism with subversive anti-European sentiment. Although New Zealand at the time lacked a vocal intelligentsia willing and able to criticise the government, according to Gordon there had always been a small minority whose 'intellectual capacity' gave it an importance 'disproportionate to its numerical strength', and he was pleased to identify with the judges, prelates and occasional statesman and politician who made up its numbers.[70] He felt the time he had spent as governor in New Zealand was the most miserable of his life, but while New Zealand was hateful to him as a governor, as a private person he believed it had more charms than almost any other country. He was leaving 'with but one regret: that he had ever been connected however passively, with the working of this government, and the spoliation of the Maoris'.[71] His ministers were sure he would never return to the country from his leave of absence and Hall told Bell they 'would give anything to see his back', for he was, according to Whitaker, 'without exception the worst man to deal with he ever met in his life; ten times worse than Grey'. Gordon knew how his ministers felt and had told Whitaker he was 'quite as anxious to be off as they were to get rid of him'.[72]

Gordon finally embarked on 24 June on HMS *Miranda*, which had been waiting in Lyttelton and Wellington for nearly two months to take him to the Pacific. He was criticised by some for having acted unconstitutionally, for example when he called Grey on Hall's resignation,[73] and by others for not having sufficiently opposed his ministers. One old friend of his, resident in New Zealand, believed that had Gordon defied his ministers they would not have resigned, 'because of their anxiety that the whole Parihaka transaction should not come before the Imperial Parliament'.[74] Gordon felt so strongly on the question that he might have done it had either the Earl of Carnarvon or Hicks-

Beach, both of whom had been so helpful to him in his work in Fiji, still been at the Colonial Office, but he did not have a sympathetic relationship with Kimberley, and believed he could expect no support from him. When Kimberley received news of the impending Parihaka crisis, he observed that 'it is a purely colonial question and we have long established the policy of not attempting any interference with the N[ew] Zealand Gov[ernmen]t whose jealousy of the slightest interference is extreme. Hitherto they have managed the native question with singular prudence and success'.[75] He was less enthusiastic about the government's handling of the native question by the time the governor left New Zealand, and minuted on a newspaper report that 'it may not have been altogether without use that he has had the courage to tell some unpleasant truths to the New Zealand colonists', and that in England the feeling was with Gordon rather than with the colonists.[76]

Before Gordon left New Zealand, Fox, who had lost his parliamentary seat in the 1881 election, submitted to him a progress report on the work of the commission issued to him on 23 December 1880 to give effect to the West Coast Settlement Act. He justified his decision to start operations south of the Waingongoro by saying that Maori there were more amenable than those under Te Whiti's influence to having their reserves defined. But with 'the failure of Te Whiti's prophecies', and the defining of reserves and issuing of crown grants to Maori south of the Waingongoro, it became 'apparent' to Fox that those north of the river were now anxious to have their reserves settled. The work was practically completed as far north as the southern boundary of the Parihaka block – yet seven months after the arrest of Te Whiti, Fox had still not managed to commence the work of defining or subdividing reserves for the Parihaka people. The government had, however, found the resources to effect the 'reduction by 5000 acres' of both the proposed Parihaka reserve and of the continuous reserve on the Waimate plains, and they had long since effected the survey of the seaward portion of the Parihaka block, and sold most of it.[77] Hall reported that this block had not sold as well as others had done, presumably because of its proximity to Parihaka and the activities of Te Whiti and his followers. 'Actual settlers did not come forward so readily and it has fallen to a greater extent into the hands of absentees.'[78] So much for the settlement of a close European population and the establishment of English homesteads and cultivations at the very doors of Parihaka.

On 29 August 1882, an Amnesty Bill was introduced to the House and it passed its second reading on 7 September with little discussion. Bryce explained that the bill was not an amnesty or a pardon in itself, but it would enable the governor in council to issue a proclamation declaring an amnesty. Bryce thought there should be a general amnesty, possibly with some exceptions, but that any amnesty required assurances of submission; Whitaker was in favour of an amnesty with no exceptions whatever. Discussion in parliament made it clear the government had an eye on Waikato, rather than Taranaki, and was again working towards the opening up of the King Country. There was a clause in the act that provided for the amnesty to extend to 'all offences and to all Maoris' or to except 'certain offences and certain Maoris', and most of the discussion dwelt on this clause, and more specifically on whether or not Te Kooti should be excepted from the amnesty.[79] The names of Te Whiti and Tohu were not mentioned. The last clause provided that nothing in the act should 'repeal or otherwise affect' any provisions in the West Coast Peace Preservation Act, and that act, which was to remain in force till the end of the 1883 session of parliament, provided that 'No court, judge, justice of the peace, gaoler, or other officer or person shall, during the continuance of this Act, discharge, bail or liberate . . . Te Whiti and Tohu . . . without an order from the Governor in Council . . . any law or statute to the contrary notwithstanding'.

Before the bill had even become law, Prendergast, as administrator of the government, sent a copy to the secretary of state, although it was to be another five months before an amnesty was actually proclaimed. He sent with it memos from Whitaker and Bryce proclaiming 'the satisfactory state of Native affairs generally'. Bryce contrasted the peaceful state of affairs with the previous year's planting season when 'the country appeared to be on the eve of war' and found the contrast so great he thought the 'Native troubles' would soon be 'well nigh forgotten'.[80]

Europeans could afford to forget since their settlement on the coast was progressing 'to a degree satisfactory beyond the most sanguine expectations', and Bryce was not concerned with the memories of those whose chiefs were in custody, whose settlement had been destroyed and whose reserves had still not been defined. Titokowaru was also not likely to forget. He had remained in prison until Manaia and a Mr Winks put up bail for him in mid July.[81] Bryce had thought Titokowaru 'the most dangerous of them all', but was satisfied the old man now intended to live 'in peace and in obedience to the law'.[82]

A group of eight northern chiefs who had not forgotten the native troubles sent three of their number to England in August 1882 to present to the Queen a memorial asking for investigation into the redress of their grievances, all of which concerned alienation or confiscation of land. One of their complaints concerned a plan 'devised by the Government to enkindle strife', by which troops were sent to Parihaka 'to capture in[n]ocent men . . . to seize their property and their money, to destroy their growing crops, to break down their houses, and commit other deeds of injustice'. They asked that Te Whiti be set at liberty and they begged the Queen to establish a Maori parliament to 'hold in check the European authorities who are endeavouring to set aside the Treaty of Waitangi'.[83]

The three chiefs who took the petition to England on behalf of their people had hoped to see the Queen's 'very countenance' and to hear her words. They were disappointed in that, but 'thanks to Lord Kimberley or Gladstone, they *did* see the Prince and Princess of Wales and were kindly treated'.[84] They presented the memorial to Kimberley who, unable to 'pass over' the colonial government, referred it back to New Zealand.[85] However, he could not help but compare the view of those who had come halfway round the world with their grievances, with that of the native minister and the premier who assured him all native troubles were settled and all but forgotten.

The colonial ministers' opinion of the memorial sent to them by Kimberley was predictable. After mulling it over for five or six weeks, Whitaker credited it not to 'the Native people of New Zealand' on whose behalf it was signed by the eight chiefs, but to Hirini Taiwhanga, a noted political activist, whom he dismissed as a Ngapuhi, a man of no rank and no importance, a man of doubtful morals and conduct. He dismissed 'the "wrongs" detailed in the memorial' with equal ease, saying that most of them pre-dated responsible government, and that a perusal of papers and documents in the Colonial Office would show 'how little reason the Maoris have to complain'. Then, forgetting his government's venial acts, he expressed the view that the 'general legislation of the Colony as to the Maoris has been more than just – it has been exceptionally favourable to them', and finished by saying that it could 'with confidence be asserted . . . that there is not . . . anything on the statute-book of the Colony, or in the conduct of the Colonial Legislature, as regards the Maoris, to which reasonable exception can be taken'.[86]

Ministers were still comfortable in the belief that many crucial papers on Parihaka had, at their request and insistence, been suppressed in England as well as New Zealand, and Hall had forecast that a fresh controversy would erupt if any of Gordon's public or private despatches were to be published first in England.[87] To their dismay, early in 1883 ministers received a copy of the Blue Book containing 'Correspondence respecting Native Affairs in New Zealand, and the Imprisonment of certain Maoris' which had been presented to the imperial parliament.[88] Whitaker hastened into print to complain to the Earl of Derby, now secretary of state, about the publication of despatches 'seriously impugning' the colonial ministry and to which the ministers had not had the opportunity to reply. They were even more disturbed by the fact that, unknown to them, Gordon had sent with his despatches voluminous clippings from the *Lyttelton Times*, 'the most uncompromising Opposition paper in the Colony', and that these had been published in the Blue Book 'authoritatively, unaccompanied by explanation'. Gordon had also regularly sent cuttings from the pro-government *New Zealand Times*, some of which were printed in the Blue Book, but they called for no comment from his late ministers.

Whitaker's memo, together with a memo from Prendergast disclaiming knowledge of Gordon's imminent return from Fiji in October 1881, were sent to the secretary of state by the new governor, Sir W. F. D. Jervois, on 27 January 1883.[89] Before presenting them to the imperial parliament, the Colonial Office sent them on to Gordon, on leave in England, for his comments. Gordon defended his action in not communicating his confidential despatches to his ministers, and went on at length to justify his other views and actions complained of by his ex-ministers. When Prendergast and the offended colonial ministers received a copy of this 'studiously insulting' letter with its 'unjustifiable and offensive' suggestions, they again took up their pens and at great length defended their wounded honour.[90]

The Colonial Office was not impressed and replied that Her Majesty's government did not consider 'the points referred to in the correspondence . . . of sufficient public interest . . . to justify the communication of further papers to Parliament on the matter'. Derby added that Gordon had been told the controversy might now 'with advantage be allowed to drop', but that if he or the ministers wished to continue their war of words they were welcome to produce their correspondence in the New Zealand parliament.[91] The colonial ministry was incensed. Atkinson, now premier, felt himself compelled to 'place on record a decided protest' against Derby's decision, and declared that the imperial government in publishing Gordon's antagonistic despatches had exceeded him in his 'unconstitutional proceedings', and had then given 'evidence of hostility to the Colonial Government by declaring their comments and replies not to be of such interest as to warrant their presentation to the Imperial parliament'. Atkinson's protest lost something of its impact before it reached Derby's eyes. Two or three changes of ministry overtook the slighted colony before a new premier, Robert Stout, found Atkinson's undated memo at the end of 1884 and dutifully sent it off 'without comment by the present Government'. Six months later, the controversy had still not been allowed to drop. Hall complained that the secretary of state had denied the right of reply to 'the gentlemen whose conduct is impugned'. He hoped his memo would at least be laid before the New Zealand parliament, where 'the character of the public men of the colony for straightforward and honourable conduct is not considered a matter of indifference'.[92]

The whole issue of suppression of information and selective publication of despatches had a wider significance than governor-minister relations or even the raising of finance on the London market. New Zealand had long had visions of a Pacific empire with New Zealand as its centre. Grey had first raised the idea in 1848 and continued to raise it over the years of his first governorship. He raised it again in the 1870s as a politician and as premier, claiming that as New Zealand understood how to manage the Maori race, the colony was ideally fitted to manage various Pacific Island groups whose annexation he urged on Britain. Even Vogel advanced the argument on similar lines, saying that once New Zealand had responsible government it had concluded 'that the plough, and the axe, and the pen were preferable agents to the sword and the rifle'.[93] The myth of New Zealand's expertise in handling native affairs was widely believed and frequently expounded. Dr M. S. Grace (Wellington) repeated it to the Legislative Council in 1880:

> It has been my pride to feel that the Colony of New Zealand alone among British dependencies has distinguished itself by the greatest impartiality and the most jealous delicacy in its public dealings with the Native race . . . whatever faults we have to reproach ourselves with, we cannot reproach ourselves with any act of voluntary injustice towards the Native race.[94]

Whitaker, Atkinson and Stout were also enthusiastic supporters of the idea of a Pacific empire, but for strategic and commercial reasons. But it would strengthen their case if the imperial government could be persuaded that New

Zealand did have the racial expertise to manage other Polynesians, and it was certainly not in their interests to have it known that their native policy was vigorously criticised by a governor who had seen it in action and was in a position to judge it. Gordon's strictures may not in the end have been without effect at the Colonial Office. Kimberley's attitude to the colonial ministers had certainly hardened, and Gladstone, an old family friend, was influenced by Gordon's experiences and views. Paul Knaplund and J. K. Chapman, twentieth century historians, both considered that Britain's refusal to allow New Zealand to take control of Fiji or to sanction Queensland's annexation of New Guinea were due in part to Gordon's lobbying.[95]

The publication of Gordon's despatches and the rest of the Parihaka papers was certainly not without effect in New Zealand. Five months after the Amnesty Act became law, but just three weeks after ministers had received the 1882 Blue Book, the governor, 'with the advice and consent of the Executive Council', proclaimed an amnesty which, subject to the provisions of the act, was to extend to 'all offences and to all Maoris' with no exceptions.[96] The provisions of the act of course excepted Te Whiti and Tohu. Early in February 1883, Bryce had hurried to the King Country to question Te Kooti face to face to determine whether or not he should be included in an amnesty. They met in Rewi's presence on 12 February and Te Kooti repeated what he had told Sheehan in March 1878: 'You did not make peace. I have made it myself . . . In 1874, I ceased strife; I have not since returned to it.' Bryce telegraphed this news to the governor and within hours the proclamation was issued.[97]

A few days later, Bryce decided the time had also come to release Te Whiti and Tohu – not because the food at Parihaka had run out, but because it 'would come in well with the amnesty and we ought to have time to rearrest if necessary before Assembly meets'. Cabinet agreed in principle, but wished first to confer with Fox. He thought the chiefs should not be released until the surveys on the Parihaka block were complete, while the Cabinet thought the continuation of the survey under Te Whiti's nose 'would be a good test whether he has any thought of giving further trouble, or is likely to be induced to do so'. They finally decided on immediate release on the grounds that it would be 'more than ever difficult to justify . . . detention after the issue of the amnesty'.[98] But by then the amnesty was not their only concern. It was almost two weeks since they had had the governor inform the Colonial Office that he had 'this day granted permission to Te Whiti and Tohu to return to their own home at

Parihaka'.[99] The two chiefs were not informed of the fact until 7 March, when Ward received a telegram ordering him to advise them they would be freed 'in a few days'. Asked if they had anything to say or wanted anything done, they simply said, 'the Government sent us here, and they can bring us back or not as they think fit'. They were permitted a last visit to their friends at the pa, then were lectured by Mr Dive of the Native Office who told them 'the Government were going to bury the past, and let them go back free men; but that they hoped no more meetings would be held, and that both of them would cease raising strife in the land'. Te Whiti understood the government's idea of freedom and told him: 'The shirt I wear is the Government's'. He also understood his people and added: 'If the grasshoppers find good new grass they will come; nothing will prevent them'. They were loaded onto the *Stella* on 8 March en route to Opunake with 'nearly £30 worth of clothing etc . . . as a tohu aroha . . . a gift in loving forgiveness from the Government to them both'.[100]

At dawn on 9 March 1883 the two chiefs, moved as at no other time during the term of their captivity, greeted Taranaki, their tapu mountain. Te Whiti was 'very silent, but much agitated', while Tohu 'came on deck, chanting . . . a song of welcome to the mountain'. There was a crowd of some 40 Europeans and 20 Maori on shore to welcome them, but when an old man began the traditional greetings, Te Whiti, feeling himself contaminated by association with the government, replied briefly: 'When this rotten stuff is cleaned from underneath my feet I will stand as a man before you all, and open my mouth; it is shut today. Salutations to you all'. Colonel Roberts, sent to drive them back to Parihaka, received them 'very courteously, and legally took possession of them' from Ward.[101] Such was their freedom.

Exile in the South Island had evidently not brought Te Whiti to 'a proper frame of mind' and it certainly had not diminished his mana, for three months later Parris reported that he was 'idolised by his followers' and Parihaka was undoubtedly 'the centre of attraction again'. There was a 'constant course of visiting and communicating with the place' and large supplies of food were being sent there from north and south, supplies which Parris thought the contributors could ill afford. But he found no amount of reasoning would induce the people to abandon their old custom of gathering and feasting, a habit universally condemned by Europeans, who viewed it simply in economic and not in social terms. Parris decided there were no political overtones to the gatherings, and when parliament opened a few days later the governor's speech suggested that ministers were of the same view. Noting that Te Whiti and Tohu had been released from custody and allowed to return to Parihaka, the governor observed there was no indication that this concession would lead to 'the renewal of dangerous proceedings' on the part of the west coast tribes.[102]

However, before the session closed Bryce had passed the West Coast Peace Preservation Continuance Act, just a simple one clause act 'to continue for another year the West Coast Peace Preservation Act of last session'. This he found necessary because 'the infatuation of the natives on that Coast with respect to their prophet Te Whiti continues in a wonderful manner, so much so that when the monthly Sabbath comes round there is a very strong attempt on the part of numerous Natives to hold meetings at Parihaka'. Bryce had just prevented the August hui from taking place and he wanted the legal power to go on preventing any such riotous assemblies 'for a short time longer'. Bryce's supporters were still ready to condemn Te Whiti 'and other insane fanatics like him' and insist that if the House was not given this power blood would again be shed on the west coast. But several members would not support any extension of the act on the grounds that it was unjust and unnecessary, and they might as well pass an act 'to prevent the assembling of the Salvation Army in Dunedin or Wellington'. Bryce's opponents asked what danger there could be in such meetings when the west coast tribes, as members had recently been assured, were the recipients 'of wonderful benevolence' and 'countless blessings' and had been 'enriched . . . for ever' by the receipt of valuable reserves. But the main opposition to the bill came from those members who could not accept the injustice of restricting those who had given 'no evidence of any desire to disturb the public peace', when the ministry had just extended a free pardon to Te Kooti, 'the man of blood, the man guilty of the vilest atrocities'.[103]

Bryce's trump card was Te Mahuki, a Ngatimaniapoto follower of Te Whiti who at the end of March 1883 had been arrested in the King Country for capturing Hursthouse and his survey party.[104] Hursthouse had been rescued by Te Kooti, and some members felt this showed that the policy of pardoning Te Kooti had paid off and a similar policy of trust should be applied to Te Whiti. Bryce, however, was sure that as Te Mahuki's followers were also followers of Te Whiti the House would be encouraging a rise in fanaticism if it refused to grant the government the lawful power to prevent meetings at Parihaka by the 'gentle means' embodied in his bill. The seal was put on the bill in the Council on 3 September by J. C. Richmond, who declared that the aim and object of all the government's recent actions had been to 'protect the Natives against themselves', and that 'no harm whatever' had arisen by imprisoning Te Whiti and Tohu who had returned to Parihaka 'none the worse either in body or in mind for their very light captivity'.[105]

Bryce's bill did not drive the west coast tribes to further rebellion, but neither did it intimidate them. In his annual report on the natives of his district, Parris noted the people were 'as much as ever under the influence of Te Whiti' and that this influence extended beyond the west coast to many parts of both the North and South Islands. He felt their enforced sojourn in the South Island had wrought 'a wonderful change' on Te Whiti and Tohu as regards the 'mode of entertaining visitors', for they no longer limited the feast to traditional foods or those which they themselves produced, as they had done previously.[106] At Parihaka in March 1884, a professional cook had provided an elaborate banquet of 'Beef, mutton, pork, sucking-pig, geese, pies (meat and fruit) . . . fancy biscuits, almonds, raisins and figs, jellies . . . champagne, and several other sorts of wines, ale and porter'. About 100 Europeans were present at that assembly, but since they were not aboriginal natives of New Zealand they were not debarred from Parihaka under the terms of the West Coast Peace Preservation Act, and they were welcomed by Te Whiti who was 'civil and polite to all'. Parris, who was not a guest at the feast, was very indignant about this squandering by Maori of their meagre resources on feasting and hospitality, which he saw as a 'fanatical imposition for no other object than to foster the vanity of an ambitious pretender'.[107]

Parris was obviously displeased to find Te Whiti unrepentant and unreformed by his period in captivity, and he reverted to his old terminology, condemning Te Whiti once more for fostering 'superstitious fanaticism', 'arrogating to himself Divine authority', and allowing Parihaka to become a place of refuge for criminals. Te Whiti's great crime in Parris' eyes was his continuing to think and act like a Maori – giving hospitality, sharing resources, seeing himself not as an individual but as part of a group, albeit leader of that group and responsible for its collective welfare; and even for seeing that welfare not in economic, but in social and spiritual terms. The best efforts to make Te Whiti appreciate the superiority of Europeans and their ways had failed, as had the best efforts to destroy his mana and abase him in the eyes of his followers. Parris admitted that as long as the West Coast Peace Preservation Act remained in force there would be periodical attempts to visit Parihaka by those from both north and south who sought the 'human and Divine' teaching of Te Whiti and Tohu. It was all beyond his comprehension. 'These two individuals are a mystery, their wide-spread influence is a mystery, and how so many devoted followers can be induced to disregard their own true interest to serve them is a mystery.'[108] The real mystery is that one who had known the Maori people as long and as well as Parris had done should wonder that they preferred Maori values and the Maori way of life, which they could still find with Te Whiti, to European ones.

Bryce did not attempt to renew or extend the act in the following parliamentary session, his last as native minister, and when the Atkinson ministry fell in August 1884 the act finally lapsed. Now that more than 50 Maori could once again 'assemble together in public meeting' on the west coast, instead of the people going to Parihaka to celebrate the event, Parihaka went to the people. Te Whiti and Tohu would organise an orderly group of 1,500 or 2,000 of their followers and send them off in Titokowaru's care to visit the whole district, as far north as Pukearuhe and as far south as Patea. A joyous procession of chanting, poi-swinging Maori, proclaiming their identity and celebrating the mana of their chiefs, would progress from village to village, and as they left after an overnight stay their hitherto hosts would swell the numbers of the travelling party and help consume the 'immense' quantities of food provided locally or sent by friends of Te Whiti and Tohu in Nelson or by the 'rabid Te Whiti-ites' in the Chathams.[109] On arrival in Patea they presented their hosts with 'a large number of Maori presents, such as greenstones', many of them made by the ploughmen and fencers during their captivity in the South Island. Wilfred Rennell, of the New Plymouth Native Office, explained that a 'very intelligent Native chief' had told him these journeyings were to establish peace among Maori now that peace had been 'firmly established between Europeans and Natives' – but his own opinion was that it was 'a way of passing their idle time'.[110] In Taranaki, where the people were 'almost to a man' followers of Te Whiti and Tohu, such gatherings were less likely to be about banishing old enmities than about expressing solidarity over a shared grievance: confiscation of their land.

Grievances were not confined to Taranaki. European politicians could continue to assure the Colonial Office that no promise remained unfulfilled and no grievance remained unrequited, but Maori did not share this view and, unable to obtain satisfaction at home, they turned again directly to England. The four

Maori members of parliament, representing their tribes whom they had 'consulted on this subject', wrote to the Aborigines Protection Society asking them to bring their 'wrongs under the notice of the Queen and Parliament' and telling them that the following year Tawhiao would travel to England himself to petition the Queen. The immediate cause of their dissatisfaction was the opening up of the King Country 'to all that we have striven to preserve it from', but they also complained of the working of the Native Land Courts and of the never-ending land laws which each year took the control of more land out of their hands.[111] The letter was referred first to the Colonial Office and then back to the New Zealand government, and Bryce felt obliged to make 'a few observations' on it, despite the 'inconvenience in being required to make an official memorandum on such a communication', which was nothing more than 'an attack made from an irresponsible quarter in London, prompted . . . by some tenth-rate politician in New Zealand, with probably a petty grievance against the Government'. Bryce apparently considered the Maori members incapable of thinking for themselves and declared the letter could not really have emanated from them since it professed a sympathy with the King movement which none of the putative writers would profess. He sought to destroy the credibility of the Maori members' letter by attempting to convince the Colonial Office that whatever importance might be 'attached in the abstract' to the statements it contained, it should not be added to by the 'assumption that these statements really embody the feelings of the Native representatives'. He then declared sanctimoniously that Maori were 'in no way subjected to oppression, and . . . that no possible appeal to the New Zealand Assembly could be so certain of consideration as an appeal for justice to the Maoris or protection for them against oppression'.[112] Bryce as usual believed he knew what was good for Maori, and was sure that if any one of them expressed a word of dissatisfaction he did so mistakenly and at the instigation of scheming Europeans.

In June 1883, three months after Te Whiti's return to Parihaka, Fox was able to report to Governor Jervois that the Parihaka reserve had at last been marked out on the ground. Fox cited difficulty in surveying the land 'intended' for natives on the west coast as one reason for his work being in arrears. Many of the reserves were in 'extremely rugged country, broken by deep and wide gullies, and covered by extremely heavy forest', which rendered the surveys 'more arduous, and consequently more protracted' than he had expected.[113] He

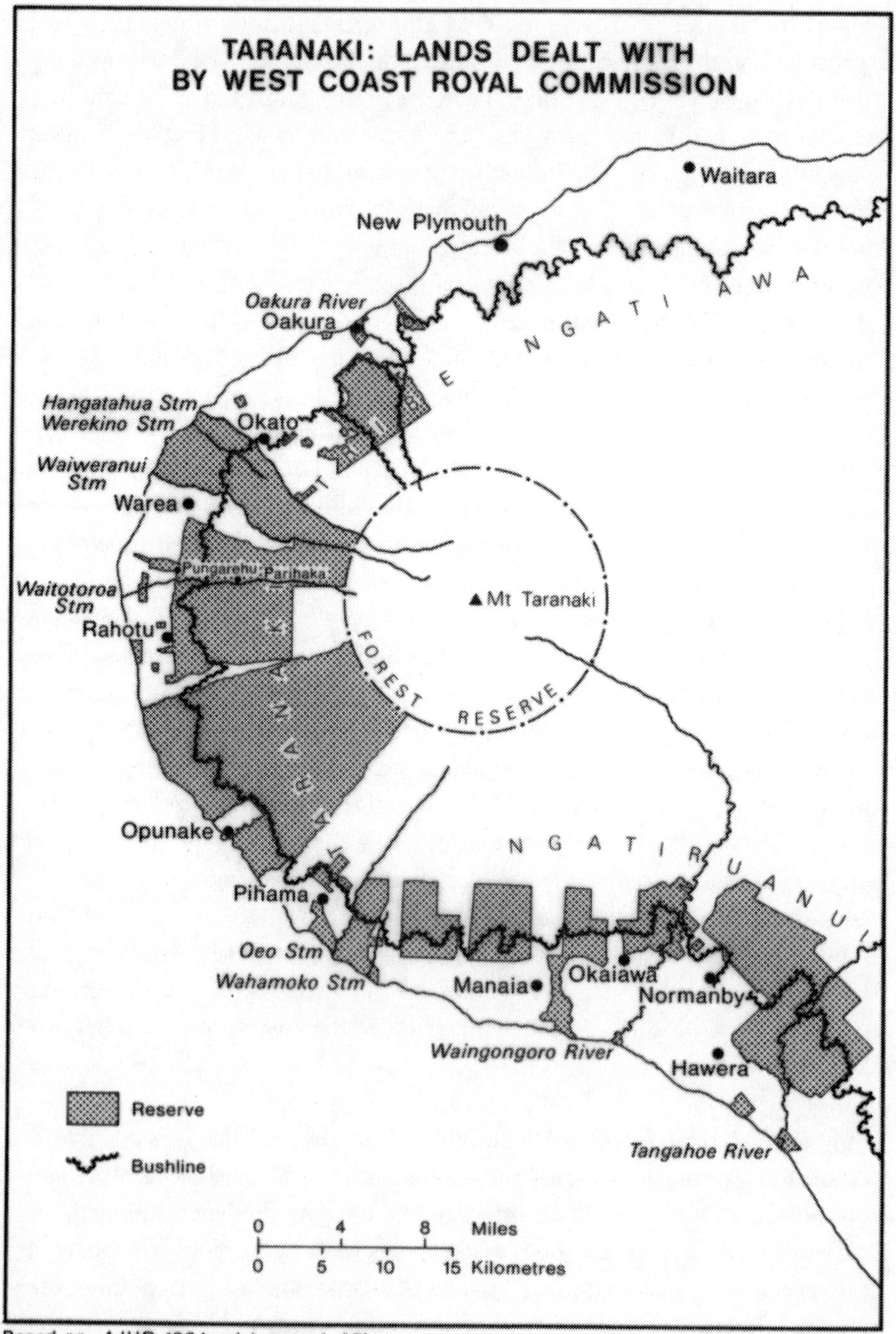

Based on: AJHR 1884 vol 1, sess 1, A5b

should not have been surprised. Fox knew, if anyone knew, that the most open and accessible land had long ago been surveyed and granted or sold to Europeans. Even Ngatirahiri of Waitara, who were 'always loyal' and who had fought with the British, had had to be content with a reserve of which one-quarter was open land and three-quarters in very rough bush, since their ancestral land had been given to military settlers – who 'had become as a large rock deeply embedded, which there was no power to remove'. Not surprisingly, Ngatirahiri became 'devoted adherents of Te Whiti'.[114]

A year later, Fox finally reported the completion of his work as a west coast commissioner. Considerable misgivings had been expressed in parliament about the length of time it had taken to complete the work and the fact that the whole question was in the hands of one man 'who is the supreme arbiter – who gives land to whom he likes – who deals with everything as he likes' – and who settled all things in secret court. It was felt to be 'not desirable that a single gentleman . . . should have so large a power' on the west coast. Many petitions had been sent to the House complaining of great injustice inflicted upon individuals through Fox's awards, but no one had any redress for their grievances because the Public Petitions Committee or Native Affairs Committee which received them invariably referred them back to the commissioner.[115]

Fox did not concern himself with such petty criticism but made much of the praise Grey had lavished on him when the original reports were presented to parliament four years earlier, and claimed that he had given effect 'to the very letter, as far as possible' to the recommendations which he and Bell had then made. He congratulated himself that 'no single promise, great or small, actual or implied' remained unfulfilled, and no complication remained unsolved. This ensured that every Maori with any right to confiscated land on the west coast had his name inscribed on a crown grant and would thus have 'a settled homestead and the means of maintenance, and in many cases a considerable pecuniary income besides'. This income was to come from land leased to Europeans which was 'surplus' to personal requirements, and since over 5,000 grantees would share about 200,000 acres,[116] or fractionally over 38 acres each, their requirements for personal use were obviously considered to be minimal – even less, in fact, than the statutory provision of 50 acres per head.

Whitaker enlarged on the more than '250,000 acres' of reserves which when leased would probably return about £10,000 per year, reduced only by 'comparatively small costs of survey and administration', and concluded that the government had 'promoted the material interests of the Natives' in a most handsome manner.[117] Bryce thought Maori were beginning to realise that government action was in their interests – or at least they accepted it as inevitable and had abandoned all thought of obstruction. He wanted the letting of reserves 'pressed to completion, in the interests alike of the Native owners, the occupying settlers and the colony'. The land had not, after all, been set aside *for* Maori, but for the 'benefit' of Maori, and even then Bryce had grave misgivings about these extensive reserves, whose value now exceeded that of all the confiscated lands at the time of confiscation, being set aside in the interest of the owners. He doubted such 'ample' provision was altogether wise, since it would 'provide means sufficient to keep these Natives in a state of idleness in perpetuity'.[118] However, he preferred this alternative to that of having Maori land lying in a state of idleness in perpetuity. The land was a valuable commodity, but only in the hands of Europeans. Bryce was convinced that his solution had been the right one.

Fox had a rather different view. He felt that much of the credit for the present satisfactory state of affairs was his own, and he expressed his regret that a similar pacific solution to the native difficulty had not been found in the past. He informed the governor that the idea of a 'mixed Commission' was not new in 1879. He had suggested such a commission to examine the Waitara question in December 1861 when he was premier and native minister, but first Tarapipipi had declined the proposition and then it was 'rejected, somewhat contumeliously' by the followers of the Maori king at the Peria meeting in October 1862. Fox deluded himself that he could have brought a pacific solution to the colony's troubles in 1862 as he believed he had now done in 1884, and he claimed that by refusing his offer Maori had 'removed from the Government the responsibility for the disasters which followed during the several years of continuous wars'. However, he considered that the award of these just and ample reserves had now removed all traces of dissatisfaction from the Maori mind and all reason for disaffection, and that amicable relations between the races had, by his efforts, now 'been restored never again to be disturbed'.[119]

While the principal European actors in the west coast drama each congratulated himself on having at last solved the native problem, Maori were obviously far from satisfied with the solution presented to them. After the breakup of Parihaka and Te Whiti's arrest, Fox had gradually gained the grudging cooperation of every hapu on the coast 'except that which occupied the Parihaka block'. Te Whiti's people remained aloof to the end, uncowed and unsubmissive. From the start, they declined to accept money derived from the enforced leasing of their land. They had no interest in being the richest natives on the coast or in being maintained in a state of idleness. Any money they received they wished to earn by their werawera, by the sweat of their brow. Rennell reported that owing to their 'peculiar ideas' government officials had found difficulty in apportioning the rent monies, but 'very shortly' those willing to receive rents would get their shares and he had no doubt the others would then gradually alter their minds when they saw the 'advantages' they would incur.[120] He was wrong; in the twentieth century there were still Parihaka people who steadfastly refused rent money, denying to the last the government's right to lease the land Fox had told them would be theirs and their children's forever.

One month after Fox had declared that amicable relations had been restored between the races, Tawhiao was in England on the visit the Maori members of parliament had spoken of the year before. He and four other chiefs representing tribes from a wide area of the North Island crossed the great ocean of Kiwa in another effort to seek redress of their grievances from the Queen. The memorial they presented made five requests: that the Queen grant her Maori people their own government; that she appoint a Maori commissioner to act as a mediator between Maori and European in matters concerning the leasing and selling of Maori land; that Maori taxes be used for Maori purposes; that European judges in the Native Land Court be replaced by Maori ones; and that the lands wrongly obtained by the government be returned to the Maori people. They quoted wrongs done them over the years, all over the island, including those done in Taranaki between 1879 when the government 'began to seize the land without pretext' and 1884 when 'Te Whiti and party were . . . still under some restraining law of the Government'.[121]

This was the third time in three years that leading chiefs had turned to their Queen to seek the justice denied them by the colonial government and it was indicative of a deep malaise within the Maori community, a malaise which the government refused to recognise or address. Once more Te Wheoro was one of the signatories. When the 'leading chief' of the 'most loyal Natives in the colony', who supposedly had had 'his land claims, as a loyal chief, superabundantly recognised by the Government and the Compensation Courts', became disillusioned and turned away from the European government and towards those seeking separate Maori government, it was surely time for ministers of the day to take notice.[122]

Yet once more the appeal fell on deaf ears. When the petition was referred back to Jervois, ministers took six months to reply; they put the delay down to the desire of the native minister, Ballance, to visit the Maori districts before furnishing Jervois with a memo on the subject. It might be wondered what took them so long. They dismissed the allegations of the petition as 'unsubstantial', and declared the policy of all the native land acts was to maintain the 'laws, customs and usages of the Natives', which showed in fact the natives could not really have any grievances. They did 'not deem it necessary to point out the unreasonableness and absurdity' of a request for a Maori parliament; and referred the secretary of state back to Whitaker's memo of 12 December 1882, which 'specially dealt with a petition very similar to the one now under consideration', and to Bryce's memo of 11 January 1884, 'referring to the alleged ill-treatment of the Maories'. Finally, they declared that 'Ministers do not consider that there is any allegation in this petition that has not been before the Imperial Government, replied to by the Colony, and dealt with before'.[123]

There seemed to be no way through for the Maori people. Europeans were determined they knew what was best for Maori, and when Maori demurred their protests were dismissed as groundless. To do otherwise would be to admit that European action had been founded on a false premise. Each tribe had to find its own way through, and out of the search for self-determination grew the Kotahitanga movement among the kupapa tribes and in the north. When the King movement chiefs became disillusioned by their failure to obtain help directly from England, they too associated themselves to some extent with the aims of Kotahitanga.

Te Whiti's tactic was simply to continue to ignore the government, to rebuild Parihaka, and to maintain the old values and the old way of life as well as he could with the meagre land resources available to him. Far from suffering mate through imprisonment, his influence was stronger than ever. 'Natives in other districts may make light of Te Whiti and his doings, but none of them ever come within reach of his influence, but are soon, more or less, his admirers and supporters.'[124] Te Whiti's influence was still supra-tribal because he was a bulwark against the individualism Europeans sought to impose on Maori, and he offered a positive alternative to the destruction of the Maori way of life caused by the encroachment of European civilisation. At Parihaka the old values were reinforced, the old ways maintained as far as possible. Europeans were impressed by the signs of 'progress' they saw in the village, but disturbed and bewildered by the rejection of some of their most cherished institutions such as European education and religion. The question of Te Whiti's influence over his people remained a mystery to Europeans because they could not appreciate that many Maori would choose Maori values in preference to European ones and that adherence to Te Whiti allowed them to maintain their identity as Maori. The question of Te Whiti's influence over his people was a question of mana.

CHAPTER EIGHT

A Question of Mana

THE INFLUENCE OF TE WHITI AND TOHU LIVES ON. ON 5 NOVEMBER 1981, several thousand people gathered on the marae at Parihaka to celebrate their identity as a people and to acclaim the mana of their chiefs. It was this mana the government had sought to extinguish a hundred years earlier when they destroyed the village and imprisoned Te Whiti and Tohu. They did not destroy Parihaka to get the land. Since confiscated land was *ipso facto* crown land, the government already possessed it and felt they could do what they liked with it. Their ownership of the land was not, in their view, in question. What was in question was mana. Europeans were concerned about their superiority and dominance which, it seemed to them, could be assured only by destroying Te Whiti's mana. As long as he remained at Parihaka he constituted a threat to European supremacy in that he offered his people an alternative to the way of life Europeans sought to impose on them.

Te Whiti, on the other hand, was concerned not with his mana tangata, but with mana whenua, not with promoting his own standing, but with ensuring the wellbeing of his community through retention of the land. This the government continually denied, claiming that no amount of reserves would satisfy him, that his sole concern was his own mana, and that he meant once more to make the Maori people dominant throughout the land. By labelling him a deluded prophet and a self-seeking madman, they could deny his legitimate grievances and justify their attempts to 'destroy' his mana tangata and force him to submit to European domination.

The act of confiscation had extinguished native title and the government did indeed possess the land, but Europeans had been in no position in the 1860s to occupy the confiscated lands on the west coast. They had bitten off more than they could chew and in the end had permitted and indeed encouraged the defeated tribes to return and occupy their ancestral lands; they had then paid money and issued deeds of cession to certain chiefs in an effort to induce them to relinquish their mana whenua. Maori confusion over the status of the confiscation was understandable, but as the compensation money was paid from a fund set aside for the acquisition of native title, the issue was apparently no more clear-cut to the Europeans. They felt they could not enforce the confiscation north of the Waingongoro because Titokowaru and his people had returned to the Waimate plains, but they would not abandon it because the immigration and public works policies were rapidly increasing the demand for land for settlement. When it appeared to the government that Titokowaru's mana toa, his warrior status, had been surrendered in return for takoha, they judged the moment opportune to possess themselves of the desirable and fertile Waimate plains. It was ironic that it was Grey as governor who had proclaimed the confiscation – for punishment – in 1865, and Grey as premier who would attempt to enforce it – for profit – in 1878. His failure to take into account the reality of the situation – the years of unfulfilled promises, the presence at Parihaka of those whose legitimate claims had never been recognised – ensured the failure of the government's precipitate action in attempting to do what it liked with the land.

While the west coast commissioners were in no doubt that the question of reserves was basic to the settlement of the 'native difficulty', Bryce was adamant that no mere adjustment of reserves would solve the problems on the coast. Fox had insisted that nothing be done till adequate reserves were marked out on the ground, yet when the Waimate plains were surveyed and advertised for sale, no reserves had been made there for Ngatiruanui; when Bryce invaded and destroyed Parihaka, no reserves had been delineated in the Parihaka block. The survey for sale of the seaward Parihaka block, the best arable land, was the ultimate provocation, calculated to force Te Whiti to give in or resist. In the end, the 'reasons' for the failure to make reserves were nothing but excuses. Failure to make them stemmed from a deep-seated aversion to land remaining in Maori hands and thus allowing the traditional owners a certain degree of separateness and independence. It was an axiom of the time that only by assimilating to European culture could Maori survive, so destruction of the old way of life was held to be in Maori's own interests. The race was widely believed to be in a state of moral, spiritual and psychological collapse following defeat in war, and the people therefore were thought to be ready and willing to accept European solutions to Maori problems. The Europeans' cherished myths about their superior values and way of life led to the expectation that their settlement of the country would elevate the Maori community, but Te Whiti's lack of desire for money or anything the Europeans had to offer, his scorn for their values and progress, were a reproach, an accusation of failure, to the Europeans' civilising mission. When the people at Parihaka appeared to thrive in their isolation from the European world, when they refused to be subordinated according to the edicts of social Darwinism, the very laws of nature were perceived to be under attack. The only acceptable explanation for their behaviour was that they were suffering a mental epidemic.

Victorian notions of racial and cultural superiority meant that a partnership between Maori and European was an impossibility: it was domination or nothing. Te Whiti and Tohu and their people could not be allowed a separate existence on their ancestral land but must suffer the encroachment of a destructive European culture and learn to accept its values. Te Whiti's besetting sin in European eyes was that he rejected their proffered civilisation and accepted only those facets of European culture, especially its technology, that appeared to be in the interests of his people. The very fact of Parihaka's prosperity had to be denied and Maori agricultural skills overlooked. When correspondents from 'notorious opposition newspapers' reported the extensive acreages of flourishing crops surrounding Parihaka, the 'ministerial organs' described them as further evidence of madness, as wasted effort, far in excess of any possible needs of the people at Parihaka; or more menacingly as another indication of Maori intention to take over the whole of New Zealand and drive the Europeans into the sea.

The government's treatment of Te Whiti was an orchestrated campaign to destroy his mana; Tohu they took little notice of at all. Ministers were concerned that by communicating with Te Whiti they would compromise their dignity. Since they were convinced that their recognition of him would increase his mana in the eyes of his followers, they studiously ignored him or at least avoided direct contact, and when contact was unavoidable they sent underlings to treat with him. Only when it was too late, and then with an eye to British opinion, did they allow the native minister to go to Parihaka and talk to Te Whiti directly. Yet all through the crisis years, they maintained official contact with Titokowaru and spent time, money and energy in conciliating him. The government feared Titokowaru's mana toa, which he had long since surrendered, yet sought to destroy Te Whiti's mana tangata which he exercised in the interests of peace. They convinced themselves that he was a deluded fanatic and, in order to explain his hold over his allegedly warlike followers, they too had to be seen as deluded and infatuated, beguiled by Te Whiti's prophecies and bewitched by his spell. But peace is a positive injunction, and since Te Whiti's followers did not overthrow him or abandon him, but waited patiently for his return from exile, it must be accepted that his hold over them was a positive, not a negative one. They did not need his 'mystical oratory' to keep them peaceful. They needed it to strengthen their resolve and give them hope; to keep them from despair and European-induced demoralisation perhaps, but not to keep them from murdering the poor Taranaki settlers in their beds.

The government feared Te Whiti's followers would do his every bidding. They did, but not in the way the government expected. Instead of rising in a body to effect the disappearance of the Europeans 'like a swish from the face of the country', they ploughed and fenced and cultivated their ancestral land with great determination and persistence. Instead of murdering Europeans they planted melons, and they were pouri when the settlers formed committees and pressured the government to provide them with arms. Instead of attacking the armed constabulary they willingly suffered arrest and went to prison. This was a new kind of warfare, and one the government found disconcerting and financially embarrassing. It could have been ended at any time, had they been prepared to recognise Te Whiti's mana by dealing with him directly and by allowing him to retain the cultivations of his ancestors, the seaward Parihaka block. It was not greed for land but cultural arrogance that drove them. They had the Waimate plains, the land the Taranaki settlers had always coveted, but even after they had surveyed and sold all but a few reserves in the seaward Parihaka block, they continued their efforts to destroy Te Whiti's mana, a symbol, in their eyes, of mana motuhake, of Maori identity, separateness, independence. They might have saved their efforts. Neither imprisonment, nor the loss of the land, nor finally the death of both Te Whiti and Tohu in 1907, caused their followers to forsake them, and their teaching has been given expression over the years in Taranaki's continuing commitment to non-violence.

Until the time of Te Whiti's and Tohu's arrest, their reviled followers had many opportunities for violence on a grand scale, yet violence never did eventuate. Maori were not fools. It was twelve years since any of them had borne arms, twelve years in which European might had multiplied around them. It did not take a build up in the armed constabulary in their district to persuade those who had fought previously that they would be no match for the European if they turned back to violence. War offered them sure defeat and further confiscation. They could now renounce that option because they had an acceptable alternative: the non-violent resistance advocated by Te Whiti and Tohu which threw the government into confusion and which enhanced their sense of identity by emphasising their moral superiority and offering them the hope of retaining their ancestral land. When the surveyors were removed from the plains, Maori armed themselves with drays and good humour; at the time of the ploughing, they armed themselves with ploughs; at the fencing, with green branches; at the cultivating, with ko; and on invasion day with aroha. But the settlers armed themselves with guns, and threatened violence if the government did not put down these demonstrations of Maori arrogance and independence. Settler pressure forced Grey's hand; their representatives, Bryce and Atkinson, helped force Hall's. It was the settlers who threatened violence, but Maori who were arrested – and since the colony's judges could not be relied upon to manipulate the law, the legislators found it expedient to introduce legislation which applied only to certain Maori and to certain offences – those which offended certain settlers. There was no semblance of equality before these laws.

Although Te Whiti's concern was not with his mana tangata, his personal mana, but with mana whenua, the mana associated with the land, his pacific resistance to European claims as to the validity of the confiscation served to enhance his mana tangata in the eyes of his followers, and as long as they looked to him and not to the government, he was perceived as a living threat and a nuisance. Whether or not he was seen as a physical threat, he was certainly seen as a moral one. While settlers with memories of earlier wars pressured the government for protection from those they still claimed were savages and fanatics, their real concern was for their supremacy, not their survival. But they couched their protests in terms of fear of physical violence, and their representatives in parliament turned this to good effect to pass legislation designed to put an end to Maori independence on the west coast. While governments preached sovereignty and obedience to the rule of law, they practised domination and subjugation, and justified their actions by proclaiming that their repressive legislation would save Maori from their madness and infatuation. Had Maori been acknowledged as sane instead of mad, their grievances would have had to be considered legitimate and properly investigated. As it was, no government was ever prepared to allow the legality of the confiscation to be questioned officially, and the legislation passed by the Grey, Hall and Whitaker ministries making trial of the Maori protesters unnecessary ensured the question was never raised in a court of law.

Te Whiti's sanity was judged by the government from the reports of a few of their agents and interpreters, and by the settlers from the reports of their local newspaper's correspondents. In neither case, by common admission, was Te Whiti understood. Since his oratory was unintelligible to Europeans, and to many Maori, it was credited with ridiculous and mysterious qualities. The expectation that his speech would be mystical and obscure led to his message being ignored when it was unacceptably intelligible. He was generally credited with preaching peace, but not being able to maintain it. When things were peaceful on the coast, the monthly meetings at Parihaka were accepted as a useful safety valve, allowing Maori to expend their energy and emotions in feasting and oratory rather than obstruction to the work of colonisation. When Maori took the initiative, they were supposedly bent on annihilating the Europeans and returning the country to Maori control. Bryce was the greatest offender against truth and logic, saying Te Whiti dreamed of unbounded power as the supreme ruler of the west coast and of New Zealand, indeed of the whole world. His colleagues who passed his obnoxious legislation were equally offenders against justice. Although Bryce and Sheehan were opposites in many ways, they were equally insensitive to Maori needs, and strangely in accord with regard to the repressive legislation each introduced.

While successive governments, ministers and individual Europeans were bent on destroying Te Whiti's mana, they were busily engaged in attempts to enhance their own. In an era of personal rather than party politics, the small colonial stage was full of contenders for the limelight. The dissension between the west coast commissioners and the native minister was not the only contest for pre-eminence in west coast matters. European rivalry and dissension existed at several levels: ministerial, departmental, and individual. Any number of Europeans saw themselves as ideally placed to solve the problems associated with the enforcement of the confiscation, and one by one they fell out of favour with both Fox and Bryce. The dichotomous Mr Fox spoke now as commissioner, now as politician; now highlighting the legitimate grievances of Maori, now voting in favour of their imprisonment for daring to protest those grievances. Fox agreed with no one, in the end not even with himself. His abrupt change of course from first insisting on the importance of reserves for the Parihaka people to then ignoring the question altogether until *after* the return of Te Whiti and Tohu from exile, was not his only about-face in a long political career. Nor did it prevent him from claiming that it was his work as a commissioner in allotting just and ample reserves to the people that had been the means of solving all the problems on the coast. Bryce was equally adamant that the victory was his, for the opposite reason: he had ignored Maori claims and settled a 'close European population' on the coast.

The dissension between Gordon and his ministers was ten times worse than that between Grey and his, according to Whitaker, who as attorney-general advising both governors was doubtless in a position to judge. Gordon's attitude to Pacific peoples was unusual for his time, and was not such as to inspire the confidence of a colonial ministry bent on establishing the supremacy of the white race. Gordon's ideals were far too lofty for the likes of Bryce and Sheehan, Atkinson and Whitaker. Unlike other governors, Gordon was not content to accept ministerial explanations, especially when couched in Bryce's extravagant language, and he did what he could to inform himself and the Colonial Office of the realities of the situation. If there was one thing that united government and opposition it was their wariness of imperial interference in colonial affairs, and the aim of each succeeding ministry was to present themselves to the Colonial Office as successful managers of native affairs, to the British public as just and humanitarian rulers, and to the financiers as worthy recipients of loans. It was therefore essential to their pride and their pocket that only their version of events reached the other side of the world.

Individual Europeans had their own reasons for seeking prominence in west coast affairs: to enhance their status, to ensure re-election, to get land, even to 'meet a certain liability next week'. Bryce was anxious to make his name as the saviour of the west coast; Fox was convinced that but for Maori intransigence he could have found a pacific solution to the colony's problems many years before and was determined to make his mark this time; Atkinson had fostered the belief that he was the only possible colonial treasurer, and was intent on making political capital out of the native difficulty to get himself re-elected and to get loan money spent in Taranaki; Whitaker wanted the freedom to speculate in Maori lands, but was anxious about the colony's good name and financial standing in Britain. Rolleston was one who did not seek prominence but had it thrust upon him and he evidently did not relish the role he was called upon to play.

Thompson and Croumbie-Brown performed singular functions in the west coast drama. As an alternative source of information on the progress of events they constituted a threat to the government propaganda machine. As long as their reports had a favourable tinge their efforts were tolerated, but their first dissentient words brought their summary dismissal. They had sweet revenge on 5 November 1881. These two Europeans, among the most reviled on the coast, constitute practically the sole source of information on events surrounding the invasion of Parihaka. Unhappily, they are also the most cited sources on Te Whiti's utterances. Croumbie-Brown's words are taken as gospel, Te Whiti's gospel; his interpreter, he who was never told anything straight at Parihaka, does not usually get a mention.

The government credited Thompson with greater influence over Te Whiti than he possessed. It was all part of the assumption of the time that Maori could not think for themselves but took their cues from evilly disposed Europeans, Fox's harpies and rogues who infested the coast. Nor were Maori credited with the capacity to undertake a sustained campaign of non-violent resistance to gain their ends. Political protest was an unacceptable explanation for Maori actions; madness and infatuation were not. There was a sense of desperation about the way the government emphasised the fanaticism of the west coast people, a desperation to mask the real cause of the disturbances, to ignore the legitimacy of the grievances.

The government never ceased proclaiming that Te Whiti's hold on his people was due to infatuation and a blind belief in his prophecies, but it was government injustice, not infatuation, that built Te Whiti's following. For years they claimed that his power was waning and that his people were about to abandon him because of the non-fulfilment of his prophecies. But it did not happen; the prophecies were apparently more evident to Europeans than to Maori. When the government could not win Te Whiti's cooperation, or buy him, or entice his followers away, they sought acceptable explanations for straightforward protests such as the ploughing and fencing. According to Sheehan, Te Whiti turned the surveyors off the plains because he claimed that he and his people constituted the parliament of New Zealand and would decide what should happen in the land; he sent his men to plough because he had promised that he would return all the confiscated land in the country to its rightful owners. Bryce maintained that, although there was no opposition offered to the construction of main roads or the erection of the telegraph line or the surveying of the continuous reserve, the fencers had set to work when the coast road cut through their cultivations because Te Whiti had persuaded them to have faith in him as a great prophet and a god. In each case, the government's answer was to arrest the protesters and hold them without trial in the South Island, the local Siberia, supposedly in their own best interests, but in reality so that the government could, without opposition, proceed with their policy of settling Europeans on disputed land. Hall credited the spring planting and fencing on the seaward Parihaka block to Te Whiti's fanatical obstinacy and sought to overcome it by goading the people into providing the government with a good *casus belli*. When none eventuated, the government agonised over the best way of bringing about 'the inevitable collision' and hit on the expedient of labelling Parihaka's peaceable inhabitants a riotous mob who could be arrested and dispersed.

The government did not take an overwhelming military force to Parihaka because they took the threat of resistance seriously, but because they were obliged to pretend they did. They knew there were no fortifications at Parihaka, no weapons, no hostility, no intention to fight. Te Whiti was a nuisance to them, and a financial embarrassment, but they had no lawful reason to arrest him – in fact Whitaker hoped they could find one and would not have to make one. So it was necessary to magnify the outrage, to stress Te Whiti's prophetic utterances and the infatuation of his deluded followers, and persuade the public that he was a serious threat to the peace of the colony. Talk of the 'front' and the 'enemy' put their policies into perspective. The nation, indeed the world, was to understand that they were not dealing with a simple protest over legitimate grievances. This was a national movement, rebellion against the Queen, an uprising against the constituted government of the country, to be put down with all the heroism and patriotism with which the colonists credited themselves.

But it was an even deeper, more emotive, more compelling reason that brought about the patriotic rush to arms of the Nelson City Rifles, the Thames Rifle Rangers, the Wairoa Light Horse, the Wellington Naval Brigade, the Taranaki Mounted Rifles – and all those others from all parts of the country who were given offence when the government had to admit it did not need their offers of service. Te Whiti had spurned European civilisation, he had chosen to remain Maori, he had asserted his mana, and this insult had to be avenged lest the power of the European be dragged through the dust. When Europeans had the upper hand the talk was simply of subordinating the Maori population; in times of threat the talk was of exterminating the savages. If the rhetoric was veiled, that aim was certainly implied. Parihaka was to be obliterated, merged into a road. The sentiment was apt. Since Roman times, roads had been symbolic of the dominance of a conquering power.

The perceived danger from Te Whiti and his deluded followers would thus warrant the employment of an overwhelming military force and justify the sacking of Parihaka and the arrest of its leaders – and by banning the press and issuing highly selective communiqués the world was to be kept in the dark as to the true situation. It was only thanks to the 'precious correspondent' of the 'most uncompromising opposition newspaper in the colony' that it became known to the world that the government's prophecies and policies were founded on a false premise, and that Te Whiti's hold on his followers was based not on infatuation, a negative force, but on aroha, a positive one.

Politicians had more than an eye on British opinion. They were posturing on a world stage, proclaiming their respect and concern for Maori and their fitness to manage Polynesian races. But the thinness of the veneer was only too evident. Sentiments had not changed much in twenty years, and the rush of volunteers showed that it was probably true, as Gordon said, that nine-tenths of the colony were in favour of the government's Parihaka policy. Even so, the ministries which attempted to destroy Te Whiti's mana were not able to put their policies in place without European as well as Maori opposition. Not all those who voted in favour of the repressive legislation were really in favour of it, but for various reasons they allowed political or financial expediency to take precedence over their concern for justice. And not all of those who voted against the legislation actually took the part of Maori. As the debates in parliament show, many members believed it was in the Maori's best interests that Parihaka be broken up, but they voted against injustice, against double standards, and especially against the dangerous peacetime precedent of suspending *habeas corpus*. Those who did take the Maori part, who did stand up to be counted, were few enough, but their protests were genuine and sustained, and they joined that intellectual minority in the colony amongst whom Gordon was pleased to count himself. The minority view was generally reviled, and had it not been for Gordon's despatches and the *Lyttelton Times* it would scarcely have been heard.

Te Whiti was an astute political opponent of the government, but there was a limit to what any Maori could do in the 1870s and 1880s to halt the tide of European encroachment. It is to the credit of Te Whiti and Tohu that they managed for fourteen years to keep at bay the civilisation supposed to provide their salvation, and to maintain the integrity of their community; and it is to their followers' credit that they retained their spirit in the face of such adversity and even in the absence in exile of their revered leaders. Confiscation was a grievous wrong, but it gave the Taranaki tribes a unity, a common identity as a people which sustained them through their ordeals, a strong identity which they continued to maintain in the face of relentless settler pressure over the years.

It was not to the government's credit that they claimed they were acting in Maori interests when, for reasons of political and financial expediency, they were acting in European interests. They imprisoned political protesters on the grounds that they were a menace, since their fanaticism might cause the *settlers* to take up arms. They denied them the justice of a trial, lest it be shown in court that the confiscation of their land was indeed invalid. They refused to recognise Te Whiti's right to reserves, but were determined he would recognise their right to grant or withhold them. They destroyed the most prosperous Maori village in the country, at a time when Maori needed encouragement to re-establish themselves after the wars. They ruined acres of growing crops and brought hardship and privation to hundreds of tribespeople, and especially to their children. They could find no charge to level at the two leaders but they imprisoned them regardless, and fed them a forced diet of European might and technology to try to convince them to cease thinking and acting like Maori. Then, to prevent criticism at home and abroad, and with an eye to their reservoir of overseas finance, they attempted to suppress those sources of information which exposed and were critical of their actions. They amnestied ex-rebels, whom they still feared, in order to gain access to the King Country, yet exempted from the amnesty those who had not been in rebellion but whose ancestral lands they had already occupied. They ignored all the promises from the past and the recommendations of the West Coast Commission, and made no reserves for the Parihaka people until after the return of their leaders from imprisonment; and then, to add insult to injury, they vested those meagre reserves in the Public Trustee and leased them to Europeans. And finally, with cynical disregard for justice, they indemnified themselves for all their illegal acts. The road to Parihaka was a long one, and it was not to the government's credit that they marched on it with booted feet.

The government's handling of the west coast situation was typical of a colonial government pressured by settlers convinced of their superiority and bent on forcing Maori to submit to European domination. Settler prejudice died hard. Even after the sale of the seaward Parihaka block and the breaking up of Parihaka, there were still those who were not satisfied with having got the land, and throughout the 1880s new settler racism was expressed in calls for an increase in the armed constabulary as a protection against the threatening attitude of local natives. The English settlers, whose homesteads, fences, and cultivations at the very doors of Parihaka were to be the surest guarantee of peace, did their best to create new Maori scares, and the Taranaki press, through its settler correspondents, still complained about the impostor Te Whiti and the large number of unwashed natives of bad character inhabiting Parihaka. But with Atkinson and Bryce out of office, settler agitation received little official attention, and the one policeman stationed in the district served to assure European and Maori equally of protection from cattle theft and trespass.

Te Whiti continued his show of autonomy long after any such challenge to European supremacy could hope to succeed. But it was a stand for Taranaki, and a stand for mana motuhake. Taranaki's grievances were finally investigated by the 1926 Royal Commission which was appointed to inquire into claims arising from land confiscation. The commission reported that when war was declared against Wi Kingi and his people they were not in rebellion against the Queen and had committed no crime, and that even those Taranaki Maori who had been in arms after 1 January 1863 ought not to have been punished by the confiscation of *any* of their lands. The commissioners judged an annual payment of £5,000 to be adequate compensation for the injustice of the confiscation, and advised that the sum of £300 be paid as acknowledgement of the injury done the Parihaka people by the destruction of their village and growing crops and the theft of their stock, personal belongings and taonga, or treasures. This totally inadequate compensation is a continuing source of grievance to the wronged Taranaki people, but in the end Te Whiti's mana triumphed and his stand was wholly vindicated when the confiscation he had challenged so long and so tenaciously was shown to be invalid.

NOTES

PREFACE

1 Hayden White, *Tropics of Discourse: Essays in Cultural Criticism*, Baltimore, 1978, pp27–50.

INTRODUCTION

1 *Daily News* 17 Oct 1991, p1.
2 Interim Response of Crown Counsel to Claims, 29 Nov 1995, Wai 143, doc 2.108, pp4–5.
3 *The Taranaki Report: Kaupapa Tuatahi*, Waitangi Tribunal Report, Wai 143, Wellington, 1996, pp13, 308, 309, 311.
4 Hazel Riseborough, 'Parihaka and the Historians', *Te Niho o Te Atiawa Parihaka Seminars* no. 1, 1993.
5 Te Miringa Hohaia, Gregory O'Brien and Lara Strongman, eds, *Parihaka: The Art of Passive Resistance*, Wellington, 2001, pp192, 204, 206.
6 ibid pp 43–65.

CHAPTER ONE

1 C. S. Lewis, quoted in *New Zealand Listener* 31 May 1986, p78.
2 W. H. Oliver, *The Story of New Zealand*, London, 1960, p255.
3 William Greenwood, *Riemenschneider of Warea*, Wellington, 1967, pp6, 18.
4 LE 1/1863/106.
5 LE 1/1879/3. Rev. T. G. Hammond used these reports for a paper he wrote in the 1880s when he was stationed in the Hokianga; 'Te Whiti and Parihaka', Acc. 73.28, A.T.L.
6 James Cowan, *The New Zealand Wars: A History of the Maori Campaigns and the Pioneering Period* [1923], vol II, Wellington, 1956, pp476–91; *Hero Stories of New Zealand*, Wellington, 1935, p245. (An almost identical version was published as 'Famous New Zealanders: Te Whiti of Taranaki. The Story of a Patriot and Peacemaker', *New Zealand Railways Magazine* 1 Oct 1934, pp17–21).
7 W. B., Otorohanga [William Baucke], *Where the White Man Treads* [1905], Auckland, 1928, pp164–65.
8 G. W. Rusden, *History of New Zealand*, vol III, London, 1883; Dick Scott, *The Parihaka Story*, Auckland, 1954; *Ask That Mountain: The Story of Parihaka*, Auckland, 1975; Judith Bassett, 'Review of *Ask That Mountain: The Story of Parihaka*, by Dick Scott', *New Zealand Journal of History* 9, 2, 1975, p191.
9 Libel trial heard before Baron Huddleston and a special jury in the Queen's Bench Division of the High Court of Justice in London in March 1886, *Bryce v Rusden*, London, 1886, pp5–6, 31; Rusden to Mantell 1 Sept 1883, Rusden t/s letters. Unknown to Rusden and his advisers, Bryce had the transcript of the trial printed in London for 'distribution among his friends'. It was supposedly not for sale but was readily bought in New Zealand, though not in England; Rusden to Mantell 20 Dec 1887, 13 March 1888, Rusden t/s letters. Rusden later brought out his own account of the trial and of his 1887 appeal on the grounds of

excessive damages; [G. W. Rusden] *Tragedies in New Zealand in 1868 and 1881. Discussed in England in 1886 and 1887*, London, 1888.

10 Bryce later agreed to accept only £2,531 as indemnity, plus costs of £1,144.

11 See e.g. 'The Parihaka Affair: Interesting Letter from the Hon. John Bryce', letter to the editor, *Press* 4 Feb 1903; John Bryce, 'Fanaticism in the Maori Race', ibid 23 March 1903; 'Maori Fanaticism', ibid 25 March 1903; 'The Constabulary at Parihaka', ibid 28 March 1903.

12 William Pember Reeves, *The Long White Cloud: Ao Tea Roa* [1898], Auckland, 1973, pp225–26. See also Reeves Medium Clipping Book pp1–8.

13 Report on Confiscated Native Lands and other Grievances 29 June 1927, AJHR 1928 G7 pp32–33.

14 James Cowan, *The Maoris of New Zealand*, Christchurch, 1910, pp335–36; *Hero Stories* pp236–46; 'Famous New Zealanders'.

15 J. C. Beaglehole, *New Zealand: A Short History*, London, 1936, p40.

16 J. B. Condliffe and W. T. G. Airey, *A Short History of New Zealand*, Auckland, 6th edn 1938, pp137–38; 7th edn 1953.

17 W. P. Morrell and D. O. W. Hall, *A History of New Zealand Life*, Christchurch, 1957, pp158–61.

18 J. K. Hunn, *Report on the Department of Maori Affairs*, Wellington, 1961.

19 Keith Sinclair, *A History of New Zealand* [1959], Harmondsworth, 1969, pp147–48. The section on Parihaka is unchanged in the revised and enlarged edition of 1980.

20 Oliver pp253–56.

21 See e.g. Bernard Gadd, 'The Teachings of Te Whiti O Rongomai, 1831–1907', *Journal of the Polynesian Society* 75, 4, 1966, pp445–57; Daniel P. Lyons, 'An Analysis of Three Maori Prophet Movements', in I. H. Kawharu, ed., *Conflict and Compromise: Essays on the Maori since Colonization*, Wellington, 1975, pp64–66.

22 Apirana T. Ngata and I. L. G. Sutherland, 'Religious Influences', in I. L. G. Sutherland, ed., *The Maori People Today: A General Survey*, Christchurch, 1940, p362.

23 E. H. Ackerknecht, quoted in Raeburn Lange, 'Changes in Rarotongan Attitudes toward Health and Disease: Historical Factors in the Development of a Mid-Twentieth-Century Understanding', *Pacific Studies* 10, 1, 1986, p30.

24 Scott *Ask That Mountain* p7.

25 John A. Williams, *Politics of the New Zealand Maori: Protest and Cooperation, 1891–1909*, Auckland, 1969, pp37–40.

26 Alan Ward, *A Show of Justice: Racial 'Amalgamation' in Nineteenth Century New Zealand*, Auckland, 1973, pp236, 274, 279–80, 284–85.

27 Keri Kaa's felicitous phrase.

28 Harry Dansey, *Te Raukura: The Feathers of the Albatross*, Auckland, 1974. See also K. R. Howe, 'The Fate of the "Savage" in Pacific Historiography'. *New Zealand Journal of History* 11, 2, 1977, pp152–54, on indigenous writers' use of drama, poetry and fiction in preference to western style historical writing to express their view of the past.

29 'Leave it to us to write our own narratives.' Keri Kaa, 'Review of Michael King's *Maori*', *New Zealand Listener* 24 Sept 1983, pp98–99.

30 See e.g. NZPD 1882 xli pp119, 557.

31 AJLC 1882 No.9 p4.

32 R. M. Ross, 'The Autochthonous New Zealand Soil', in Peter Munz, ed., *The Feel of Truth: Essays in New Zealand and Pacific History*, Wellington, 1969, p49.

33 See e.g. AJHR 1882 G1 p10; Peter Buck, 'The Taranaki Maoris: Te Whiti and Parihaka', *Te Aute College*

Students' Association Conference, Papers and Addresses, Dec 1897, in J. B. Condliffe, *Te Rangi Hiroa: The Life of Sir Peter Buck*, Christchurch, 1971, p43; Cowan *Hero Stories* p245.

CHAPTER TWO

1 Tamati Ngapora, 1872, quoted in M. P. K. Sorrenson, 'Maori and Pakeha', in W. H. Oliver with B. R. Williams, eds, *The Oxford History of New Zealand*, Wellington, 1981, p187.

2 *Gazette* 17 Dec 1864, 31 Jan and 5 Sept 1865.

3 William Gisborne, *New Zealand Rulers and Statesmen 1840 to 1885*, London, 1886, pp211–12; AJHR 1863 E2 p20.

4 Domett memo 23 May 1863, AJHR 1863 E7a pp7–8; Domett memo 24 June 1863, AJHR 1863 E7 p8.

5 *Gazette* 15 July 1863.

6 AJHR 1863 A8 pp1–4; AJHR 1863 A8a pp1–12; Cardwell despatch 26 April 1864, AJHR 1864 App to E2 p20.

7 Domett memo 31 July 1863, AJHR 1863, A8 pp2–4.

8 AJHR 1864 App to E2 p18; J. Rutherford, *Sir George Grey, K.C.B., 1812–1898: A Study in Colonial Government*, London, 1961, p192.

9 Grey despatch 29 Aug 1863, AJHR 1863 A8 p1. The conditions of service are laid down in Domett's memo of 3 Aug 1863, ibid pp4–7.

10 ibid p8.

11 AJHR 1863 A8a p7.

12 Henry Sewell, *The New Zealand Native Rebellion: Letter to Lord Lyttelton*, Auckland, 1864, pp43–44.

13 AJHR 1864 App to E2 pp4, 12, 13.

14 ibid pp15, 17–18.

15 ibid p18.

16 NZPD 1861–63 pp782–85, 825.

17 AJHR 1928 G7 p11.

18 There was no clause in the act suspending its operations and the secretary of state required that the colonial government enact legislation to limit its duration. The New Zealand Settlements Amendment Act of 1864 provided that the act should lapse on 3 Dec 1865. The New Zealand Settlements Amendment and Continuance Act of 1865 made the 1863 act perpetual but provided that no districts could be proclaimed, or land taken for settlement, after 3 Dec 1867; NZPD 1864–66 pp100–01, 263; AJHR 1864 App to E2 p22, AJHR 1865 A6 p18, ibid A1 p26.

19 AJHR 1864 A1 p5; NZPD 1861–63 pp847, 848.

20 AJHR 1864 E2 pp30–31; Whitaker memo 29 Feb 1864, ibid p31.

21 AJHR 1864 App to E2 p19; AJHR 1864 E2 pp16–17.

22 AJHR 1864 E2 pp17–20. The society was not convinced and in reply said 'The truth is that confiscation is persisted in because the colonists want the land, and they would rather that the last Maori should cease to exist than forgo their insatiable cupidity'; quoted in A. J. Harrop, *England and the Maori Wars*, London, 1937, p209.

23 See e.g. William Fox, *The Six Colonies of New Zealand*, London, 1851, pp54–56; William Fox, *The War in New Zealand*, London, 1866, pp15, 256, 258.

24 FitzGerald's happy phrase for the struggle of wits, or if that was too flattering an expression, of pens, between the governor and the 'memorandummies'; NZPD 1864–66 pp127–28.

25 Rutherford p506.

26 Fox *Six Colonies* p120; Rutherford p239.

27 AJHR 1883 A3 pp60–63; Fox *Six Colonies* and *War*.

28 AJHR 1864 E5 p12; Rutherford p282; Alfred Saunders, *History of New Zealand*, vol II, Christchurch, 1899, p112.

29 R. C. J. Stone, *Makers of Fortune: A*

Colonial Business Community and its Fall, Auckland, 1973, pp9, 174.

30 AJHR 1864 E2 pp35–46. For an amended version of the original draft see Irish University Press series of British Parliamentary Papers, Colonies, New Zealand, (hereafter IUP), vol 14, Shannon, 1969, pp19–20.

31 Whitaker memo 10 May 1864, AJHR 1864 E2 p40.

32 Grey memo 11 May 1864, ibid pp40–41; Whitaker memo 17 May 1864, ibid pp41–43; Whitaker memo 3 June 1864, ibid p46.

33 Grey memo 25 May 1864, ibid p44; Whitaker memo 3 June 1864, ibid p46.

34 Whitaker memo 30 May 1864, ibid p55; Grey memo 17 June 1864, ibid.

35 Cardwell despatch 26 April 1864, AJHR 1864 App to E2 pp20–22.

36 Grey despatch 22 Jan 1846, IUP vol 5, pp392–93; James Belich, *The New Zealand Wars and the Victorian Interpretation of Racial Conflict*, Auckland, 1986, p65.

37 AJHR 1864 E2 pp58–59.

38 Whitaker memo 2 Aug 1864, AJHR 1864 E2c p22.

39 Grey despatch 26 Aug 1864, AJHR 1864 E5 pp8–9. For Whitaker's view of this despatch see ibid E2 pp97–100.

40 For the proclamation and the sparring match between Grey and Whitaker which ensued see AJHR 1864 E2 pp89–97.

41 ibid pp95, 111.

42 AJHR 1864 E2a p9; Grey memo 10 Oct 1864, ibid p10.

43 ibid p25.

44 See e.g. Reader Wood memo 19 Nov 1864, AJHR 1864 E2c pp16–19.

45 *Gazette* 17 Dec 1864.

46 Alan D. Ward, 'The Origins of the Anglo-Maori Wars: A Reconsideration', *New Zealand Journal of History* 1, 2, 1967, p156; Jeanine Williams, 'Frederick Weld: A Political Biography', PhD thesis, University of Auckland, 1973, pp157–58, 167–69; Grey memo 30 Sept 1864, AJHR 1864 E2 p95; Harrop p406; Rutherford pp573–75; Weld memo 22 Nov 1864, AJHR 1864 A2; NZPD 1863–64 pp13–15; C. M. Sealy, 'A Study of the Policy of Land Confiscation as Applied in the District of Taranaki', MA thesis, University of New Zealand, 1949, p31.

47 Rusden *History* vol II p273; Sinclair *History* p143. See also Williams thesis pp176–79.

48 Cardwell despatch 27 March 1865, AJHR 1865 A6 p16; Weld memo 11 Aug 1865, AJHR 1865 A1 p26.

49 FitzGerald memo 30 Aug 1865, AJHR 1879, A8 p3; Weld memo 2 Sept 1865, AJHR 1865 A1 pp26–27.

50 *Gazette* 5 Sept 1865.

CHAPTER THREE

1 NZPD 1872 xiii pp471–77; AJHR 1873 C4a pp1–2; AJHR 1880 G2 ppxiii, xvii, 36–38; AJHR 1882 G5a p2.

2 AJHR 1880 G2 pxvii.

3 AJHR 1879 A8 pp3–5.

4 AJHR 1872 C4 pp26–27.

5 NZPD 1872 xii p640.

6 AJHR 1879 A8 p6.

7 NZPD 1872 xii p639.

8 ibid p167.

9 NZPD 1872 xiii p154; Wi Parata to McDonnell 12 Sept 1872, AJHR 1880 G2 App A p6.

10 NZPD 1872 xiii pp431, 467, 469–70; Reports of Select Committee on Native Affairs no.7, 25 Sept 1872, AJHR 1872 H11 p4.

11 NZPD 1872 xiii p471.

12 There is a suggestion that he was prepared to use Hone Mohi Tawhai as a mediator between himself and the government; AJHR 1880 G2 pxix. The only correspondence concerning the 'messenger sent by Te Whiti' that has survived suggests

simply that Te Whiti invited Ngapuhi to the March 1872 hui at Parihaka; McLean to Tawhai 30 March 1872, MA 4/78. It seems unlikely that Te Whiti should surrender his mana by asking either Tawhai or Ngapuhi to act as a mediator for him. In any case the government was not prepared to recognise his mana by negotiating with him.

13 For conflicting views see Parris report 23 March 1870, AJHR 1870 A16 p18: 'Te Whiti is one of the few who never embraced Hauhauism'; Bowen despatch 6 Oct 1870, AJHR 1871 A1 p50: 'Te Whiti . . . now professes . . . to be a prophet of the Hauhau creed'; West Coast Commissioners' statement, AJHR 1880 G2 pviii:
'. . . men like Te Whiti . . . who never were in arms against the Queen'; Hadfield to Gordon 12 Nov 1881, AJHR 1888 A1 p3: 'Neither he nor Tohu nor any of his people, about 250, including women and children, ever took part in the rebellion'. Cowan's informant Te Kahu Pukoro as a twelve-year-old boy saw Te Whiti and Tohu at Sentry Hill, but they carried tokotoko, not guns; Cowan *Wars* p23.

14 Hadfield to Gordon 12 Nov 1881, AJHR 1888 A1 p3.

15 European perceptions of individual Maori had a lot to do with appearances. Te Whiti was described as having 'almost European features', like those of a half-caste or a Spaniard, and he was compared favourably with the darker skinned Tohu; Rusden *History* vol III p240; S. J. Bryant, 'Te Whiti O Rongomai: A Reassessment', MA extended essay, University of Canterbury, 1978, pp33–34. Even so, to the settler mind at least, there was little to choose between one Maori and another, and by popular reasoning Te Whiti was associated with Tohu, who was sometimes confused with Titokowaru, whose exploits were equated with those of Te Kooti.

16 Knollys report 31 Dec 1880, AJHR 1881 A1 p25.

17 AJHR 1869 A10 pp45–47, A13 p22; Belich chapter 12.

18 Parris to McLean 23 Oct 1869, McLean Mss 494. Even in the period of 'uneasy peace' before Titokowaru's war, the west coast tribes controlled the passage of Europeans by the coast road; see e.g. AJHR 1867 A21 p3.

19 Parris report 23 March 1870, AJHR 1870 A16 pp18–19.

20 Parris to McLean 12 August 1870, McLean Mss 494.

21 Bowen despatch 6 Oct 1870, AJHR 1871 A1 p50; AJHR 1871 F6b pp5–10; Parris to McLean 25 Sept 1870, McLean Mss 494.

22 AJHR 1880 G2 ppxxxviii, 31; AJHR 1884 A5a pp2–3; AJHR 1872 C4 pp27–28.

23 AJHR 1868 A8 pp41–42; Belich pp235–36.

24 Parris report 6 July 1872, AJHR 1872 F3 p13.

25 NZPD 1872 xii p639.

26 AJHR 1872 F3 p13.

27 Saunders pp386, 401; *Timaru Herald* quoted in *Patea Mail* 30 Oct 1878.

28 W. J. Parker, 'John Sheehan, Native Minister and Colonial', MA thesis, University of Auckland, 1963, pp88, 117–18; A. Ward *Show of Justice* p280.

29 AJHR 1878 G1 p14.

30 See e.g. NZPD 1877 xxvii pp230–31; Sharron Mary Cole, 'The Repudiation Movement: A Study of the Maori Land Protest Movement in Hawkes Bay in the 1870's', MA thesis, Massey University, 1977, pp69–85, 97–99; Parker thesis pp116, 125–26; R. C. J. Stone, 'The Maori Lands Question and the Fall of the Grey Government, 1879', *New Zealand Journal of History* 1, 1, 1967, pp52–54.

31 NZPD 1877 xxvii pp232–33.

32 See e.g. NZPD 1877 xxvii p233, ibid 1878 xxix p221; Alfred K. Newman, 'A Study of the Causes leading to the Extinction of the Maori', *Transactions and Proceedings of the New Zealand Institute* 14, 1881, pp459–77; Te Rangi Hiroa, 'The Passing of the Maori', *Transactions and Proceedings of the New Zealand Institute* 55, 1924, pp362–75; M. P. K. Sorrenson, *Maori Origins and Migrations: The Genesis of Some Pakeha Myths and Legends*, Auckland, 1979, pp73, 75, 83–84.

33 NZPD 1877 xxvii p239.

34 AJHR 1878 G3 pp1–3, 18–21; Rutherford pp607–09.

35 The following section is based on accounts from the *New Zealander*, *Taranaki Herald* and *New Zealand Herald* reprinted in AJHR 1878 G3 pp41–70.

36 On paper, at least, Teira 'and others' were the official hosts. This was a convenient fiction which enabled Brown (with Sheehan's approval) to charge the costs of the meeting to the confiscated lands account; AJHR 1880 G2 pp88–91.

37 Cooper minute 25 Dec 1871, approved by McLean 26 Dec 1871, AJHR 1880 G2 pxvii.

38 AJHR 1880 G2 pxvii.

39 ibid ppxxiii, xli–xliii.

40 ibid p72.

41 Brown to McLean 21 June 1876, McLean Mss 178.

42 Brown to McLean 11 Oct 1876, ibid; R. S. Thompson to Brown 6 Aug 1878, LE 1/1879/3.

43 AJHR 1880 G2 pxxvii.

44 Thompson to Brown 10 Jan 1879, LE 1/1879/3.

45 A. Ward *Show of Justice* p237; Judith Bassett, *Sir Henry Atkinson 1831–1892*, Auckland, 1975, p28.

46 No stigma over land deals ever attached to Sheehan while in office, although his later handling of the Patetere purchase was another matter. See e.g. Parker thesis pp153, 160, 182–85.

47 G. H. Scholefield, ed., *A Dictionary of New Zealand Biography*, vol I, Wellington, 1940, pp98–99, and *Newspapers in New Zealand*, Wellington, 1958, pp2, 129–30.

48 D. W. Hinch, 'General Elections in Taranaki 1879–1884', MA thesis, Victoria University of Wellington, 1968, p141. Hinch said Brown was always in debt and the files of the *Taranaki News* are incomplete as he sold them to raise money; ibid p140.

49 A. Ward *Show of Justice* p259; Brown to McLean 24 March and 11 May 1870, McLean Mss 178.

50 Brown to McLean 21 June 1876, McLean Mss 178.

51 AJHR 1877 G1 p13; AJHR 1876 G1 p31.

52 See e.g AJHR 1864 App to E2 p7; AJHR 1878 G3 p54.

53 AJHR 1880 G2 p50.

54 ibid pxxv.

55 In the House on 9 Aug 1879, Sheehan claimed that 'twelve months ago' he had offered Te Whiti funds with which to contest his right to the land in a court of law. Grey claimed the offer was made to Bob Erangi (Ngarongomate), not Te Whiti; NZPD 1879 xxxi p557. There is no official record that any such offer was ever made.

56 AJHR 1880 G2 p49.

57 ibid p72.

58 ibid pp68–69, 47.

59 ibid p69.

60 Brown report 10 Aug 1878, AJHR 1878 G5 p1.

61 NZPD 1872 xiii p431. See also Ione Margaret Bremer, 'The Early Development of the Patea-Waverley District: A Study of the Problems of Settling Confiscated Land', MA thesis, Victoria University of Wellington, 1962, pp126–27; and on intra-departmental rivalry see A. Ward *Show of Justice* p259.

62 Brown report 10 Aug 1878, AJHR 1878 G5 p1.
63 AJHR 1878 G5 p1. The chief's name is variously written Te Ika, Te Iki, Te Ike.
64 Dillon Bell 'was impressed with a feeling of great anxiety' when he read Brown's report of 10 August 1878 when it was finally laid on the table of the House on 2 October of that year. He felt McLean's policy 'was going to be hastily reversed by taking forcible possession of the land'; NZPD 1879 xxxi p152.
65 Brown report 10 Aug 1878, AJHR 1878 G5 pp1, 2; AJHR 1880 G2 pxlvii.
66 NZPD 1878 xxviii pp102–03.
67 Brown report 10 Aug 1878, AJHR 1878 G5 p2.
68 Brown to Sheehan 21 Aug 1878, AJHR 1881 G5 pp15–16. His claim was summarily dismissed by Fox as worthless since, among other things, 'he never did complete the surveys, nor peaceably or otherwise acquire the Plains'; Fox report 22 April 1881, ibid p15.
69 See correspondence regarding the incident dated 21 Sept to 10 Nov 1878 in AJHR 1878 G11 and 1879 G4. See also Parris report 23 May 1882, AJHR 1882 G1 pp11–12.
70 He had been 'a brave and daring scout for McDonnell in 1869–70; McDonnell did not regard his killing of McLean . . . as murder'; A. Ward *Show of Justice* fn22 p346.
71 He was warned of an approaching search party one day in the bush by Kimble Bent and Pakanga of Ngatimaniapoto; James Cowan, *The Adventures of Kimble Bent: A Story of Wild Life in the New Zealand Bush*, Christchurch, 1911, pp313–17.

CHAPTER FOUR

1 Sheehan memo 14 April 1879, AJHR 1879 Sess I C4 p4.
2 Evidence of Humphries, Chief Surveyor, 15 March 1880, AJHR 1880 G2 p69.
3 Finnerty to Humphries 18 March 1880, ibid App E p7.
4 Evidence of Humphries 15 March 1880, AJHR 1880 G2 pp69–70. Opposition to surveying of confiscated land was not new. Wi Kingi te Rangitake had sent women to pull up survey pegs at Waitara in February 1860; Rutherford p449. In 1866–67 the surveys south of the Waingongoro were continually interrupted; Bremer thesis p24; Rutherford p551. In 1866 the Pirirakau people of Tauranga turned back surveyors and in early 1867 exchanged fire with the military on the confiscation boundary; Belich p210; Evelyn Stokes, 'Te Raupatu O Tauranga: A Study of Land Transactions and Race Relations at Tauranga 1864–1886', *Occasional Paper, Centre for Maori Studies and Research, University of Waikato*, No 3, 1978, p32.
5 Evidence of Finnerty, Assistant Surveyor, 23 March 1880, AJHR 1880 G2 p81.
6 Brown report 22 July 1879, AJHR 1879 Sess II G7.
7 ibid.
8 Sheehan memo 14 April 1879, AJHR 1879 Sess I C4 pp1–5.
9 NZPD 1879 xxxi pp44–45.
10 For a contrary view see Parker thesis pp173–78.
11 Parris report 15 May 1882, AJHR 1882 G1 p9.
12 AJHR 1880 G2 pp70–71.
13 Brown report 2 April 1879, AJHR 1879 Sess I C4 p10.
14 *Patea Mail* 29 March 1879.
15 AJHR 1880 G2 pp69, 73, 74.
16 Fox memo on 'The Final Payments of "Takoha" ' 7 June 1883, AJHR 1883 G3 p25.
17 Brown evidence 16 March 1880, AJHR 1880 G2 pp73–74; NZPD 1879 xxxi p187.

[18] AJHR 1880 G2 passim.
[19] ibid p47.
[20] ibid pxi.
[21] Brown report 2 April 1879, AJHR 1879 Sess I C4 p10.
[22] For details of the controversy over the sale of the plains between the government and the Taranaki Land Board, who legally controlled the confiscated land, see AJHR 1880 G2 ppxxx–xxxii, 64–68.
[23] ibid ppxxvii, xxviii, 47.
[24] Bell to Hall 14 April 1879, Hall Mss vol 37.
[25] Sheehan memo 14 April 1879, AJHR 1879 Sess I C4 p1.
[26] AJHR 1880 G2 p74.
[27] A. Ward *Show of Justice* pp207–08, 237–38, 340 fn3. As a land purchase officer in the Thames district in the late 1860s Mackay was paid 'threepence per acre on 468,358 acres and twopence per acre on 307,079 acres' amounting to £8,413-9-4, in addition to whatever he earned from his private buying conducted at the same time; Native Affairs Committee petition no.326/1880, LE 1/1880/6.
[28] AJHR 1880 G2 App A pp9–12.
[29] Mackay report 14 April 1879, AJHR 1879 Sess I C4 pp6–8.
[30] Blake's mother was Ngamahanga, a Taranaki hapu, and he was married at one time to Takiora Grey, who was 'nearly taken from him' and given to Brown.
[31] Mackay and Blake to Sheehan 4 April 1879, AJHR 1880 G2 App A pp9–12.
[32] NZPD 1879 xxxi p185.
[33] Sheehan to Mackay 5 April 1879, AJHR 1880 G2 App A p12.
[34] AJHR 1880 G2 p66.
[35] Sheehan memo 14 April 1879, AJHR 1879 Sess I C4 p1.
[36] ibid pp2–4; AJHR 1880 G2 pli.
[37] AJHR 1880 G2 p72; AJHR 1879 Sess I C4 p3; AJHR 1880 G2 App A part II p2.
[38] Parris report 6 July 1872, AJHR 1872 F3 p13; Brown report 23 May 1876, AJHR 1876 G1 p32.
[39] Sheehan memo 14 April 1879, AJHR 1879 Sess I C4 p3. For official European reports of Te Whiti's supposed religious beliefs see e.g. AJHR 1870 A16 p18, 1871 F6b p8, 1872 F3a p24, 1876 G1 p32, 1879 Sess I C4 p7.
[40] Pihama had long been bought off by the government; A. Ward *Show of Justice* p266; AJHR 1881 G11 pp1–2. He was the source, via Bryce, of many myths about Te Whiti; see e.g. Bryce 'Fanaticism in the Maori Race'.
[41] *Patea Mail* 26 March 1879.
[42] AJHR 1880 G2 App A pp9–12; AJHR 1879 Sess I C4 pp6–8.
[43] Sheehan to Mackay 5 April 1879, AJHR 1880 G2 App A p12.
[44] NZPD 1880 xxxvi p298.
[45] Mackay to Sheehan 6 May 1879, AJHR 1880 G2 App A p13.
[46] Mackay to Sheehan 14 April 1879, AJHR 1879 Sess I C4 p8; Mackay to Sheehan 6 May 1879, AJHR 1880 G2 App A p13.
[47] NZPD 1882 xli p142.
[48] LE 1/1879/3.
[49] AJHR 1878 G3 p51.
[50] Thompson to Brown 19 May 1879, LE 1/1879/3; Thompson to Roberts 23 Aug 1880, ibid.
[51] Te Whiti disputed the *validity*, not the *legality* of the confiscation. He had talked to Mackay in terms of conquest and occupation, of unfulfilled promises and the inconsistency of government officials, not in terms of legality with its implications of recourse to European law. His faith in the law might be judged from his remark that if he was to surrender Hiroki for trial by the Supreme Court, the court should sit on the marae at Parihaka.
[52] Thompson to Brown 19 May 1879, LE 1/1879/3. The Marquis of Normanby had left New Zealand on

20 February 1879; Sir Hercules Robinson arrived on 27 March.
53 ibid; Brown to Grey 25 June 1879, PM 6/2.
54 Quoted in *Taranaki News* 3 May 1879.
55 AJHR 1880 G2 pxxx.
56 The newspapers gave the settler's name as Courtney; some official papers gave it as Courtenay.
57 May correspondence, LE 1/1879/135.
58 ibid.
59 Editorial, *Taranaki News* 31 May 1879, *New Zealand Herald* 29 May 1879.
60 AJHR 1880 G2 ppxxxix, 52.
61 Crown grants had been issued to Europeans in the district, but not to Maori.
62 Extract from *Taranaki Herald* 2 June 1879, in May correspondence, LE 1/1879/135.
63 See e.g. Bremer thesis chapter 5.
64 Oliver *Story* p255.
65 Bryce memo 9 Sept 1882, AJHR 1883 A1 p5.
66 Extract from *Taranaki Herald* 5 June 1879, in May correspondence, LE 1/1879/135.
67 Brown report 11 June 1879, AJHR 1879 Sess I G1 p20.
68 ibid G6.
69 *Taranaki News* 7 June 1879.
70 June correspondence, LE 1/1879/135.
71 See e.g. Stone 'The Maori Lands Question' pp56–60.
72 AJHR 1879 Sess I G2 pp15–16; NZPD 1879 xxxi p73.
73 See e.g. correspondence May, June, July 1879, LE 1/1879/135.
74 Stone 'The Maori Lands Question' p56.
75 June correspondence, LE 1/1879/135.
76 *Patea Mail* 7 June 1879.
77 *New Zealand Herald* 5 and 28 June 1879.
78 Extract from *Taranaki Herald* 2 June 1879, in May correspondence, LE 1/1879/135.
79 NZPD 1880 xxxvi p312.
80 June correspondence, LE 1/1879/135; Brown to Grey 25 June 1879, PM 6/2.
81 June correspondence, LE 1/1879/135.
82 ibid. See also telegrams from Grey to civil and military officers, PM 6/2.
83 Brown to Sheehan 2 July 1879, transmitting Katene's report of the meeting, July correspondence, LE 1/1879/135. It was not Mr Barrow that Titokowaru had in mind to cook, but a midday kai for his ploughmen.
84 Brown to Sheehan 3 July 1879, ibid.
85 *Taranaki News* 5 July 1879.
86 As many as 34 ploughed in one day and 180 were arrested in all; 'Epitome of Events', compiled from *Taranaki Herald*, MA 4/31.
87 *Taranaki News* 26 July 1879. Te Mahuki, of Ngatimaniapoto, achieved notoriety in March 1883 when he captured Hursthouse whom Bryce had sent to survey the railway route through the King Country; *New Zealand Herald* 27 March 1883, reprinted in IUP vol 17 pp91–95. See also Wilkinson report 11 June 1883, AJHR 1883 G1 pp5–6.
88 *Taranaki News* 2 Aug 1879.
89 Mackay report 29 July 1879, AJHR 1879 Sess I G10 pp1–2.
90 *Gazette* 18 Sept 1879.
91 Mackay report 29 July 1879, AJHR 1879 Sess I G10 p2.
92 See e.g. Rutherford pp618–21; Saunders pp403–05; Stone 'The Maori Lands Question' pp64–65; T. G. Wilson, 'The Grey Government 1877–9: An Episode in the Rise of Liberalism in New Zealand', *Auckland University College Bulletin* No 45, History Series No 5, 1954, pp36–40.
93 AJHR 1879 A9: NZPD 1879 xxxi p83.
94 Saunders p406.
95 NZPD 1879 xxxi pp72–75. Brown

demonstrated his powers of prophecy when he wrote to Mantell on 5 Nov 1879; 'Sheehan . . . has many good points but he also has many bad ones, and his surroundings are worse still. I do not think it will be long before he kills himself by his excesses, which his fall will cause him to give way to altogether'; Mantell Mss 250. Sheehan died of double pneumonia in June 1885, just short of his 41st birthday; Parker thesis p199.

96 Grey and Normanby had had a very strained relationship. Normanby thought Grey 'without any exception, the man *least to be trusted* that I have ever met', G26/1; Rutherford pp604–06, 624. Normanby was doubtless instrumental in the question of Fox's knighthood.

97 NZPD 1879 xxxi pp80–83.

98 ibid p153.

99 ibid pp184–85.

100 ibid pp184, 186. Mackay found Te Whiti 'uncommonly sharp when he came to talk business'; newspaper report quoted in Rusden *History* vol III p 265.

101 NZPD 1879 xxxi pp528–29, 530.

102 'Epitome of Events' 14 July 1879, MA 4/31; AJHR 1880 G2 pxxxix.

103 Bryce to Hall 8 Jan 1880, Hall Mss vol 41; see also Bryce to Matakatea 4 October 1880, AJHR 1881 G7 P4.

104 NZPD 1879 xxxi p541.

105 ibid pp538ff, 551ff.

106 Even worse than this bill was the Peace Preservation Bill introduced at the same time. It passed the House without debate or division but caused consternation in the Council where Dillon Bell called it an invitation to war and an 'outrage upon our civilization'. He successfully moved to have the bill shelved at its second reading; NZPD 1879 xxxi p544.

107 ibid p553.

108 A. Ward 'Origins' p160; R. F. Irvine and O. T. J. Alpers, *The Progress of New Zealand in the Century*, London, 1902, p304.

109 In the Taranaki election campaign much was made of the 'menace of Parihaka' by the more militant candidates. The fact that moderates not militants were elected had more to do with the overriding importance of other issues than with that of forcing Te Whiti to accept European supremacy by militant or moderate means. For a somewhat different view see Hinch thesis pp92–93.

CHAPTER FIVE

1 Te Whiti 18 May 1880, LE 1/1879/3.

2 Rutherford pp624–28; Saunders pp407–18; Stone 'The Maori Lands Question' pp66–70; Wilson pp41–59.

3 Saunders pp391, 408, 418.

4 NZPD 1879 xxxii pp4, 358.

5 ibid p359.

6 Rusden *History* vol III pp285–86. These remarks were made much of by the prosecuting counsel in the Bryce v Rusden libel trial; *Bryce v Rusden* pp10–11.

7 Scholefield *Dictionary* vol I pp109, 111; A. Ward *Show of Justice* p293.

8 NZPD 1879 xxxii p415.

9 ibid p4; Panui 26 Aug 1879, MA 24/20.

10 See e.g. Blake memo 4 April 1879, AJHR 1879 Sess I C4 p9.

11 *Taranaki News* 20 Sept 1879.

12 Thompson to Whitmore 19 Sept 1879, LE 1/1879/135; Thompson to Sheehan 19 Sept 1879, LE 1/1879/3.

13 Thompson to Sheehan 22 Sept 1879, LE 1/1879/3. The voice of the ploughmen was indeed heard. Their 'proceedings . . . undoubtedly led to the appointment of the Royal Commission, and that Commission at once recognised the existence of the grievances . . . which, except for that Commission, would probably be

yet undealt with'; Gordon report 26 Feb 1881, AJHR 1882 A8 p10.

14 Thompson to Brown 10 Nov 1879, LE 1/1879/3.

15 ibid.

16 Thompson to Bryce 19 Nov 1879, ibid; Brown to Bryce 2 Dec 1879, MA 2/17.

17 Thompson to Bryce 19 Dec 1879, LE 1/1879/3.

18 Sheehan wrote him a sort of testimonial for his 'honest and valuable services' and regretted he and Brown had not seen to the increase in salary months before; Sheehan to Thompson 13 Dec 1879, ibid.

19 Bryce had threatened the House with his resignation by saying he would 'not like to take the responsibility of remaining in office' if they decreed that the trials were to be held as scheduled; NZPD 1879 xxxiv p798.

20 NZPD 1879 xxxiv pp621, 796, 797.

21 ibid pp621, 793, 794.

22 ibid p863.

23 ibid pp864–65.

24 As early as 1869 Rolleston had proposed a commission to inquire into relations between the races. For the dismissive comments of Fox and Bell on the proposal see NZPD 1869 vi pp65, 66, 79–81.

25 Scholefield *Dictionary* vol I pp56–61.

26 AJHR 1880 G2 App A pp1–2.

27 The reporting date was later extended. The First Report is dated 15 March, the Second Report 14 July and the Third Report 5 August 1880.

28 AJHR 1880 G2 App A pp2–3.

29 In the event so few Maori appeared before the commissioners that decisions about reserves were made for them in their absence.

30 Witness the conclusions of the West Coast Commission, and of the 1926 Sim Commission; AJHR 1880 G2; AJHR 1928 G7.

31 *Gazette* 24 Dec 1879.

32 Bryce to Hall 8 Jan 1880, Hall Mss vol 41. Ninety-one prisoners went to Dunedin, 39 to Hokitika; NZPD 1880 xxxv p229.

33 NZPD 1880 xxxvi p354. See also a letter signed by 'Renata Kawepo and the Ngatikahungunu Tribe' and 'Karanamate Kapukaiotu and the whole of the Ngatiraukawa Tribe' printed in the pro-government *New Zealand Times* and reprinted in translation in the *Patea Mail* 25 Feb 1880.

34 See e.g. Edward Ellison, 'Sacred Stone Links Taranaki and Otago', *Historic Places* 19, 1987, pp7–11.

35 Hall to Bryce and Fox to Bell 28 Jan 1880, Hall Mss vol 41.

36 NZPD 1880 xxxvi pp293–95. See also ibid pp313–15.

37 *Patea Mail* 4 Feb 1880.

38 Fox to Hall 31 Jan 1880, Hall Mss vol 41.

39 Hall to Fox 3 March 1880, Hall Mss vol 4.

40 UPA report 23 March 1881 of Bryce speech in explanation of his resignation, enclosed in Gordon despatch 23 April 1881, IUP vol 16 p475.

41 Robinson confidential despatch 29 Dec 1879, G 26/1.

42 Robinson confidential despatch 31 Jan 1880, ibid.

43 *Patea Mail* 17 Jan 1880.

44 NZPD 1880 xxxv p309.

45 Bryce to Robinson quoted in Robinson confidential despatch 25 Feb 1880, G 26/1.

46 Thompson to Roberts 29 Feb 1880, reporting a conversation with the commissioners and adding a 'suitable message' (generosity repaid by generosity) to go with the return gift; LE 1/1879/3.

47 Thompson to Roberts 24 Feb 1880, ibid; Roberts to Bryce 24 Feb 1880, AJHR 1883 A4 p18.

48 Thompson to Bryce 25 and 26 Feb 1880, LE 1/1879/3. Again Thompson had read his man. Bryce

later admitted publicly that he did 'strongly desire' to associate his name with the settlement of the west coast difficulty; UPA report enclosed in Gordon despatch 23 April 1881, IUP vol 16 p477.

49 Bryce to Thompson 27 Feb 1880, LE 1/1879/3.

50 The commission sat at Oeo, Hawera, Waitara, Patea and New Plymouth between 11 February and 30 March, and in Wellington on 12 May and 3 June. The commissioners also corresponded with ministers and officials past and present in an effort to get to the bottom of the 'alleged promises'. Stafford suggested 'Wi Tako has . . . of all the Maoris the most knowledge as to promises alleged to have been made by Ministers with respect to the confiscated lands on the West Coast'; AJHR 1880 G2 App A p18. Wi Tako was not called to give evidence before the commissioners.

51 Hall to Bell 16 Feb 1880, Hall Mss vol 3.

52 Te Whiti was reported to be 'perfectly indifferent' to the commission and when told it would sit at Oeo, to have said 'Yes, they are doing that for the purpose of catching the Maoris as they return from Parihaka as they cannot catch them otherwise'; *Lyttelton Times* quoted in *Patea Mail* 28 Feb 1880.

53 AJHR 1880 G2 p7.

54 AJHR 1880 G2 pxlvii; Fox, 'Notes on the Treaty of Waitangi; The New Zealand Settlements Acts; Proclamations of Confiscation etc', undated but enclosed with Hall memo to governor 14 Feb 1881, G 17/8.

55 Katene of Weriweri told the commissioners that had Te Whiti called the meetings and appointed the commission they would have seen 'what a large number of Natives would have attended'; AJHR 1880 G2 p4.

56 ibid p33.

57 Bryce to Hall 19 March 1880, Hall Mss vol 41; Hall to Bryce 19 March 1880, ibid vol 4.

58 'Te Whiti has shown no feeling of dislike or bitterness towards our race. On the contrary, whether at the summit of his prosperity, and when he might naturally consider himself to be master of the situation; or, when his endurance was tried to the uttermost by the near approach of our forces to Parihaka, everyone was freely admitted to his settlement, and treated there with the utmost courtesy'; Parris report 15 May 1882, AJHR 1882 G1 p11.

59 *Patea Mail* 27 March 1880.

60 Thompson to Roberts 1, 5 and 30 April 1880, LE 1/1879/3.

61 *Taranaki News* 20 March 1880.

62 West Coast Commission First Report, AJHR 1880 G2 ppv–x.

63 Hall to Bryce and Hall to Fox 2 April 1880, Hall to Atkinson 3 April 1880, Hall Mss vol 4; Atkinson to commissioners 18 March 1880, G. H. Scholefield, ed., *The Richmond-Atkinson Papers*, vol II, Wellington, 1960, p476.

64 NZPD 1881 x1 p733; Atkinson to Hall 5 April 1880 quoting telegram from Bryce, Scholefield *R-A Papers* p477; Hall to Fox 3 March 1880, Hall Mss vol 4.

65 Bryce 'Fanaticism in the Maori Race'.

66 Hall to Fox 26 March 1880, Hall Mss vol 4; Thompson to Roberts 30 April 1880, LE 1/1879/3.

67 Atkinson to Hall 5 April 1880 quoting Parris telegram, Scholefield *R-A Papers* p477.

68 *The Bulletin* (Sydney) 25 March 1905; *Patea Mail* 24 Jan 1880; Croumbie-Brown to Hall 1 and 7 Nov 1879, Hall Mss vol 37.

69 Croumbie-Brown to Hall 13 Nov 1879, Hall Mss vol 37.

70 'Report on Position etc, etc, of

Parihaka, the Stronghold of Te Whiti', 10 Nov 1879, AC 3528 P 79.

71 Hall to Rolleston 4 Jan 1880, Hall Mss vol 27. According to the *Lyttelton Times* of 30 March 1881 the government had correspondents attached to both the armed constabulary and the West Coast Commission so that they might furnish the Christchurch *Press* and 'other Ministerial organs' with 'approved reports'.

72 Hall to Fox 20 Feb 1880, Hall Mss vol 3.

73 Hall to Fox 3 March 1880, Hall Mss vol 4; Fox to Hall 6 Nov 1880, ibid vol 39.

74 NZPD 1880 xxxvi pp298–99.

75 Robinson confidential despatch 24 April 1880, G 26/1; Brown report 18 May 1880, AJHR 1880 G4 p17.

76 Bryce memo 21 May 1880, enclosed in Robinson confidential despatch 22 May 1880, G 26/1.

77 Thompson to Roberts 19 May 1880, LE 1/1879/3.

78 First Report 15 March 1880, AJHR 1880 G2 pvii.

79 Thompson to Roberts 19 June 1880, LE 1/1879/3.

80 Bryce 'Fanaticism in the Maori Race'.

81 *Gazette* 1 April and 1 July 1880.

82 NZPD 1880 xxxv pp308–09. The Second Report of the West Coast Commission reviewed the history of European-Maori relations and events on the west coast which had led to the troubles which existed there; AJHR 1880 G2 ppxi–xliv and appendices.

83 Robinson despatch 14 Aug 1880, IUP vol 16 p361.

84 This 'official' view of Te Whiti's status derived from Pihama's assessment of the situation. In 1880 he told Bryce 'I am a great chief . . . Te Whiti is not a great chief'; Bryce 'Fanaticism in the Maori Race'.

85 NZPD 1880 xxxvi pp284ff, 326.

86 Hall to Fox 26 March 1880, Hall Mss vol 4.

87 NZPD 1880 xxxvi pp285, 297–98, 305, 306, 308–09.

88 *Taranaki Herald* 24 Sept 1880, report on the trial of the fencers, reprinted in IUP vol 16 p369.

89 Gordon report 26 Feb 1881, AJHR 1882 A8 p9. Bryce sent a very different account to Robinson on 13 Aug 1880; IUP vol 16 pp361–62. The original version of Bryce's report (MA 4/30) contains an unsubstantiated statement that Te Whetu was 'a very violent man and a reputed murderer'. This remark served to influence Robinson's thinking, but was not repeated in the printed version. See also NZPD 1880 xxxvi p519.

90 *Patea County Mail* 29 July 1880.

91 AJHR 1880 G2 plxii; Gordon report 26 Feb 1881, AJHR 1882 A8 p10; *Taranaki News* 24 July 1880; Robinson to Kimberley 14 Dec 1880, AJHR 1883 A5 p3.

92 Bryce to governor 13 Aug 1880, IUP vol 16 p361.

93 Robinson to Kimberley 14 Dec 1880, AJHR 1883 A5 p3.

94 NZPD 1880 xxxvii pp17–26.

95 West Coast Commission Third Report 5 Aug 1880, AJHR 1880 G2 ppxlv–lxiv.

96 NZPD 1880 xxxvii p79.

97 It was not so clear. In April 1879 nothing had been said to Te Whiti and his people 'of an authoritative character as to the intentions of the Government with reference to their particular tribal estate'; Sheehan memo 14 April 1879, AJHR 1879 Sess I C4 p3. See AJHR 1880 G2 App A part II for disagreement between Grey and Sheehan on the question of the restoration of the Parihaka block.

98 AJHR 1880 G2 ppli, liii.

99 Bryce to governor 13 Aug 1880, IUP vol 16, p362.

100 Gordon report 26 Feb 1881, AJHR 1882 A8 p8.
101 Robinson to Kimberley 14 Dec 1880, AJHR 1883 A5 p3.
102 NZPD 1880 xxxvii pp480–83.
103 ibid pp486–91, 528.
104 *Taranaki Herald* 23, 24 and 25 Sept 1880, enclosed with Prendergast despatch 9 Oct 1880, IUP vol 16 pp366–75.
105 Hall to Bryce 24 June 1880, Hall Mss vol 4.
106 Bryce to Hall 22 Sept and 5 Dec 1880, Hall Mss vol 41.
107 Hall to Atkinson 14 Sept transmitting Whitaker's telegram to Hall of 13 Sept 1880, Hall Mss folio 297.
108 Hall to Whitaker 23 Sept 1880, Hall Mss vol 41; Whitaker to Hall 30 Sept 1880, ibid.
109 *Taranaki News* 25 Sept 1880.
110 Thompson to Roberts 19 Sept 1880, LE 1/1879/3.
111 Bryce to Hall 2 Oct 1880, Hall Mss vol 41; Hall to Bryce 3 Oct 1880, ibid vol 5.
112 Bryce to Matakatea 4 Oct 1880, AJHR 1881 G7 pp4–5.
113 NZPD 1879 xxxi p222.
114 NZPD 1879 xxxiv p789.
115 A big group assembled to welcome him and his companions, twenty-five in all, when the *Hinemoa* reached New Plymouth. There was a karanga from the shore, they were welcomed by Maori and Europeans alike, and wept over at a formal hui at the Native Office; *New Zealand Times* 9 Oct 1880.
116 Thompson to Roberts 23 Aug and 17 Oct 1880, LE 1/1879/3.
117 'I am heartily glad you have at last got rid of that fellow Thompson. I never could understand what Bryce kept him on for. I feel satisfied that he has been playing the traitor all along and been one of Te Whiti's evil genii'; Fox to Hall 6 Nov 1880, Hall Mss vol 39.
118 *Patea County Mail* 2 Dec 1880.
119 Thompson to Bryce 27 Oct 1880, LE 1/1879/3. See also NZPD 1881 xxxviii p296, ibid xl p570. In the early 1900s Thompson was proprietor, editor and for most part writer of the *Maori Record*, a monthly journal published from July 1905 to June 1907, 'devoted to the advancement of the Maori people' and which placed their 'grievances, desires and aspirations . . . before their European fellow-subjects'; *Maori Record* Aug 1905. Thompson died in Aug 1907; *Hawera Star* 22 July 1983.
120 See e.g. Hall to Gordon 22 Dec 1880, AJHR 1881 A1 p21; Parris report 15 May 1882, AJHR 1882 G1 p10.
121 The government of the day had employed the same device with Wi Kingi te Rangitake; Sim report 29 June 1927, AJHR 1928 G7 p7.
122 Fox to Hall 30 Sept 1880, Hall Mss vol 39. On 14 July 1881 the reports were still not translated. Hutchison said in the House he had ascertained from the Maori members that Te Whiti only knew of the reports 'by scraps, and by little bits now and again; that English friends who understood Maori, had told him pieces . . . but he did not know exactly and fully' their contents; and Hutchison moved that they be translated, printed and circulated without delay. The motion was agreed to; NZPD 1881 xxxviii p479.
123 Hall to Fox 18 Oct 1880, Hall Mss vol 5.
124 Hall to Bell 2 Nov 1880, ibid; Hall to Gordon 22 Dec 1880, AJHR 1881 A1 p21.
125 Fox to Hall 6 Nov 1880, Hall Mss vol 39.
126 Parris report 19 Nov 1880, AJHR 1881 A1 pp22–23.

CHAPTER SIX

1 Michel Quoist, *Prayers of Life*, Dublin, 1963, p8.

2 J. K. Chapman, *The Career of Arthur Hamilton Gordon, First Lord Stanmore, 1829–1912*, Toronto, 1964, chapter 6. See also Peter France, 'The Founding of an Orthodoxy: Sir Arthur Gordon and the Doctrine of the Fijian Way of Life', *Journal of the Polynesian Society* 77, 1, 1968, pp6–10.

3 Parris report 19 Nov 1880, AJHR 1881 A1 p23.

4 Hall to Vogel 14 Aug 1880, Hall Mss vol 4; Hall to Vogel 6 and 30 Dec 1880, ibid vol 5.

5 Fox to Hall 6 Nov 1880, Hall Mss vol 39.

6 Brown to Mantell 18 Feb 1880, Mantell Mss 250.

7 Rolleston diary 2 Oct 1881.

8 Quoted in *New Zealand Herald* 20 Jan 1881.

9 See e.g. Bell to premier 3 Nov 1881, PM 5/1; Bell to premier 9 Feb 1883, MA 23/1 83/102; R. M. Dalziel, *The Origins of New Zealand Diplomacy: The Agent-General in London 1870–1905*, Wellington, 1975, pp95, 109, 112.

10 AJHR 1881 G5 p7.

11 Hall to Bell 12 Dec 1880, Hall Mss vol 5.

12 Bryce to Hall 11 and 24 Nov 1880, Hall Mss vol 41; *New Zealand Herald* 24 Nov 1880.

13 Kimberley to administrator 22 Oct 1880, AJHR 1881 G7 pp1–2; Gordon to Kimberley 29 Dec 1880, ibid p2.

14 Rolleston memo 24 Dec 1880, ibid pp2–4. The 'notorious Bradlaugh', an atheist, refused 'to take the oath before taking his seat in the House of Commons . . . [His] mission is to publish obscene books for which he has been put and properly into prison'; *Taranaki News* 7 Aug 1880. Bradlaugh's supposed informant was 'nearly the greatest blackguard in the Colony. Not long since he passed several months in . . . gaol . . . for a false and malicious libel. . . . He is aided by some Pakeha-Maori lawyers who would find it very profitable to have a trip to England to argue before the Privy Council the illegality of Confiscation'; Hall to Vogel 30 Dec 1880, Hall Mss vol 5. Hall was not so reticent in correspondence with Bell: 'If he knew who and what Sherrin is, even Bradlaugh would not act on his information'; 18 May 1881, ibid vol 28.

15 Bryce memo 20 Dec 1880, AJHR 1881 G7 pp5–8. Nearly a quarter of a century later, in the 'bright light of the twentieth century', Bryce still described Te Whiti as a madman and fanatic; Bryce 'Fanaticism in the Maori Race'.

16 The Colonial Office also asked Robinson, then in England, to supply them with his observations 'relative to the detention of the Maori prisoners'. Robinson's reply was less virulent than Bryce's, but much of the same ilk; AJHR 1883 A5 pp1–4. When it was later read out in court, Bryce, on oath, said Robinson (who was in New Zealand for 17 months) had been in the country 'a good while . . . about three years . . . more than that . . . over four years speaking roundly'; *Bryce v Rusden* p66. His memory was not so defective when it came to Gordon who did not share his ideas. He remembered he had been in the country for 'about 18 months or two years'; ibid p183.

17 Gordon confidential despatch 31 Dec 1880, G 26/1.

18 Gordon despatch 31 Dec 1880, enclosing Hall memo 22 Dec 1880 and draft letter, AJHR 1881 A1 pp20–22.

19 Hall to Gordon 22 Dec 1880 and Gordon to Te Whiti, AJHR 1881 A1

pp21–22. The Maori version of Gordon to Te Whiti, dated 22 Dec, is in MA 4/85. Te Whiti was reported to have said that if he met the governor at any place named in the letter, it would be in a 'hidden place'; Hursthouse to Atkinson 28 Dec 1880, Hursthouse Telegraph Books 1880–82.

20 Hall to Bell 28 Jan 1881, Hall Mss vol 6.

21 Rolleston diary 2 Oct 1881.

22 Every 'Maori expert' of the time had his own interpretation of this cryptic statement; see e.g. Fox report 3 June 1884, AJHR 1884 Sess I A5b p4. There is a helpful discussion on the role of cooked food in F. Allan Hanson and Louise Hanson, *Counterpoint in Maori Culture*, London, 1983, pp94–97. The raw tuber is imbued with mauri (life essence) and therefore has the potential for tupu (development); it signifies the influence of atua (the divine), and is therefore tapu. Cooking destroys the potential for tupu, renders it noa (without tapu) and signifies mate (lifelessness). Cooked food *attracts* tapu, it does not repel it. It renders noa that with which it comes in contact and itself becomes highly tapu, but being mate has lost its potential for tupu. Te Whiti was saying that discussion in that state could not be profitable; no tupu could ensue.

23 In other words, if the governor possessed the mana to restore the mauri to the potato there could still be potential for tupu. The situation could be reversed were a man of mana to visit, and prove his mana in courtesy, fairness, ability to negotiate.

24 Hall to Atkinson 27 Dec 1880, Hall Mss vol 5; Hall to Bryce 29 and 30 Dec 1880, ibid.

25 Bryce 'Fanaticism in the Maori Race'. See also NZPD 1882 xli p110.

26 Knollys to Gordon 31 Dec 1880, AJHR 1881 A1 pp23–26. Te Whiti had set great store by the governor's going to Parihaka. A special house was built there to accommodate him, and his letter to Te Whiti was discovered in it later when the village was being destroyed on Bryce's orders; *Lyttelton Times* 22 Nov 1881.

27 Knollys to Gordon 31 Dec 1880, AJHR 1881 A1 p26.

28 'Just what I expected,' said Hall. 'If the Archangel Gabriel went on his knees to Te Whiti he would get nothing out of him'; Hall to Bell 28 Jan 1881, Hall Mss vol 6.

29 Gordon confidential despatch 31 Dec 1880, G 26/1.

30 IUP vol 16 p477.

31 Hall to Bryce 29 Dec 1880, Hall Mss vol 5; Bryce to Hall 8 Jan 1881 enclosing letter of 5 Dec 1880, ibid vol 41.

32 Hall to Rolleston 28 Dec 1880, Hall Mss vol 5.

33 Undated press cutting attached to Bryce's letter of resignation, Hall Mss vol 41; Gordon confidential despatch 12 Jan 1881, G 26/1.

34 Oliver to Hall 25 Dec 1880, Hall Mss vol 41; Whitaker to Hall 16 Feb 1881, ibid.

35 *Lyttelton Times* 7 Jan 1881.

36 Gordon to Kimberley 12 Jan 1881, AJHR 1881 A1 pp26–27.

37 NZPD 1881 xxxviii pp122–23; Bryce to Gordon 10 June 1882, AJHR 1883 A4 p25. Hall defended the ministry, saying they were only responsible for the governor's actions 'so far as that action is taken on the advice of the Ministers', but the governor's despatches 'were matters over which Ministers had no control' since he was responsible for them to the secretary of state; NZPD 1881 xxxviii pp123, 148. A year later the government made strenuous efforts to control the governor's despatches.

38 UPA report 23 March 1881, IUP vol 16 pp475–76.
39 ibid p477.
40 Hall to Bell 28 Jan and 18 April 1881, Hall Mss vol 6.
41 Gordon report 26 Feb 1881, AJHR 1882 A8 p1; Gordon despatch 21 May 1881, G 25/13.
42 Hall to Vogel and Hall to Bell 28 Jan 1881, Hall Mss vol 6; Hall to Bell 18 April 1881, ibid.
43 Speech delivered at Leeston Town Hall 27 May 1881, in John Hall, *Speeches Delivered out of Parliament by the Honourable Sir John Hall, K.C.M.G.*, Christchurch, 1911, pp46–47.
44 MA 4/31.
45 *Gazette* 20 Jan 1881; Gordon report 26 Feb 1881, AJHR 1882 A8 p11.
46 Hall to Gordon 6 April 1881 and Gordon despatch 14 April 1881, IUP vol 16 p474.
47 *Lyttelton Times* 14 Jan 1881.
48 Such a *volte face* was not unique in Fox's career. See e.g. Gisborne p213; Claudia Orange, *The Treaty of Waitangi*, Wellington, 1987, pp152, 160.
49 Fox report 17 June 1881, AJHR 1881 G5 pp1–2; AJHR 1880 G2 pix; Fox report 2 June 1882, AJHR 1882 G5 p1. This reasoning was based on a false premise — that because the Parihaka people objected to their land being surveyed for sale, they would also object to the defining of their reserves.
50 Fox panui March 1881, AJHR 1881 G5 p4.
51 AJHR 1880 G2 pplxiv, liv.
52 ibid plviii.
53 *New Zealand Herald* 20 Dec 1880, 19 Jan and 19 Feb 1881.
54 *Taranaki News* 19 and 26 March 1881.
55 Hall to Rolleston 8 April 1881, Hall Mss vol 6.
56 *Taranaki News* 7 May 1881; Gordon despatch 23 May 1881, AJHR 1882 A8 p18.
57 Gordon to secretary of state 3 June 1881, AJHR 1882 A8 p18; NZPD 1881 xxxviii p1.
58 *Lyttelton Times* 26, 28, 30 March and 6 April 1881.
59 *Timaru Herald* quoted in *Taranaki News* 16 April 1881.
60 Bryce to Hall 13 April 1881; Hall Mss vol 41.
61 *Taranaki News* 18 and 25 June 1881.
62 Hall to Bell 18 May 1881, Hall Mss vol 28; Hall memo 19 May and 15 June 1881, AJHR 1882 A8 pp12–15. Hall repeated a claim often made that Grey had told Te Whiti the government would pay for all questions to be investigated in a court of law. Grey had already denied this in the House; NZPD 1879 xxxi p557. See also *Bryce v Rusden* p199.
63 Gordon confidential despatch 18 June 1881, G 26/1.
64 Gordon to Hall 12 July 1881, AJHR 1882 A8 pp15–16; Gordon despatch 16 July 1881, ibid pp16–17.
65 Hall memo 13 July 1881, ibid p16; Iona McIntosh, 'Sir Arthur Hamilton Gordon: Attitudes to and Influence on New Zealand Relations with the United Kingdom 1880–1882', MA thesis, University of Otago, 1968, p33.
66 Hall to Bell 13 Aug 1881, Hall Mss vol 28.
67 Fox report 3 June 1884, AJHR 1884 A5b p4.
68 Rolleston memo 24 Oct 1881, AJHR 1883 A4 p4.
69 *Taranaki News* 20 Aug 1881.
70 Parris report 15 May 1882, AJHR 1882 G1 p10.
71 Bryce described these 'formidable weapons' as 'great heavy sticks six or seven feet long with a club at the end'. Grey thought 'these clubs and weapons whose might and length have been made so much of were nothing but the flower-stalks of the New Zealand flax-plant';

NZPD 1882 xli pp114, 116.

72 Rolleston memo 24 Oct 1881, AJHR 1883 A4 pp4–5; New Zealand Constabulary annual report 31 May 1882, AJHR 1882 H14 p2. John Mackintosh Roberts was born in India and had been in New Zealand since 1855. He joined the Forest Rangers in 1863, was von Tempsky's subaltern in the Waikato, and fought with McDonnell at Te Ngutu o te Manu and with Whitmore at Moturoa and in the Urewera; Cowan *Wars* p479. The passage of twelve years must have affected his view of what constituted a serious situation.

73 New Zealand Constabulary annual report 31 May 1881, AJHR 1881 H18 p2.

74 Hall memo 25 Jan 1881, Hall Mss vol 6; NZPD 1881 xl p793.

75 Hall to Bell 10 Sept 1881, Hall Mss vol 28.

76 Paul Knaplund, 'Sir Arthur Gordon and New Zealand, 1880–1882', *Pacific Historical Review* 28, 1959, pp163–64; Chapman pp224, 228.

77 Gordon to Hall 5 Sept 1881, IUP vol 17 pp58–59; Hall to Gordon 6 Sept 1881, ibid p59; AJHR 1882 A4 pp1–3.

78 ibid p60.

79 Hall to Bell 10 Sept 1881, Hall Mss vol 28.

80 Scholefield *Dictionary* vol II p184; Wi Parata v the Bishop of Wellington (1877) NZJR 72, quoted in Legal Research Foundation Inc., Seminar, 'A Bill of Rights for New Zealand,' Aug 1985, pp180–81. See also Orange pp186–87.

81 The first amendment to the act came in 1883 and there were another seven amendments in the next nineteen years.

82 NZPD 1881 xl pp695, 696, 728.

83 ibid pp730, 732, 735, 792; AJHR 1880 G2 plxiii.

84 *New Zealand Herald* 19 Sept 1881; NZPD 1881 xl p639. At 31 March 1880 the constabulary force stood at 996, a year later it had been reduced to 717, of whom 522 were in Taranaki, and by 5 Nov 1881 it had risen to 1,088 of whom 828 were in Taranaki; New Zealand Constabulary annual reports 31 May 1881, AJHR 1881 H18 pp1–2, and 31 May 1882, AJHR 1882 H14 p1.

85 Copy of Prendergast to Gordon 16 Sept 1881 in Gordon to Mantell 6 Sept 1883, Mantell Mss 287. Gordon later said had he received that letter alone, and no warning from Murray that 'Ministers were about to take advantage of my absence to precipitate a crisis in Native affairs' he would probably have gone on from Fiji to the Solomons as originally planned; Gordon to Colonial Office 31 March 1883, AJHR 1884 Sess II A5 p3.

86 Prendergast memo 27 Jan 1883, AJHR 1883 A4 p29. Hall agreed that 'as a matter of courtesy, the Premier might well inform an absent Governor of any matter of importance occurring in the colony, which would or might affect his movements'; Hall memo 22 Feb 1883, ibid p28. Whitaker's view was that 'it would have been not only irregular but improper' had ministers communicated with an absent governor when an administrator was in office; Whitaker memo 25 Jan 1883, ibid p27.

87 AJHR 1883 A4 pp6–7.

88 *New Zealand Herald* 19 Sept 1881; *Taranaki News* 24 Sept 1881.

89 *New Zealand Herald* 20 Sept 1881.

90 Hursthouse to premier 17 Oct 1880, and Hursthouse to native minister 17 Sept 1881, Hursthouse Telegraph Books 1880–82.

91 *New Zealand Herald* 24 Sept 1881. R. S. Thompson generally interpreted for Croumbie-Brown.

92 NZPD 1881 xl pp793, 838.

93 Rolleston to Atkinson 23 and 25

Sept 1881, Scholefield *R-A Papers* pp489, 490; Rolleston memo 24 Oct 1881, AJHR 1883 A4 p5.

94 Hall to Bell 1 Oct 1881, Hall Mss vol 28.

95 Atkinson to H. R. Richmond 27 Sept 1881, Scholefield *R-A Papers* p492.

96 *Taranaki Herald* quoted in *New Zealand Herald* 26 Sept 1881.

97 Rolleston to Hall 28 Sept 1881, Scholefield *R-A Papers* pp492–93.

98 *New Zealand Herald* 27, 28 and 29 Sept 1881.

99 Rolleston diary 30 Sept 1881.

100 Hall to Whitaker 1 Oct 1881, Hall Mss folio 296; Hall to Bell 3 Nov 1881, ibid vol 7.

101 *New Zealand Herald* 30 Sept and 1 Oct 1881.

102 Mackay's visit to Parihaka in April 1879 is another.

103 Rolleston diary 2 Oct 1881.

104 It might be compared with Mackay's telegram of his interview with Te Whiti and his official report, the expurgated version, written ten days later at Sheehan's request; AJHR 1880 G2 App A pp9–12, and AJHR 1879 C4 pp6–8.

105 Hall to Whitaker 14 Oct 1881, Hall Mss folio 296.

106 Rolleston report 24 Oct 1881, AJHR 1883 A4 p6.

107 Rosamond Rolleston, *William and Mary Rolleston: An Informal Biography*, Wellington, 1971, pp86, 89–91.

108 Rolleston to Te Whiti 10 Oct 1881, AJHR 1883 A4 p6.

109 Hall to Whitaker 1 and 14 Oct 1881, Hall Mss folio 296; Whitaker to Hall 15 Oct 1881, ibid vol 41.

110 *Taranaki News* 15 Oct 1881; *New Zealand Herald* 15 Oct 1881.

111 Bryce to Rolleston 12 Oct 1881, Scholefield *R-A Papers* pp494–95.

112 Hall memo 19 Oct 1881, AJHR 1882 A8b p1; Rolleston diary 19 Oct 1881. The 'good authority' was probably Katene.

113 See Rusden *History* vol III p396, and fn 129 below.

114 Hall to Whitaker 17 Oct 1881, Hall Mss folio 296.

115 Hall to Whitaker 17 Oct 1881, ibid.

116 Hall to Fox 18 Oct 1881, Hall Mss vol 7; Fox to Hall 19 Oct 1881; ibid vol 41.

117 It was Parris who finally decided just what reserves the government intended to give the Parihaka people. He was directed to select whatever reserves in the seaward Parihaka block 'were necessary to give effect to the intentions of the Commissioners and all his proposals were adopted'; Hall to Bell 3 Nov 1881, Hall Mss vol 7.

118 ibid.

119 Whitaker to Hall 18 Oct 1881, Hall Mss folio 296.

120 Hall to Whitaker 19 Oct 1881, ibid.

121 Hall to Whitaker 20 Oct 1881, Hall Mss folio 296; Hall to Bryce 20 Oct 1881, ibid vol 7; Hall to Bell 22 Oct 1881, PM 5/1.

122 Hall to Whitaker 20 and 21 Oct 1881, Hall Mss folio 296.

123 Gordon memo 20 Oct 1881, AJHR 1883 A4 p1.

124 Hall to Whitaker 20 Oct 1881, Hall Mss vol 7.

125 Minutes of Executive Council 20, 21 and 26 Oct 1881, EC 1/9a; Hall to Bell 3 Nov 1881, Hall Mss vol 7.

126 Quoted in Chapman p250.

127 Hall to Bell 3 Nov 1881, Hall Mss vol 7.

128 Gordon to Colonial Office 31 March 1883, AJHR 1884 Sess II A5 p3; Hall to Whitaker 24 Oct 1881, Hall Mss folio 296.

129 Rusden was sure that Gordon's imminent return was known 'wheresoever a telegraph line existed and was used'. He had been told by the commodore of the Australian station that on arrival in Sydney on 15 October the *Gunga* had reported Gordon's departure from Suva for Wellington in the *Emerald* on 7

October. Rusden thought Hall and Prendergast would both 'make good Russians'; Rusden to Mantell 25 Dec 1881, 20 Feb 1882, and 6 May 1885, Rusden t/s letters. Fieldhouse thought ministers did not know, but that in any case it was 'a curious story whose significance has been greatly exaggerated'; D. K. Fieldhouse, 'Sir Arthur Gordon and the Parihaka Crisis, 1880–1882', *Historical Studies Australia and New Zealand* 10, 37, 1961, p43. It was obviously significant to ministers. They were still proclaiming their innocence in print two years later.

130 Murray memo 20 Oct 1881, AJHR 1884 Sess II A5 pp4–5. See also Hall to Whitaker 21 Oct 1881, Hall Mss folio 296.

131 Hall to Whitaker 22 Feb 1883, AJHR 1883 A4 p28; Prendergast memos 27 Jan 1883, ibid p30, and 14 Sept 1883, AJHR 1884 Sess II A5 p6. Gordon felt that if Hall and Prendergast could claim no 'official' knowledge it was because they had 'no desire to seek for information which would have made it certain'; Gordon to Colonial Office 31 March 1883, AJHR 1884 Sess II A5 p4.

132 AJHR 1883 A4 pp19, 27; British Parliamentary Papers 1882 xlvi c.3382, reprinted in IUP vol 16 pp349–639.

133 AJHR 1882 A8b pp1–2. The *New Zealand Herald* of 20 October called it 'virtually a Proclamation of war' for Te Whiti would probably 'not deign to notice it', while the offer of 'abundant land' to those who left him would not 'induce a single man to desert'.

134 Butler to Rolleston 22 Oct 1881, AJHR 1883 A4 pp3–4.

135 Christchurch *Press* quoted in *New Zealand Herald* 31 Oct 1881; *Taranaki News* 29 Oct 1881; *Timaru Herald* quoted in ibid.

136 *Lyttelton Times* 21 Oct and 3 Nov 1881.

137 Hall to Bell 3 Nov 1881, Hall Mss vol 7.

138 Gordon to Hall 3 Nov 1881, AJHR 1883 A4 pp7–8; *Gazette Extraordinary* 28 Oct 1881.

139 Hall to Bell 3 Nov 1881, Hall to Fox 1 Nov 1881, Hall Mss vol 7.

140 Hall to Whitaker 27 Oct 1881, Hall Mss folio 296.

141 Whitaker to Hall and Hall to Whitaker 28 Oct 1881, ibid; Whitaker to Hall 29 Oct 1881, ibid.

142 Bryce report 1 Nov 1881, AJHR 1883 A4 pp9–10.

143 *New Zealand Herald* 2 Nov quoting *Evening Post* 1 Nov 1881.

144 Hall to Fox 1 Nov 1881, Hall Mss vol 7; Bryce to Hall 26 Oct 1881, IUP vol 16 p572.

145 *Taranaki News* 5 Nov 1881, *New Zealand Herald* 5 Nov 1881.

146 AJHR 1883 A4 p2.

147 Hall to Bryce n.d., Hall Mss vol 7.

148 Reports from correspondents of the *Lyttelton Times*, reprinted in IUP vol 16 pp551, 546.

149 Gordon to secretary of state 5 Nov 1881, AJHR 1883 A4 p10; Gordon despatch 3 Dec 1881, ibid p11.

150 See IUP vol 16 pp541–71, 572–613.

151 He was no longer shirking but was in the thick of the fray. 'Splendid day', he telegraphed back to Hall. 'Reached Parihaka bout 9am. Found marae crammed. . . . Natives dressed in holiday attire. Apparently no intention of resistance'; ibid p573. He can hardly have been surprised.

152 New Zealand Constabulary annual report 31 May 1882, AJHR 1882 H14 p3. The last of the volunteers was withdrawn on 18 Nov and on 23 Nov the armed constabulary force was reduced.

153 Tuke later took exception to Croumbie-Brown's reporting and said his words were 'If any man *uses* a tomahawk, use your revolver'.

Croumbie-Brown noted this was the only exception taken to the correctness of his report; IUP vol 16 p600.

154 *Lyttelton Times* reports reprinted in IUP vol 16 pp546–48, 573–77.

155 *Lyttelton Times* 9 Nov 1881.

156 Fox to Hall 7 Nov 1881, Hall Mss vol 41.

157 *Lyttelton Times* 9 Nov 1881.

158 Bryce to Rolleston 12 Nov 1881, IUP vol 16 p589.

159 Fox to Hall 6 Nov 1881, Hall Mss vol 41.

160 Quoted in IUP vol 16 pp543–44.

161 *New Zealand Times* 2 Dec 1881.

162 Bryce to Hall 11 Nov 1881, IUP vol 16 p588; Bryce to Rolleston 13 and 15 Nov 1881, ibid pp595, 596.

163 Press Association report, ibid p611. In the next session of parliament Bryce told the House he had pulled up the potatoes at two places 'where the Maori had kept a sentry over the road for eighteen months to watch the crops . . . which had the effect of dispersing the guard for the first time'; NZPD 1882 xli p116.

164 Variously spelled Puahoaho, Puawheawhe, Puhouhou.

165 IUP vol 16 pp608–10.

166 ibid p603; Bryce to Rolleston 19 Nov 1881, ibid p609; Bryce speech on 25th anniversary of 'Parihaka Day', *Chronicle* 6 Nov 1906.

167 Rolleston to Bryce 19 Nov 1881, Rolleston Mss 50.

168 *Lyttelton Times* 22 Nov 1881.

169 IUP vol 16 p602.

170 Bryce to Rolleston 20, 21 and 22 Nov 1881, ibid pp609–10.

171 Parris report 15 May 1882, AJHR 1882 G1 p11.

172 *New Zealand Times* 2 Dec 1881, reprinted in IUP vol 16 p543.

173 Quoted in *Taranaki News* 26 Nov 1881.

174 See e.g. M. P. K. Sorrenson, 'Land Purchase Methods and their Effect on Maori Population, 1865–1901', *Journal of the Polynesian Society* 65, 3, 1956, pp193–98.

CHAPTER SEVEN

1 Tohu 29 June 1885, AJHR 1885 G8 p1.

2 Hinch thesis pp119–25, 165–66. Hinch's view, that 'almost overnight' and with the election still a month away 'Parihaka ceased to dominate the province's outlook' and was scarcely again mentioned in campaigning, contrasts with Bassett's view that the 'Parihaka crisis . . . was one of the main issues in the 1881 election in Egmont'; Bassett *Atkinson* p92.

3 Hall to Bell 5 Nov 1881, Hall Mss vol 28; Hall *Speeches* pp78–79.

4 Hall to Bell 1 Dec 1881, Hall Mss vol 7.

5 'Mine is the land, mine the people. This shall be the paramount struggle of this generation . . .' AJLC 1882 No9 pp4, 7, 9; *Lyttelton Times* 14, 15 and 16 Nov 1881, reprinted in IUP vol 16 pp589–95; Rawson, R. M. to minister of justice 26 June 1882, enclosing the *Budget* 19 Nov 1881, J 1/1882/1311.

6 AJLC 1882 No 9 pp5, 6, 9.

7 This was probably in response to Hursthouse's complaint that he did not know 'what land is reserved or to be reserved for Maoris on seaward side of road'; Hursthouse to Rolleston 18 June 1881, Hursthouse Telegraph Books 1880–82.

8 Rawson to minister of justice 26 June 1882, J 1/1882/1311.

9 Rolleston to Bryce 19 Nov 1881, Rolleston Mss 50.

10 AJLC 1882 No9 pp8–9.

11 See e.g. the ploughman who did not 'understand writing now', p89 above. Also Piripiri and Pene who took a large contract for fencing from a European settler in the Chathams and gave 'their word as Te Whiti

men but would not sign an agreement'; entry for 12 Feb 1885, *Diary of E. R. Chudleigh 1862–1921: Chatham Islands*. E. C. Richards, ed., Christchurch, 1950, p332.

12 *Lyttelton Times* 16 Nov 1881.

13 IUP vol 16 pp558–59, 611–13.

14 Hall to Bryce 30 Jan 1882, Hall Mss vol 27.

15 Hall to Fox 12 March 1882, ibid; Hall to Bell 25 March 1882, ibid vol 8.

16 Hall to Bell 29 Dec 1881, Hall Mss vol 7; Hall to Gordon 23 Dec 1881, ibid vol 27; Hall to Bryce 30 Jan 1882, ibid. Ngatihaumiti were considered loyal throughout the war and were given a 'solemn promise' that none of their land would be confiscated; AJHR 1880 G2 pxxxix. Fifteen years later when they finally protested because their title to the land had never been confirmed, they were labelled 'presumed loyal' and threatened with 're-confiscation'. Fox argued that 'neither in law nor in equity' was reconfiscation of any of this block justified by the fact that Matakatea had been arrested for 'supposed complicity with Te Whiti's ploughmen' and that many of his hapu were 'sympathisers' with Te Whiti; Fox report 2 June 1882, AJHR 1882 G5 p3.

17 Mair report 29 May 1880, AJHR 1880 G4a pp1–2.

18 Bryce to Rolleston 12 Jan 1882, Rolleston Mss 30; Rolleston to Bryce 12 Jan 1882, ibid 50.

19 *New Zealand Herald* 14, 20 and 30 Jan 1882.

20 ibid 1 Feb 1882; Hall to Bell 25 March 1882, Hall Mss vol 8.

21 *Evening Post* quoted in *New Zealand Herald* 30 Jan 1882.

22 Hall to Rolleston 3 Feb 1882, Rolleston Mss 37.

23 Bryce to Rolleston 27 Feb 1882, Rolleston Mss 30.

24 History is the richer for his absence. A great deal of information was passed orally between ministers but Whitaker had necessarily to 'confer' by mail or telegraph and the meticulous Hall carefully preserved some telling communications.

25 Hall to Bell 19 April 1882, Hall Mss vol 8; Atkinson to Wakefield 11 April 1882, Scholefield *R-A Papers* p507; Gordon despatch 22 April 1882, G 25/13; Gordon confidential despatch 22 April 1882, G 26/1. Hall found himself well enough to attend the session of 1882 and did not resign his seat in the House until February 1883.

26 Gordon despatch 22 April 1882, G 25/13; Hall to Bell 19 April 1882, Hall Mss vol 8.

27 Gordon to Kimberley 3 Dec 1881, G 25/13; Kimberley to Gordon 3 Feb 1882, G 2/2.

28 LE 1/1882/150.

29 Telegrams between Roberts and Bryce 13–18 April 1882, AJHR 1882 G3 pp1–2; New Zealand Constabulary annual report 31 May 1882, AJHR 1882 H14 p4.

30 Hall to Bell 20 April 1882, Hall Mss vol 8.

31 Parris reported in May that 'Their faith in Te Whiti is as strong as ever, and they talk of a re-union being near at hand'; Parris report 15 May 1882, AJHR 1882 G1 p11.

32 Gordon despatch 20 May 1882 enclosing cuttings from *New Zealand Times* 10 May 1882, IUP vol 16 pp630–31. Titokowaru was discharged under that act but was held for want of sureties to keep the peace.

33 Hall to Bell 18 May 1882, Hall Mss vol 8.

34 J 1/1882/1183.

35 *Gazette* 15 June 1882; NZPD 1882 xli p253.

36 NZPD 1882 xli pp5, 117, 554; Whitaker memo 21 March 1883, AJHR 1883 A8 p4.

37 IUP vol 17 p45; Hall to Bell 17 June 1882, Hall Mss vol 8.

38 NZPD 1882 xli pp107–16, 126.

39 ibid pp282–83; Atkinson to Parris 27 and 29 May 1882, Scholefield *R-A Papers* p511.

40 NZPD 1882 xli pp113, 117, 140–44. Rolleston did not speak in any debate on any of Bryce's contentious west coast legislation between 1879 and 1883, and he brought in only one bill of his own in 1881 — the West Coast Settlement Reserves Bill — which he introduced with but a few dozen words.

41 ibid p158. Of the major European actors in the Parihaka 'affair', Prendergast, Hall, Whitaker and Atkinson all received knighthoods, some sooner, some later. Bryce and Rolleston did not.

42 ibid p279.

43 ibid pp375–76.

44 ibid p383.

45 See John P. Ward, *Wanderings with the Maori Prophets Te Whiti and Tohu*, Nelson, 1883, for an account of their eleven month stay in the South Island. Bryce described Ward as 'in reality an attendant' upon Te Whiti and Tohu; Bryce to Prendergast 9 Sept 1882, AJHR 1883 A1 p5.

46 Dick to Beetham and Dick to gaoler 20 May 1882, J 43/2; Hall to Bell 18 May 1882, Hall Mss vol 8.

47 Bryce to Prendergast 9 Sept 1882, AJHR 1883 A1 p5.

48 J. P. Ward pp41, 76. Ward judged Te Whiti to be 'just like all the rest of his countrymen — a senseless block of wood'; ibid p54.

49 ibid p72.

50 Parris report 6 July 1872, AJHR 1872 F3 p13.

51 J. P. Ward pp80–81.

52 ibid pp112–15. Te Whiti's lack of interest in material riches was unwittingly borne out by a remark of Bryce's. When asked whether it was true that the homes of Te Whiti and Tohu had been pulled down and their wives and families left without a roof over their heads, he said he did not know 'whether Te Whiti's whare was one of those pulled down; but if so it was a very good thing for Mrs Te Whiti, because the whare she resided in was one of the oldest, smallest and most unwholesome in the whole village'; NZPD 1882 xli p438.

53 *Gazette* 3 Aug 1882.

54 Bryce to Whitaker 15 July 1882, G 17/8.

55 J. P. Ward pp126–28.

56 ibid p124.

57 NZPD 1881 xxxviii p479.

58 Riemenschneider was said to have read 'the whole of the Commission's reports' to Te Whiti and Tohu as a 'final step' in trying to persuade them to submit to the government's proclamation of October 1881; Rolleston diary 25 Oct 1881.

59 Parris report 15 May 1882, AJHR 1882 G1 p11.

60 NZPD 1882 xli pp119, 378, 563.

61 Whitaker to Gordon 27 May 1882, AJHR 1883 A4 p19; Gordon to ministers 8 June 1882, ibid pp20–21.

62 AJHR 1882 A8 pp12–15; AJHR 1883 A4 pp12–18.

63 He told Bell the fewer that were presented to the House of Commons the better, and continually exhorted him to 'take up the Colony's cause' with the British public and counteract adverse publicity which maligned the colonial settlers; Hall to Bell 20 April 1882, Hall Mss vol 8.

64 Hall to Bell 17 June 1882, ibid.

65 Gordon to Mantell 10 and 14 June 1882, Mantell Mss 287.

66 NZPD 1882 xli pp428–29.

67 Gordon confidential despatch 14 June 1882, G 26/1.

68 Knaplund 'Gordon and New Zealand' p169; Rusden *History* vol III p364. Hicks-Beach had asked

Rusden to draw up a question for him to put to parliament about the papers; Rusden to Mantell 11 Aug 1885, Rusden t/s letters.

69 Gordon confidential despatches 20 Jan and 22 April 1882, G 26/1.

70 Gordon despatch 3 Dec 1881, AJHR 1883 A4 p12; Gordon to Colonial Office 31 March 1883, AJHR 1884 Sess II A5 pp2–3.

71 Gordon to Gladstone 21 Jan 1882, quoted in Knaplund 'Gordon and New Zealand' p170; Gordon to Mantell 6 Sept 1883, Mantell Mss 287; Gordon to Selborne 20 Jan 1882, quoted in Chapman p260.

72 Hall to Bell 17 June 1882, Hall Mss vol 8.

73 Hall thought he 'acted within his rights' but whether his action 'as a matter of constitutional practice and precedent was wise and proper' was another matter; Hall to Fox 27 Aug 1882, Hall Mss vol 27.

74 Bakewell to Gordon 17 July 1882, quoted in Chapman pp260–61.

75 Kimberley minute 31 Oct 1881 on Gordon confidential despatch of 9 Sept 1881, quoted in ibid p247.

76 Kimberley minute 4 Sept 1882 on *New Zealand Times* monthly news summary for July 1882, ibid pp261–62. See also Robert Stout, 'Governor Gordon and the Maoris: A Chapter of New Zealand History', *Melbourne Review* 8, 1883, pp182–83.

77 Fox report 2 June 1882, AJHR 1882 G5 pp1–3.

78 Hall to Gordon 3 Feb 1882, Hall Mss vol 27.

79 NZPD 1882 xliii pp853–55, 911–15. See also John Hellyer Carr, 'A Study of European Responses to the Pardon of Te Kooti in 1883 and to his Intended Return to Poverty Bay in 1889', BA (Hons) research exercise, Massey University, 1975, pp14–16.

80 Prendergast despatch 9 Sept 1882, AJHR 1883 A1 p4; Bryce memo 9 Sept 1882, ibid pp4–5.

81 MA 2/19 82/2136a.

82 Bryce memo 9 Sept 1882, AJHR 1883 A1 p5.

83 AJHR 1883 A6 pp1–4.

84 Rusden to Mantell 23 Aug 1882, Rusden t/s letters.

85 AJHR 1883 A6 pp3–4.

86 Whitaker memo 12 Dec 1882, ibid pp5–6.

87 Hall to Bell 20 April 1882, Hall Mss vol 8.

88 Whitaker memo 25 Jan 1883, AJHR 1883 A4 p27. The 1882 Blue Book is reprinted in IUP vol 16 pp349–639.

89 AJHR 1883 A4 pp27–31.

90 Gordon to Colonial Office 31 March 1883, AJHR 1884 Sess II A5 pp1–5; Prendergast memo 14 Sept 1883 and Whitaker memo 21 Sept 1883, ibid pp5–8.

91 Derby to Jervois 10 Dec 1883, ibid p8.

92 Stout memo 7 Nov 1884, AJHR 1884 Sess II A5 p9; Stout memo 26 May 1885 forwarding Hall memo of Jan 1885 sent to Stout in May by Atkinson, AJHR 1885 G4a p1.

93 AJHR 1877 A10 pp6–7; AJHR 1874 A3 p11.

94 NZPD 1880 xxxvii pp535–36.

95 Paul Knaplund, 'Sir Arthur Gordon on the New Guinea Question, 1883', *Historical Studies Australia and New Zealand* 7, 27, 1956, pp328–33; Knaplund 'Gordon and New Zealand', pp171–72; Chapman p263. See also Angus Ross, *New Zealand Aspirations in the Pacific in the Nineteenth Century*, Oxford, 1964, pp131–48; Angus Ross, 'Maori and Polynesian: Race and Politics', in J. D. Freeman and W. R. Geddes, eds, *Anthropology in the South Seas*, New Plymouth, 1959, pp221–33. Ross argued that New Zealand had 'a special aptitude for handling islanders' but admitted this was largely due to the efforts of 'outstanding Maori leaders' such as

Carroll, Pomare and Ngata. The argument cannot be advanced that New Zealand politicians and administrators had this skill in the nineteenth century — although Whitmore and Richmond were still prepared in 1883 to claim they had, despite all that had passed in the previous two or three years; NZPD 1883 xliv pp142, 146.

96 *Gazette Extraordinary* 13 Feb 1883.

97 Bryce report 13 Feb 1883, AJHR 1883 A8 p5.

98 Bryce to Atkinson 17 Feb 1883, PM 3/2; Atkinson to Fox 20 Feb and 3 March 1883, ibid.

99 Jervois despatch 19 Feb 1883, AJHR 1883 A8 p1.

100 J. P. Ward pp132–33.

101 ibid p134.

102 Parris report 9 June 1883, AJHR 1883 G1a pp10–11; NZPD 1883 xliv p2.

103 NZPD 1883 xlvi pp157–59, 162–63.

104 IUP vol 17 pp77–81.

105 NZPD 1883 xlvi pp164–65, 480.

106 According to Thompson the change from traditional to non-traditional foods dated from 1879 when the land sellers, te hunga he, were permitted to go to Parihaka and were encouraged to spend their ill-gotten gains on flour, tea, rice and tobacco, which replaced 'taro, kumera, honey, hua-hua, paratawiti and hinau'; Thompson to Sheehan 4 May 1879, LE 1/1879/3.

107 Parris report 12 May 1884, AJHR 1884 Sess II G1 p21.

108 ibid.

109 Deighton report 13 June 1885, AJHR 1885 G2 p21. In Feb 1885 a European in the Chathams noted some 2,000 tuna drying and another 5,000 in drays drawn by 14 bullocks, and thought there would be 'quite 20,000 eels in all for Te Whiti'; Chudleigh *Diary* p332.

110 Rennell report 13 April 1885, AJHR 1885 G2 p20.

111 Te Wheoro, Tawhai, Tomoana and Taiaroa to secretary, Aborigines Protection Society 16 July 1883, AJHR 1884 Sess I A2 p14.

112 Bryce memo 11 Jan 1884, AJHR 1884 Sess I A1 pp11–12.

113 Fox reports 7 June 1883, AJHR 1883 G3 p1; and 2 June 1882, AJHR 1882 G5 p2. Bryce talked of 'A large number of reserves of the very best land', about eighty acres for every man, woman and child, enough to keep them in idleness in perpetuity; *Bryce v Rusden* p182.

114 AJHR 1880 G2 pplv, 31–22; AJHR 1883 G3 p2; AJHR 1884 Sess I A5a pp2–6.

115 NZPD 1882 xli p146, ibid 1883 xlvi p158. On R. S. Thompson's claims on behalf of his wife see Lewis to Thompson 19 Jan 1882, MA 4/33; Whitaker memo 22 April 1882, G 17/8; Prendergast to colonial secretary 29 Aug 1882, G 25/13.

116 Fox report 3 June 1884, AJHR 1884 Sess I A5b pp1–3.

117 Whitaker memo 21 March 1883, AJHR 1883 A8 p4.

118 Bryce memo 13 Feb 1883, ibid p3.

119 Fox report 3 June 1884, AJHR 1884 Sess I A5b p5.

120 Rennell report 13 April 1885, AJHR 1885 G2 p20.

121 AJHR 1885 A2 pp3–5.

122 NZPD 1877 xxvii p233; Bryce memo 11 Jan 1884, AJHR 1884 Sess I A1 p11.

123 Stout memo 12 March 1885, AJHR 1885 A1 p32.

124 Rennell report 13 April 1885, AJHR 1885 G2 p21.

BIBLIOGRAPHY

PRIMARY SOURCES

I Unpublished

Alpers Mss; MS Papers 86, Alexander Turnbull Library.
Hall Mss; MS Papers 1784, Alexander Turnbull Library.
Hammond, T. G., 'Te Whiti and Parihaka', Acc. 73.28, Alexander Turnbull Library.
Hursthouse Telegraph Books, Taranaki Museum.
Mantell Mss; MS Papers 83, Alexander Turnbull Library.
McLean Mss; MS Papers 32, Alexander Turnbull Library.
Reeves Medium Clipping Book, Alexander Turnbull Library.
Rolleston Diary, Alexander Turnbull Library.
Rolleston Mss; MS Papers 446, Alexander Turnbull Library.
Rusden t/s letters, Auckland Institute and Museum Library.

Armed Constabulary archives (AC P), National Archives.
Executive Council Minutes (EC), National Archives.
Governors' archives (G), National Archives.
Justice Department archives (J), National Archives.
Legislative archives (LE), National Archives.
Maori Affairs Department archives (MA), National Archives.
Prime Ministers' archives (PM), National Archives.

II Official Published

Appendices to the Journals of the House of Representatives (AJHR).
Appendices to the Journals of the Legislative Council (AJLC).
British Parliamentary Papers, Colonies, New Zealand, Irish University Press series (IUP).
New Zealand Government Gazette (*Gazette*).
New Zealand Parliamentary Debates (NZPD).

III Newspapers

Budget.

Chronicle.
Evening Post.
Hawera Star.
Lyttelton Times.
Maori Record.
New Zealander.
New Zealand Graphic.
New Zealand Herald.
New Zealand Times.
Patea (County) Mail.
Press.
Taranaki Herald.
Taranaki News.
The Bulletin (Sydney).
Timaru Herald.

IV Books and Articles

[Bell, F. D., Frederick Whitaker, Thomas Gore Browne] *Notes on Sir William Martin's Pamphlet entitled 'The Taranaki Question'*, Auckland 1861.
Brookes, E. S., *Frontier Life: Taranaki, New Zealand*, Auckland 1892.
Bryce, John, 'Fanaticism in the Maori Race', *Press* 23 March 1903.
Bryce, John, 'Maori Fanaticism', *Press* 25 March 1903.
Bryce, John, 'The Constabulary at Parihaka', *Press* 28 March 1903.
Bryce v Rusden, Queen's Bench Division, High Court of Justice, London, 1886.
Buck, Peter, 'The Taranaki Maoris: Te Whiti and Parihaka', *Te Aute College Students' Association Conference, Papers and Addresses*, December 1897, in J. B. Condliffe, *Te Rangi Hiroa: The Life of Sir Peter Buck*, Christchurch, 1971, pp40–45.
Chudleigh, E. R., *Diary of E. R. Chudleigh 1862–1921: Chatham Islands*, E. C. Richards, ed., Christchurch, 1950.
Cowan, James, 'Famous New Zealanders: Te Whiti of Taranaki. The Story of a Patriot and Peacemaker', *New Zealand Railways Magazine* 1 Oct 1934, pp17–21.
Cowan, James, *Hero Stories of New Zealand*, Wellington, 1935, pp236–46.
Fox, William, *The Six Colonies of New Zealand*, London, 1851.
Fox, William, *The War in New Zealand*, London, 1866.
Gisborne, William, *New Zealand Rulers and Statesmen 1840–1885*, London, 1886.
Gudgeon, Thomas Wayth, *The Defenders of New Zealand*, Auckland, 1887.
Hadfield, Octavius, *One of England's Little Wars*, London, 1860.
Hadfield, Octavius, *A Sequel to 'One of England's Little Wars'*, London, 1861.
Hadfield, Octavius, *The Second Year of One of England's Little Wars*, London, 1861.
Hall, John, *Speeches Delivered out of Parliament by the Honourable Sir John Hall, K.C.M.G.*, Christchurch, 1911.
Irvine, R. F. and O. T. J. Alpers, *The Progress of New Zealand in the Century*, London, 1902.
Martin, Sir William, *The Taranaki Question*, Auckland, 1860.
'Matangi, Rawiri', 'Te Whiti, The Prophet of Parihaka', *New Zealand Times* 29 March 1899, in W. D. McIntyre and W. J. Gardner, eds, *Speeches and Documents on New Zealand History*, Oxford, 1971, pp158–62.
McDonnell, Thomas, 'A Maori History: Being a Native Account of the Pakeha-Maori

Wars in New Zealand', as related to McDonnell by Kowhai Ngutu Kaka, in T. W. Gudgeon, *The Defenders of New Zealand*, Auckland, 1887, pp493–556.

Newman, Alfred K., 'A Study of the Causes leading to the Extinction of the Maori', *Transactions and Proceedings of the New Zealand Institute* 14, 1881, pp459–77.

Rees, William Lee and Lily Rees, *The Life and Times of Sir George Grey, K.C.B.*, Auckland, 1892.

Reeves, William Pember, *The Long White Cloud: Ao Tea Roa* [1898], Auckland, 1973.

Richmond, J. C., *Reminiscences of a Minister for Native Affairs in New Zealand: being a corrected report in the New Zealand 'Hansard' of a speech delivered by Hon Mr J. C. Richmond in the Legislative Council on Wed, Aug. 1, 1888, in reply to defamatory passages contained in Rusden's 'History of New Zealand'*, Wellington, 1888.

Rusden, G. W., *History of New Zealand*, 3 vols, London, 1883.

[Rusden, G. W.] *Tragedies in New Zealand in 1868 and 1881. Discussed in England in 1886 and 1887*, London, 1888.

Rusden, G. W., *Aureretanga: Groans of the Maoris*, London, 1888.

Saunders, Alfred, *History of New Zealand*, vol II, Christchurch, 1899.

Scholefield, G. H., ed., *The Richmond-Atkinson Papers*, vol II, Wellington, 1960.

Seffern, W. H. J., *Chronicles of the Garden of New Zealand Known as Taranaki*, New Plymouth, 1896.

Seffern, W. H. J., 'Parihaka, Its Past and Present Aspect: The Prophet Te Whiti', *New Zealand Graphic* 22 May 1897, pp629–30.

Sewell, Henry, *The New Zealand Native Rebellion: Letter to Lord Lyttelton*, Auckland, 1864.

Stout, Robert, 'Governor Gordon and the Maoris: A Chapter of New Zealand History', *Melbourne Review* 8, 1883, pp164–85.

Vaggioli, Felice, *Storia della Nuova Zelanda e dei Suoi Abitatori*, vol II, Parma, 1896.

Ward, John P., *Wanderings with the Maori Prophets Te Whiti and Tohu*, Nelson, 1883.

W. B. Otorohanga [William Baucke], *Where the White Man Treads* [1905], Auckland, 1928.

Wells, B., *The History of Taranaki*, New Plymouth, 1878.

SECONDARY SOURCES

I Books

Allport, Gordon W., *The Nature of Prejudice*, New York, 1958.

Ballara, Angela, *Proud to be White? A Survey of Pakeha Prejudice in New Zealand*, Auckland, 1986.

Banton, Michael, *Race Relations*, New York, 1967.

Bassett, Judith, *Sir Harry Atkinson 1831–1892*, Auckland, 1975.

Beaglehole, J. C., *New Zealand: A Short History*, London, 1936.

Belich, James, *The New Zealand Wars and the Victorian Interpretation of Racial Conflict*, Auckland, 1986.

Bromley, A. P. C., *Hawera: An Outline of the Development of a New Zealand Community*, Hawera, 1981.

Burdon, R. M., *New Zealand Notables: Henry Williams, Te Whiti, Johnny Jones*, Christchurch, 1941, pp71–104.

Caselberg, John, ed., *The Voice of the Maori: A Culture Conflict Anthology*, Christchurch, 1969.

Caselberg, John, ed., *Maori is my Name: Historical Maori Writings in Translation*, Dunedin, 1975.

Chapman, J. K. *The Career of Arthur Hamilton Gordon, First Lord Stanmore, 1829–1912*, Toronto, 1964.

Charlot, John, *The Hawaiian Poetry of Religion and Politics: Some Religio-Political Concepts in Postcontact Literature*, Laie, 1985.

Clark, Paul, *'Hauhau': The Pai Marire Search for Maori Identity*, Auckland, 1975.

Coad, N. E., *New Zealand from Tasman to Massey*, Wellington, 1934.

Colless, Brian and Peter Donovan, *Religion in New Zealand Society*, Palmerston North, 1980.

Condliffe, J. B., *New Zealand in the Making: A Study of Economic and Social Development*, London, 2nd edn, 1963.

Condliffe, J. B., *Te Rangi Hiroa: The Life of Sir Peter Buck*, Christchurch, 1971.

Condliffe, J. B., and W. T. G. Airey, *A Short History of New Zealand*, Auckland, 6th edn, 1938, 7th edn, 1953.

Cowan, James, *The Maoris of New Zealand*, Christchurch, 1910.

Cowan, James, *The Adventures of Kimble Bent: A Story of Wild Life in the New Zealand Bush*, Christchurch, 1911.

Cowan, James, *The New Zealand Wars: A History of the Maori Campaigns and the Pioneering Period* [1923], vol II, Wellington, 1955.

Cowan, James, *Tales of the Maori Bush* [1934], Wellington, 1966.

Cowan, James, *Sir Donald Maclean: The Story of a New Zealand Statesman*, Dunedin, 1940.

Dalton, B. J., *War and Politics in New Zealand 1855–1870*, Sydney, 1967.

Dalziel, R. M., *The Origins of New Zealand Diplomacy: The Agent-General in London 1870–1905*, Wellington, 1975.

Dansey, Harry, *Te Raukura: The Feathers of the Albatross*, Auckland, 1974.

Greenwood, William, *Riemenschneider of Warea*, Wellington, 1967.

Hammond, T. G., *In the Beginning: The History of a Mission*, Auckland, 1915.

Hanson, F. Allan and Louise Hanson, *Counterpoint in Maori Culture*, London, 1983.

Harrop, A. J., *England and the Maori Wars*, London, 1937.

Henderson, James McL., *Ratana: The Origins and the Story of the Movement*, Wellington, 1963.

Hill, Edward, *There was a Taranaki Land League*, Wellington, 1969.

Hocken, T. M., *A Bibliography of the Literature Relating to New Zealand*, Wellington, 1909.

Houston, John, *Maori Life in Old Taranaki*, Wellington, 1965.

Howitt, W. K., *A Pioneer Looks Back: Days of Trials, Hardships and Achievements*, Auckland, 1945.

Howitt, W. K., *A Pioneer Looks Back Again: A Story of Fortitude, Courage and Achievement*, Auckland, 1947.

Hunn, J. K., *Report on the Department of Maori Affairs*, Wellington, 1961.

King, Michael, *Te Puea: A Biography*, Auckland, 1977.

Lipson, Leslie, *The Politics of Equality: New Zealand's Adventures in Democracy*, Chicago, 1948.

Lowenthal, David, *The Past is a Foreign Country*, Cambridge, 1985.

Mason, Philip, *Race Relations*, London, 1970.

Mason, Philip, *Patterns of Dominance*, London, 1971.

Miller, Harold, *New Zealand*, London, 1950.

Miller, Harold, *Race Conflict in New Zealand 1814–1865*, Auckland, 1966.

Miller, John, *Early Victorian New Zealand: A Study of Racial Tension and Social Attitudes 1839–1852*, London, 1958.

Mitcalfe, Barry, *Nine New Zealanders*, Christchurch, 1963, pp51–59.
Mol, Hans, *The Fixed and the Fickle: Religion and Identity in New Zealand*, Waterloo, Ontario, 1982.
Morley, William, *The History of Methodism in New Zealand*, Wellington, 1900.
Morrell, W. P., *Britain and New Zealand*, London, 1944.
Morrell, W. P. and D. O. W. Hall, *A History of New Zealand Life*, Christchurch, 1957.
Oliver, W. H., *The Story of New Zealand*, London, 1960.
Oliver, W. H. with B. R. Williams, eds, *The Oxford History of New Zealand*, Wellington, 1981.
Orange, Claudia, *The Treaty of Waitangi*, Wellington, 1987.
Quoist, Michel, *Prayers of Life*, Dublin, 1963.
Roberts, C. J., *Centennial History of Hawera and the Waimate Plains*, Hawera, 1939.
Rolleston, Rosamond, *William and Mary Rolleston: An Informal Biography*, Wellington, 1971.
Ross, Angus, *New Zealand Aspirations in the Pacific in the Nineteenth Century*, Oxford, 1964.
Rutherford, J., *Sir George Grey K.C.B., 1812–1898: A Study in Colonial Government*, London, 1961.
Scholefield, G. H., ed., *A Dictionary of New Zealand Biography*, 2 vols, Wellington, 1940.
Scholefield, G. H., *Notable New Zealand Statesmen*, Christchurch, 1946.
Scholefield, G. H., *Newspapers in New Zealand*, Wellington, 1958.
Scott, Dick, *The Parihaka Story*, Auckland, 1954.
Scott, Dick, *Ask That Mountain: The Story of Parihaka*, Auckland, 1975.
Shrimpton, A. W. and Alan E. Mulgan, *Maori and Pakeha: A History of New Zealand*, Christchurch, 1930.
Simpson, Tony, *Te Riri Pakeha: The White Man's Anger*, Martinborough, 1979.
Sinclair, Keith, *The Origins of the Maori Wars*, Wellington, 1961.
Sinclair, Keith, *A History of New Zealand* [1959], Harmondsworth, 1969.
Smith, Norman, *Native Custom and Law Affecting Native Land*, Wellington, 1942.
Smith, Norman, *Maori Land Law*, Wellington, 1960.
Sorrenson, Keith, *Integration or Identity?*, Auckland, 1977.
Sorrenson, M. P. K., *Maori Origins and Migrations: The Genesis of Some Pakeha Myths and Legends*, Auckland, 1979.
Spoonley, P., C. Macpherson, D. Pearson and C. Sedgwick, eds, *Tauiwi: Racism and Ethnicity in New Zealand*, Palmerston North, 1984.
Stewart, William Downie, *William Rolleston: A New Zealand Statesman*, Christchurch, 1940.
Stone, R. C. J., *Makers of Fortune: A Colonial Business Community and its Fall*, Auckland, 1973.
Turnbull, Michael, *The Changing Land: A Short History of New Zealand*, Auckland, 2nd edn, 1975.
Ward, Alan, *A Show of Justice: Racial 'Amalgamation' in Nineteenth Century New Zealand*, Auckland, 1973.
Webster, Peter, *Rua and the Maori Millennium*, Wellington, 1979.
White, Hayden, *Tropics of Discourse: Essays in Cultural Criticism*, Baltimore, 1978.
Williams, John A., *Politics of the New Zealand Maori: Protest and Cooperation, 1891–1909*, Auckland, 1969.
Winiata, Maharaia, *The Changing Role of the Leader in Maori Society: A Study in Social Change and Race Relations*, Auckland, 1967.

Wood, F. L. W., *New Zealand in the World*, Wellington, 1940.

II Articles

Bassett, Judith, 'Review of *Ask That Mountain: The Story of Parihaka* by Dick Scott', *New Zealand Journal of History* 9, 2, 1975, pp189–92.

Dening, Gregory, 'Ethnohistory in Polynesia: The Value of Ethnohistorical Evidence', *Journal of Pacific History* 1, 1966, pp23–42.

Ellison, Edward, 'Sacred Stone Links Taranaki and Otago', *Historic Places* 19, 1987, pp7–11.

Fieldhouse, D. K., 'Sir Arthur Gordon and the Parihaka Crisis, 1880–1882', *Historical Studies Australia and New Zealand* 10, 37, 1961, pp30–49.

France, Peter, 'The Founding of an Orthodoxy: Sir Arthur Gordon and the Doctrine of the Fijian Way of Life', *Journal of the Polynesian Society* 77, 1, 1968, pp6–32.

Gadd, Bernard, 'The Teachings of Te Whiti O Rongomai 1831–1907', *Journal of the Polynesian Society* 75, 4, 1966, pp445–57.

Hargreaves, R. P., 'Maori Agriculture after the Wars (1871–1886)', *Journal of the Polynesian Society* 69, 4, 1960, pp354–67.

Hargreaves, R. P., 'Maori Flour Mills South of the Auckland Province (1847–1860)', *Journal of the Polynesian Society* 71, 1, 1962, pp101–05.

Howe, K. R. 'The Fate of the "Savage" in Pacific Historiography', *New Zealand Journal of History* 11, 2, 1977, pp137–54.

Kaa, Keri, 'Review of Michael King's *Maori*', *New Zealand Listener* 24 September 1983, pp98–99.

King, Michael, 'New Zealand Oral History: Some Cultural and Methodological Considerations', *New Zealand Journal of History* 12, 2, 1978, pp104–23.

Knaplund, Paul, 'Sir Arthur Gordon on the New Guinea Question, 1883', *Historical Studies Australia and New Zealand* 7, 27, 1958, pp328–33.

Knaplund, Paul, 'Sir Arthur Gordon and Fiji: Some Gordon–Gladstone Letters', *Historical Studies Australia and New Zealand* 8, 31, 1958, pp281–96.

Knaplund, Paul, 'Sir Arthur Gordon and New Zealand, 1880–1882', *Pacific Historical Review* 28, 1959, pp155–72.

Kuschel, Rolf and Torben Monberg, 'History and Oral Traditions: A Case Study', *Journal of the Polynesian Society* 86, 1, 1977, pp85–95.

Lange, Raeburn, 'Changes in Rarotongan Attitudes toward Health and Disease: Historical Factors in the Development of a Mid-Twentieth-Century Understanding', *Pacific Studies* 10, 1, 1986, pp29–53.

Legal Research Foundation Inc., Seminar, 'A Bill of Rights for New Zealand', August 1985.

Lyons, Daniel P., 'An Analysis of Three Maori Prophet Movements', in I. H. Kawharu, ed., *Conflict and Compromise: Essays on the Maori since Colonisation*, Wellington, 1975, pp55–79.

Mol, J. J., 'Race Relations, with Special Reference to New Zealand: A Theoretical Discussion', *Journal of the Polynesian Society* 73, 4, 1964, pp375–81.

Ngata, Apirana T. and I. L. G. Sutherland, 'Religious Influences', in I. L. G. Sutherland, ed., *The Maori People Today: A General Survey*, Christchurch, 1940, pp336–73.

Parsonson, Ann, 'Parihaka — A Triumph of Maori Spirit', *New Zealand's Heritage* 4, 49, 1972, pp 1352–57.

Parsonson, Ann, 'Te Whiti — The Protector of His People', *New Zealand's Heritage* 4, 49, 1972, pp1360–63.

Ross, Angus, 'Maori and Polynesian: Race and Politics. The Racial Argument in Support of New Zealand's Interests in Polynesia', in J. D. Freeman and W. R. Geddes, eds, *Anthropology in the South Seas*, New Plymouth, 1959, pp221–33.

Ross, R. M., 'The Autochthonous New Zealand Soil', in Peter Munz, ed., *The Feel of Truth: Essays in New Zealand and Pacific History*, Wellington, 1969, pp47–59.

Schwimmer, E. G., 'The Mediator', *Journal of the Polynesian Society* 67, 4, 1958, pp335–50.

Shirres, Michael P., 'Tapu', *Journal of the Polynesian Society* 91, 1, 1982, pp29–51.

Sinclair, Keith, 'The Maori Land League: An Examination into the Source of a New Zealand Myth', *Auckland University College Bulletin* No 37, History Series No 4, 1950.

Sinclair, Keith, 'Some Historical Notes on an Atiawa Genealogy', *Journal of the Polynesian Society* 60, 1, 1951, pp55–65.

Sinclair, Keith, 'New Zealand', in Robin W. Winks, ed., *The Historiography of the British Empire-Commonwealth: Trends, Interpretations and Resources*, Durham, N.C., 1966, pp174–96.

Sinclair, Keith, 'Te Tikanga Pakeke: The Maori Anti-Land-Selling Movement in Taranaki 1849–59', in Peter Munz, ed., *The Feel of Truth: Essays in New Zealand and Pacific History*, Wellington, 1969, pp79–92.

Smith, S. Percy, 'History and Traditions of the Taranaki Coast', *Journal of the Polynesian Society* 17, 1908.

Sorrenson, M. P. K., 'Land Purchase Methods and their Effect on Maori Population, 1865–1901', *Journal of the Polynesian Society* 65, 3, 1956, pp183–99.

Sorrenson, M. P. K., 'The Politics of Land', in J. G. A. Pocock, ed., *The Maori and New Zealand Politics*, Auckland, 1965, pp21–45.

Sorrenson, M. P. K., 'Maori and Pakeha', in W. H. Oliver with B. R. Williams, eds, *The Oxford History of New Zealand*, Wellington, 1981, pp168–93.

Sorrenson, M. P. K., 'Polynesian Corpuscles and Pacific Anthropology: The Home-Made Anthropology of Sir Apirana Ngata and Sir Peter Buck', *Journal of the Polynesian Society* 98, 1, 1982, pp7–27.

Stokes, Evelyn, 'Te Raupatu O Tauranga: A Study of Land Transactions and Race Relations at Tauranga 1864–1886', *Occasional Paper, Centre for Maori Studies and Research, University of Waikato*, No 3, 1978.

Stone, R. C. J., 'The Maori Lands Question and the Fall of the Grey Government, 1879', *New Zealand Journal of History* 1, 1, 1967, pp51–74.

Te Rangi Hiroa [P. H. Buck], 'The Passing of the Maori', *Transactions and Proceedings of the New Zealand Institute* 55, 1924, pp362–75.

Ward, A. D., 'Unpublished Parliamentary Papers: A Comment on Untapped Source Material on New Zealand History', *New Zealand Journal of History* 1, 1, 1967, pp93–94.

Ward, Alan D., 'The Origins of the Anglo-Maori Wars: A Reconsideration', *New Zealand Journal of History* 1, 2, 1967, pp148–70.

Ward, Alan, 'Law and Law Enforcement on the New Zealand Frontier, 1840–1893', *New Zealand Journal of History* 5, 2, 1971, pp128–49.

Ward, Alan, 'Documenting Maori History: The Arrest of Te Kooti Rikirangi Te Turuki, 1889', *New Zealand Journal of History* 14, 1, 1980, pp25–44.

Wilson, T. G. 'The Grey Government, 1877–9: An Episode in the Rise of Liberalism in New Zealand', *Auckland University College Bulletin* No 45, History Series No 5, 1954.

III Theses

Arthur, Peter Neil, 'Te Whiti and the Land: A Case Study in the Attitudes and Opinions of Taranaki Settlers on Native Policy, 1878–1882', BA (Hons) research exercise, Massey University, 1975.

Bremer, Ione Margaret, 'The Early Development of the Patea-Waverley District: A Study of the Problems of Settling Confiscated Land', MA thesis, Victoria University of Wellington, 1962.

Bryant, S. J., 'Te Whiti O Rongomai: A Reassessment', MA extended essay, University of Canterbury, 1978.

Carr, John Hellyer, 'A Study of European Responses to the Pardon of Te Kooti in 1883 and to his Intended Return to Poverty Bay in 1889', BA (Hons) research exercise, Massey University, 1975.

Cleave, Peter, 'The Languages and Political Interests of Maori and Pakeha Communities in New Zealand During the Nineteenth Century', DPhil thesis, Oxford University, 1979.

Cole, Sharron Mary, 'The Repudiation Movement: A Study of the Maori Land Protest Movement in Hawkes Bay in the 1870s', MA thesis, Massey University, 1977.

Hinch, D.W., 'General Elections in Taranaki 1879–1884', MA thesis, Victoria University of Wellington, 1968.

McIntosh, Iona, 'Sir Arthur Hamilton Gordon: Attitudes to and Influence on New Zealand Relations with the United Kingdom 1880–1882', MA thesis, University of Otago, 1968.

McMaster, Nita M., 'Te Whiti and the Parihaka Incident', MA thesis, University of New Zealand, 1954.

Parker, W. J., 'John Sheehan, Native Minister and Colonial', MA thesis, University of Auckland, 1963.

Sealy, C. M., 'A Study of the Policy of Land Confiscation as Applied in the District of Taranaki', MA thesis, University of New Zealand, 1949.

Sinclair, Karen P., 'Maramatanga: Ideology and Social Process Among the Maori of New Zealand', PhD thesis, Brown University, 1976.

Williams, Jeanine, 'Frederick Weld: A Political Biography', PhD thesis, University of Auckland, 1973.

FURTHER READING

Hohaia, Te Miringa, Gregory O'Brien and Lara Strongman, eds, *Parihaka: The Art of Passive Resistance*, Wellington, 2001.

Keenan, Danny, 'Ma Pango Ma Whero Ka Oti' in Bronwyn Dalley and Bronwyn Labrum, eds, *Fragments: New Zealand Social and Cultural History*, Auckland, 2000, pp39–53.

Oliver, W. H. and Claudia Orange, eds, *Dictionary of New Zealand Biography*, vols I and II, Wellington, 1990 and 1993 (essays on all the major figures involved with the events at Parihaka).

Riseborough, Hazel, 'Saviours and Savages: An Italian View of the Nineteenth-Century Maori World', *Pacific Studies* 9, 3, 1986, pp153–73.

Riseborough, Hazel, 'Parihaka and the Historians', *Te Niho o Te Atiawa Parihaka Seminars* no.1, 1993.

Riseborough, Hazel, 'Caveat Historicus: Bryce *v* Rusden Revisited', *Australian Journal of Legal History* 1, 2, 1995, pp199–219.

The Taranaki Report: Kaupapa Tuatahi, Waitangi Tribunal Report, Wai 143, Wellington, 1996.

INDEX